# Asian American Fiction, History and Life Writing

# Routledge Transnational Perspectives on American Literature
EDITED BY SUSAN CASTILLO, *Kings College London*

**1. New Woman Hybridities**
Femininity, Feminism, and International Consumer Culture, 1880–1930
Edited by Ann Heilmann and Margaret Beetham

**2. Don DeLillo**
The Possibility of Fiction
Peter Boxall

**3. Toni Morrison's *Beloved***
Possible worlds
Justine Tally

**4. Fictions of the Black Atlantic in American Foundational Literature**
Gesa Mackenthun

**5. Mexican American Literature**
Elizabeth Jacobs

**6. Native American Literature**
Towards a Spatialized Reading
Helen May Dennis

**7. Transnationalism and American Literature**
Literary Translation 1773–1892
Colleen Glenney Boggs

**8. The Quest for Epic in Contemporary American Fiction**
John Updike, Philip Roth and Don DeLillo
Catherine Morley

**9. The Literary Quest for an American National Character**
Finn Pollard

**10. Asian American Fiction, History and Life Writing**
International Encounters
Helena Grice

**Related:**

**Fictions of America**
Narratives of Global Empire
Judie Newman

# Asian American Fiction, History and Life Writing
## International Encounters

### Helena Grice

Routledge
Taylor & Francis Group
New York London

First published 2009
by Routledge
711 Third Avenue, New York, NY 10017

Simultaneously published in the UK
by Routledge
2 Park Square, Milton Park, Abingdon, Oxfordshire OX14 4RN

*Routledge is an imprint of the Taylor & Francis Group, an informa business*

First issued in paperback 2011

© 2009 Helena Grice

All rights reserved. No part of this book may be reprinted or reproduced or utilised in any form or by any electronic, mechanical, or other means, now known or hereafter invented, including photocopying and recording, or in any information storage or retrieval system, without permission in writing from the publishers.

**Trademark Notice:** Product or corporate names may be trademarks or registered trademarks, and are used only for identification and explanation without intent to infringe.

*Library of Congress Cataloging in Publication Data*
Grice, Helena.
  Asian American fiction, history and life writing : international encounters / by Helena Grice.
    p. cm.—(Routledge transnational perspectives on American literature ; 10)
  Includes bibliographical references and index.
  1. American fiction—Asian American authors—History and criticism.  2. Asian Americans in literature.  3. Autobiographical fiction—History and criticism.  4. Historical fiction—History and criticism.  5. National characteristics in literature.  6. Place (Philosophy) in literature. I. Title.
  PS153.A84G747 2009
  813.009'895—dc22
                           2008046093

ISBN13: 978-0-415-38475-9 (hbk)
ISBN13: 978-0-415-80901-6 (pbk)

*In Memoriam*
*Christian Thomas Grice*
*1974–2008*

# Contents

Acknowledgments — ix

1 Reading Asian American Fiction, History and Life Writing: International Encounters — 1

2 "The Escape from Asia Tradition": Cultural Revolution Expatriate Memoirs — 11

3 Contemporary Transracial Adoption Narratives: Prospects and Perspectives — 44

4 A Secret History: American Representations of Geisha Society — 67

5 Korean Expatriate Writing and the History of the Korean Peninsula — 92

Notes — 125
Bibliography — 137
Index — 147

# Acknowledgments

No book is written in a vacuum, and *Asian American Fiction, History and Life Writing: International Encounters* is no exception. I have been fortunate to have the support and encouragement of several esteemed colleagues in my area of American studies. As the editor of this series, Professor Susan Castillo gave me the opportunity to write this book, and has been unswerving in her gentle encouragement and careful judgement. She has also become a good friend who has set such a fine example of steadily and regularly producing world-class scholarship, providing incisive leadership to the subject community in the UK and nurturing and supporting young colleagues. Professor John Thieme has also been very generous with his time and support of this project (like my others!) and I thank him again, too. Brian Boyd of the Yeong and Yeong Book Company and Koryo Books first contacted me to discuss our shared interest in transracial adoption; his generosity in sharing information and materials with me is much appreciated. I would also like to thank Adeline Yen Mah, Anhua Gao and Jung Chang for responding to my letters.

I have been fortunate because at Routledge I have had not one, but three, kind and informative editors. Thank you to Terry Clague for the opportunity, Max Novick for the encouragement and Erica Wetter for seeing me through the final stages.

An earlier version of Chapter 4 appeared as "Transracial Adoption Narratives: Prospects and Perspectives" in the journal *Meridians: Feminism, Race, Transnationalism* 5.2, in 2005. I am grateful to Indiana University Press for permission to reprint this material.

Several grants have facilitated this research. A Research Leave Grant from the Arts and Humanities Research Council in 2007–2008 made completion of the book possible. An accompanying grant to spend time at the School of Oriental and African Studies Library at the University of London was also invaluable, and I am also grateful to the wonderful and knowledgeable subject librarians there, too. The Department of English Literature at Aberystwyth University gave me sabbatical leave in 2007, and enabled me to make progress with the project. A grant from Aberystwyth University's University Research Fund enabled me to consult the C.V. Starr

East Asian Library at Columbia University in 2006 and I am grateful for this opportunity. My department head, Professor Diane Watt, has been supportive throughout, and especially in helping me through a difficult period during the writing of this book. As always, Professor Tim Woods, my chief proofreader—and also my husband—has been constantly supportive and encouraging, even when he had to correct my work. I simply could not have produced *Asian American Fiction, History and Life Writing* without him.

Thank you to Nicky, my PhD student and editorial assistant on this project, for everything she has done to help.

To my girls, Mary and Madeleine, thank you for all of the wonderful distractions. And thanks to my mother, for her constant encouragement as always.

This book is dedicated with love to my dear adopted brother Christian Thomas Grice (who was born Kristen Koslowski). Tom died too early at the age of 34 on April 18, 2008 during the completion of my writing. I thank him for instilling in me an initial interest in adoption stories, and for being a wonderful brother for 34 years.

—Helena Grice, Aberystwyth, June 2008.

# 1 Reading Asian American Fiction, History and Life Writing
## International Encounters

> At home, historical memory is an all pervading authority. It is synonymous with the native cultural tradition. Abroad, memory becomes an opportunity—however danger ridden—for a new kind of self-becoming that benefits from forcible distance.
> —Vera Schwartz

> Memoirs are perhaps the ultimate form of immersion journalism.
> —Jeffrey E. Long, *Remembered Childhoods*, (p.xv)

> In a society where values are unstable and in flux, autobiographical memory may be felt to be a "text" that is incontrovertibly knowable and claimable.
> —Janice Haaken, *Pillar of Salt: Gender, Memory, and the Perils of Looking Back*, (p.110)

> Specific events in Asian history of the twentieth century have acquired important visibility in the American collective consciousness . . . the number of biographical, autobiographical, and fictional texts and movies on these events has heightened their prominence on the American scene, leading us, once more, to appreciate the cultural work they enact in the process of raising awareness of history and inviting comprehension towards the persons who have become dislocated as a result of that history.
> —Rocío G. Davis, *Begin Here*, (p.66)

In recent years, Asian countries have been vigorously engaged in revising and contesting perceived versions of their twentieth-century historical and political encounters with other nations and peoples. From Taiwan's and South Korea's controversial rewriting of history books in order to downplay Chinese and Japanese influences respectively, to Japan's refusal to acknowledge the atrocities that its soldiers committed upon its neighbours' citizens—from the denial of Korean comfort women, back to the 1937 rape of Nanking—the questions of historical responsibility and interpretation have never been more urgent. After lying dormant for several decades, the issue of Japan's treatment of the Korean comfort women still has the potential to stir up international diplomatic difficulties between Japan and its former enemies. At the same time, the Japanese government is working energetically to recuperate the reputations of Japanese wartime Kamikaze pilots as heroes. China, Japan and North Korea are all currently engaged in a wrangle with their Asian neighbours over interpretations of post-Second World War Asian history and its legacies. Concurrently, many narratives that address the hidden atrocities perpetrated upon the Chinese and North Korean peoples under Communist regimes have been instrumental in confirming the West's perception of each as politically and socially draconian states. With the collapse of conventional, long-running Cold War structures, China and North Korea have latterly become the new cultural, political and economic targets, especially in a post-Tiananmen Square era, in the light of the current global spotlight on these countries' poor records of human rights and North Korea's perceived aggression on the global political stage. Within this political context, stories that serve to illuminate Asia's contested twentieth-century histories from personal perspectives, such as the four histories of interest in this study, assume an unprecedented importance. They act as oppositional contributions to historical interpretation and understanding, as helping to forge political identities in resistance, and as insisting upon the voicing of a discourse of human rights.

For various economic and political reasons, the last couple of decades have witnessed an enormous growth in Western interest in Asia and Asian history. One manner in which this has been manifested is the proliferation of Asian North American fictional, historical and autobiographical books about Asia's twentieth century. The prevalence of both textual and filmic representations of Vietnam, and increasingly, representations of Cambodia, are well established and have been extensively explored in critical analyses.[1] However, my concern in this book is with a different set of key Asian historical and cultural moments that have latterly become the subject of intense Western cultural scrutiny. They include China's Cultural Revolution (1966–1976) and its aftermath; the Korean War and its legacy; the heyday era of Japanese geisha culture and its subsequent decline; and the advent of China's one-child population policy and the rise of transracial, international adoption in its wake. *Asian American Fiction, History and Life Writing: International Encounters* seeks to examine and account for this contemporary cultural preoccupation with Asian subject matter, by exploring the corresponding historical–political situations that have both circumscribed and enabled greater cultural and political contact between Asia and America. This attention may be neither positive nor welcome though, and I also address the political and cultural investments and issues at stake in these interests, both at local and international levels. Through a series of case studies, that deal in turn with China, Japan and Korea, four historical phenomena, and four moments of unique inter-cultural, transnational contact, are examined via a series of commercially successful, and often critically acclaimed, fictional, historical and autobiographical narratives. In each case, the relationship between narrative—personal as well as fictional—and history, is analysed in order to demonstrate a two-way interaction, whereby the texts themselves not only provide new and often alternative perspectives on each historical instance, but may also become implicated in each cross-cultural encounter.

Each historical example has also been chosen for the manner in which it has been largely under-addressed, intentionally suppressed or misrepresented in the corresponding Asian country. As filmmaker Joan Chen commented in relation to her production of a film about China's Cultural Revolution: "It's not just another Cultural Revolution movie. This was as important to my generation and my people as the Holocaust is important to the world. Why did Oliver Stone make three Vietnam pictures? Why do people still make World War II movies?" China's censorship of unflattering portraits of life under communist rule is well documented, and so it is only from the perspective and vantage point of outside of China that many books criticising China's regime have been possible. As I discussed in some detail in my 2002 book, *Negotiating Identities*, this is especially pertinent in relation to historical accounts of the Cultural Revolution and its aftermath, which have been published both in the United States and in Britain. The 1990s and 2000s have witnessed renewed literary interest in the history of Communist China, as can be seen in the plethora of texts that 'write Red China' and revisit this history from personal perspectives. These include life writings by expatriate women born in mainland China into early generation Communist families, including Jung Chang, Rae Yang, Moying Li, Ji-Li Jiang, Anchee Min, Hong Ying, Meihong Xu, Anhua Gao, Aiping Mu and Ting-xing Ye. Many of these narratives provide a unique range of inside perspectives—especially of women's experiences—on a country that has not only undergone radical political changes throughout the twentieth century, but that has also largely been closed to the West. In these senses, I will also ask whether a new sub-genre of women's writing is emerging. For one reason or another, it has fallen to a group of expatriate women to be spokespersons for their country's history; yet as I will later somewhat tentatively suggest, it may also be that the critical reception of these recent books about Communist China is symptomatic of a cultural resurgence of "orientalism".

The Chinese government's recent displeasure at Anglo-American criticism of its one-child population policy, implemented in the 1970s, the subsequent rise in child abandonment in China and the state of China's over-crowded and under-resourced orphanages, provides the subject of my second example from China. Adopting children from overseas has increased considerably since the 1980s. As of 2000, more than 8,000 Chinese children had been adopted to families in the United States. In 1997 alone, US families adopted 13,620 international children (3,318 from China). By 1998, this figure had exceeded 4,000 (source: US Immigration and Naturalization). In the wake of this phenomenon, narratives addressing the complexities and emotional turbulence of the process of transracial international adoption have started to appear with increasing frequency in the United States. Concerns about differences between white perceptions of the world and the experiences and world view of children of colour become particularly acute in this literature and issues of identity are thrown into especially sharp focus. Among these are visible differences in appearance between adoptees and their parents, the question of how to cope with racial stereotyping and racial slur, and the chasm between an Anglo-American family heritage and an alternative ethnic and cultural background. Together, these hybrid narratives document a unique perspective upon emergent transglobal interactions and the connection of cultures especially in relation to US–China relations.

Geisha culture has also traditionally been shrouded in secrecy, which may also account for the many myths and mysteries that surround it. Only recently has the real, obscured history of the geisha been explored, as well as the contemporary life of Japan's remaining geishas. The traditionally highly regulated and very secret world of Geishahood has also recently been penetrated by a series of Western observers, including some American women who have been trained in the arts of Geishahood, and their subsequent narratives describing this experience are also explored here. American books about the history of geisha culture have proliferated in the last few years, and include Liza Dalby's *Geisha* (2000), Lesley Downer's *Geisha* (2000) and *Women of the Pleasure Quarters: The Secret History of the Geisha* (2001), Kyoko Aihara's *Geisha* (2000), and Mineko Iwasaki's *Geisha of Gion* (2002). Western fascination with the closed world of the Japanese geishas continues, as seen by the continuing popularity of historical–cultural representations (from Giacomo Puccini's *Madama Butterfly* onwards), to later fictional and filmic representations. The publishing industry's current predilection for texts about an exotic orient may account for the recent runaway success of the depiction of geisha life in Japan from the 1920s to the 1960s, entitled *Memoirs of a Geisha*. Both book (1997) and film (2005) served up a mixture of tantalising eroticism and exoticism, culminating in the account of the geisha Sayuri's *mizuage*, or deflowering, by one of her patrons. *Memoirs of a Geisha* has been phenomenally successful and thus instrumental in reviving interest in geishahood. The world of geishahood, whilst still defined by silence and mystery, has in recent years increasingly, if still cautiously, responded by granting a degree of access to outsiders, and this has spawned a new literary genre charting the history and practices of geisha culture, and the role of geisha women in contemporary Japanese society, at once anachronistic yet modern.

The combined effects of Korea's determination to forget its colonial era, the cultural shame attached to memories of years of Japanese rule, and Japan's deliberate suppression of details about its occupation, have all contributed to a lack of accounts about the years of Japanese rule. The subsequent years of civil war, and then the politically enforced split of Korea into North and South Korea, with their emergent regimes, including the repressive and isolated northern Korean regime of Kim Il Sung and Kim Il Jong, have further silenced Korean voices. Korean American historical narratives by Theresa Hak Kyung Cha, Nora Keller, Connie Kang, Helie Lee, Linda Sue Park and others, and life writing works such as Kang Chol-Hwan's *The Aquariums of Pyongyang*, Hyok Kang's *This is Paradise!*, Hyun Sook Han's *Many Lives Intertwined* and Elaine H. Kim's and Eui-Young Yu's edited collection *East to America* seek to redress this omission. In so doing, to also acknowledge specifically the human rights atrocities that people have endured and the roles played by Korea's women during this period. Most Korean American writers deal in different ways with the effects of the Japanese colonisation of Korea. Pioneer Korean American texts such as Mary Paik Lee's *Quiet Odyssey*, Margaret K. Pai's *The Dreams of Two Yi-Min* and Ronyoung Kim's *Clay Walls*, all depicted, to varying degrees, Korean American resistance to Japanese colonial rule, and protested against the racist treatment of Korean Americans by the American state, as well as imparting a strong nationalist spirit. These issues are extensively explored by Theresa Hak Kyung Cha in her influential and formative multi-genre work *Dictee* (1982), which weaves together a variety of narrative modes, including poetry, journal entries, letters and excerpts from history books. Owing partly to its complexity, *Dictee* is an intriguing as well as important text, that has been read as both protest memoir and autobiography, although it is presented here primarily as a revisionist history, as is Nora Okja Keller's historical account *Comfort Woman* (1997). Although unaddressed until the late 1980s, critical and creative attention is increasingly being paid to the untold stories of Korean military comfort women. Records and documents relating to this practice were suppressed (the Japanese government has continued to classify documents relating to comfort women), and this was coupled with an intentional amnesia on the part of many of the victims. Although in 1993 Tokyo acknowledged the atrocities inflicted upon Korean comfort women, Japanese Prime Minister Shinzo Abe contradicted this in March 2007 with an explicit denial of the sexual coercion of Korean women, and Japan has continued to be evasive with regard to the issue. Only recently have oral testimonies, fiction and life writing accounts begun to appear on the subject; apart from Keller's account, there is now also an edited collection by several former comfort women, *The True Stories of the Korean Comfort Women*, as well as some more recent memoirs, which are all explored here.

Thus, the overall aims of this study are multiple. They are to excavate and interrogate four "shrouded histories" of Asia's twentieth century via a series of fictional and life-narrative forms; to illuminate the manner in which both fictional and life writing opens a space for a human rights discourse that is often otherwise censored; to demonstrate the specific contributions made by Asian American women to the relationship between transnational literature and cultural geographies; to illustrate the challenges posed by these (mainly women) writers to the state determined and ossified versions of national Korean, Chinese and Japanese twentieth-century histories; and to acknowledge the important cultural work collectively enacted by texts in raising consciousness of these shrouded histories in a global arena. Thus this book encompasses a sustained focus upon and across the spectrum of life writing from the overtly fictional to the straightforwardly autobiographical, and the allied emphasis upon concerns with human rights, Asian–US cultural and political contact and conflict, and women's issues, reflects the principal thematic preoccupations to be found within these books' pages. As with the series in which it appears, *Asian American Fiction, History and Life Writing: International Encounters* focuses upon transnational (Asian) American narratives and the increasing impact of globalism upon American cultural production, and the increasing importance of the dynamics of (Asian) immigration and migration both in US culture and beyond its borders. I have been deliberately interdisciplinary in my focus, particularly in my excavation of buried or muted voices, although the predominant emphasis falls upon the life writing/fiction continuum. Thus, I also write here about authors who have been amongst the bestselling of their generation, such as Jung Chang, Arthur Golden, Adeline Yen Mah, Liza Dalby and Nien Cheng, whose work is not just popular and populist in achieving high sales figures and film adaptations. Increasingly, their work is attracting serious critical attention across scholarly and academic journals.

In critically examining these four key moments in Asian/American cultural contact and their subsequent representation across a range of cultural forms (the Korean War and its aftermath, the Chinese Cultural Revolution and the post-Revolution era, China's post-1970s population policy and transracial adoption, and the late-twentieth century attempts at the revivification of Geisha culture in Japan), I seek, therefore, to address the following three over-arching questions:

1. To what extent do recent Asian American life writings and fictional narratives articulate a gender-centred human rights discourse which has not hitherto been possible in other cultural or political contexts?[2]
2. In what manner have the forces of globalization and transnational exchange or contact enabled the emergence of stories of atrocity, trauma or marginalization in twentieth-century Asian history in these four case studies?
3. In what ways have women's traumatic and often sexualised experiences—namely sexual abuse, rape, indenture, and enforced prostitution—been inscribed and framed in life writings and fiction by

women of Chinese, Japanese or Korean ancestry in the second half of the twentieth century?[3]

In exploring these questions, my hope is that this book will offer a transnational perspective upon the two-way flow of cultural influence, literary and life narrative production between areas of Asia and the United States. I also aim to explore the effect of international dynamics upon the shape and development of Asian American literary and life writing production, and how dynamically various Asian American writers have responded to events beyond the geographical borders of the United States. Thus, my study mirrors contemporary movement in Asian American scholarship towards a more internationally inflected discussion, an approach akin to that taken in *Crossing Oceans: Reconfiguring Asian Literary Studies on the Pacific Rim* edited by Noelle Brada-Williams and Karen Chow (2004), with its similar exploration of transnational perspectives on Asian American literature and the manner in which writers and readers "cross oceans" in both critical and creative practice. Another study that has been influential on my own work in its approach is *Common Ground: Reimagining American History* by Gary Okihiro (2001), which advocated a revised understanding of major events in American history to include representations from an Asian American viewpoint, as I hope that I have also done here in relation to the Korean War. My hope is that this book will be an appropriate supplement to this scholarship, as well as to existing scholarship on transnationalism and literature, especially the many fine books that have appeared to date in this series on transnational American literatures, and the study of Asian American literary and life writing productions with a specific gender inflection.

## HUMAN RIGHTS, HUMAN WRONGS

> *We do need a little human rights just now, and ... literature does have a capacity to administer to that need.*
> 
> —Joseph R. Slaughter

This book does not focus upon human rights debates to the exclusion of the literary; instead it examines a body of literature that articulates and expresses these concerns. Since December 10th, 1948, when the General Assembly of the United Nations adopted and proclaimed the Universal Declaration of Human Rights, which had at its core "the promotion of universal respect for and observance of human rights and fundamental freedoms"[4], our global citizenry has become increasingly conscious and mindful of the rights of individuals regardless of state affiliation. Many of the narratives explored here document blatant trangressions of the Declaration, from freedom without distinction upon the basis of race, colour, sex, language, religion, political opinion or birth (Article 2); from freedom from slavery or servitude (Article 3); from freedom from torture (Article 4); from freedom from arbitrary arrest or detention (Article 9); from the right to be presumed innocent until proven guilty (Article 11); from freedom from attacks upon privacy, family, home, correspondence and reputation (Article 12); from freedom of movement both within and beyond one's country (Article 13); from freedom to own property and not be arbitrarily deprived of it (Article 17); from freedom of thought, conscience and religion, opinion and expression (Articles 18 and 19); from freedom not to be compelled to belong to an association (Article 20); from free choice of employment, equal pay and fair remuneration (Article 23); from the right to rest (Article 24); from special care and equal assistance for mothers and children, born within or without wedlock (Article 25). From the mass incarceration, torture, and near-starvation of families in the North Korean gulag, the enforced prostitution of Korean women to service the Japanese military, the withdrawal of almost all rights in China during the Cultural Revolution, to the coercion involved in the brutal implementation of the one-child policy across China, almost all of these rights have been violated. To a lesser degree, too, geisha society also presents us with a human rights dilemma, since we have in this existence a highly problematic model of female labour: whilst not always—or indeed often at all anymore—an indentured position, geishahood remains a highly ritualised form of gender commodification, dependent upon culturally obsolete conceptions of womanhood and identity, outdated prescriptions of female behaviour, and a degree of restriction in daily existence that would be deemed unacceptable to most in contemporary global culture.

How, though, to narrate, record and remember such historical atrocity and traumatic experience? My focus falls throughout on the processes of memorialisation, (re)narrativisation and 'writing back', and on the challenge such discourses pose to established state narratives. One aim of *Asian American Fiction, History and Life Writing* is to begin to investigate the role of the Asian American writer in the global struggle for human rights. It seeks to accomplish this by considering the relationship between writing and rights, and the extent to which former prisoners of state or victimized individuals, can best express and protest their situation in literary and life writing representation, and to consider different forms of writing that have emerged from such historical and geographical sites of imprisonment and persecution as the North Korean gulag, Japanese 'comfort stations' or China's political prisons. Several writers explored in this book turn to querying the construction of the past and the workings and function of memory in their representation of history. Several narratives insistently return to themes that illustrate the aesthetic problem of reconciling normality with horror, the displacement of consciousness of life by the imminence and pervasiveness of death and torture, and the constant violation of the coherence of the self. Many of these writers raise issues to do with aesthetics: can torture be represented 'aesthetically'? How can physical traumas performed on the body be represented in writing? Can one speak about an 'aesthetics of incarceration'? How do literary aesthetics intersect with gross violations of human rights, and how can the power of the imagination conjure up images when a writer is confronted with the dilemma of converting into literature or memoir a history too terrible to imagine and remember?

In writing about, and expressing a concern with, these vexed issues, many writers appeal to what Joseph R. Slaughter has characterised as "the continued poignancy of human rights" due to "the global increase of human rights violations over the course of the twentieth century" (*Human Rights, Inc.: The World Novel, Narrative Form and International Law*, p. 2). Yet as Slaughter goes on to show, this appeal is sometimes predicated on a somewhat vague and simplistic understanding of what actually constitutes human rights; and that there is a "language of simplicity and obviousness that pervades human rights commentary", in which "human rights are ostensibly inherent and inalienable, deducible" (*Human Rights, Inc.*, p. 3). Slaughter argues that this central issue of the "legibility of human rights" is "a question of both literacy and legislation, as much matters of literature as law" (*Human Rights, Inc.*, p. 3); and that in "an era of intense globalization, those legal and literary forms cooperate to disseminate and legitimate the norms of human rights" (ibid). I would go further. Within these pages, I argue that narrative—from life writing to fiction—opens a discursive space that both allows and enables the exploration of what exactly constitutes human rights. This exploration of the violation of human rights, in a manner not so freely available in state-sponsored discourse (the law), is also disseminated and packaged in ways that reach and influence a considerably wider readership or audience than codified statutes. I suggest that this is especially pertinent to life writing, since life writing forms are so apposite to the articulation of the intersections between individual and community, and the progression of a life story so often coincides with an encounter with the curbing of citizens' rights—schooling, freedom, marriage, childbirth and employment. That is, books can forge links and make ideological cases, where sometimes states and societies cannot. As Slaughter summarises:

> The texts we read—and how we read, teach, speak and write about them—have an effect (however unpredictable) on the possibility that the projection of a world based on human rights might become legible, articulable, and, perhaps, even commonsensical. To paraphrase H. G. Wells: if we are not reading for human rights, what are we reading for? (*Human Rights, Inc.*, p. 328)

## GLOBALISATION, FEMINISM AND ASIAN AMERICAN STUDIES: A BRIEF METHODOLOGICAL OUTLINE

Any glance at recent Asian American scholarship confirms the sense that commentators and critics alike are increasingly looking beyond the borders of the continental United States. Similarly, Asian American literatures increasingly inscribe explicit and overt links between memories, both real and imagined, and interactions with "abroad" as well as home. Recent publications, such as the creative anthology *Unrooted Childhoods: Memoirs of Growing Up Global* (2004), and the critical collection *Transnational Asian American Literature: Sites and Transits* (2006), reflect this trend. This is not a mere incidental phenomenon but a deliberate creative as well as critical writerly decision. These texts thereby also become strategic interventions in global paradigms, in eroding the distinctions between "national" and "international", "home" and "abroad", "local" and "global", "Asian" and "American".

Therefore, this book extends recent work in Asian American studies, developing arguments about its literary and cultural reception, but combining this with other interdisciplinary approaches. For example, Chapter 3 specifically builds upon research I have undertaken at the University of California–Berkeley, and the University of London's School of Oriental and African Studies, investigating transnational adoption narratives, through surveying the life narratives of Asian adoptees and those of the adoptive American parents. It also examines children's stories written for adopted children that seek to contextualise their cross-cultural ethnic experiences. Alongside such literary texts, I also examine US Federal sociological data on transnational adoption. A second approach considers life writing as a response to traumatic experiences, building upon the pioneer life writing theories of Sidonie Smith, Cathy Caruth, Kalí Tal, Janice Haaken, Suzette Henke and others. Developing the contention that life writing is an empowering form, I demonstrate the ways in which such literary forms embed a new discourse of human rights for women who have suffered very specific forms of oppression, censorship, abuse or cultural exclusion. Finally, a third approach examines various documents concerning human rights' legislation, monitoring reports, and analyses of national breaches of international law (produced by organizations such as Human Rights Watch, Amnesty International, and the Democracy Network Against the North Korean Gulag), specifically in the cases of Korea and China, as well as non-fictional testimonies of human rights' abuses. *Asian American Fiction, History and Life Writing: International Encounters*, then, proceeds from my conviction that writing—as with reading—about rights and wrongs, if not exactly enjoyable, is as empowering and didactic an experience as it can be edifying.

## 2 "The Escape from Asia Tradition"
Cultural Revolution Expatriate Memoirs

> The number of Mainland Chinese legally entering the United States has been soaring since 1978.... This growing community has found almost no voice in its newly adopted country other than through the publication of personal narratives of China's political upheavals.
>
> —Wenying Xu

> In recent years, the reading public has clearly developed a taste for accounts of suffering and hardship under Communist rule in China. Publishers have responded eagerly with memoirs chronicling family misfortune, emotional and cultural deprivation, and political victimization by a totalitarian regime. Though these accounts vary, they often reproduce a view of China's history which reinforces stereotypes and assumes ignorance on the part of their readers. Indeed, many memoirs of life in China suggest a kind of contemporary orientalism in which China appears as a radically other, despotic and brutal world.
>
> —Harriet Evans

> Observations of Cultural Revolutionary China through the narrator's perspective reveal an irrational world where many things do not make sense to someone outside the totalitarian box. This is a world where people are divided into inherited classes and pitted against each other like mad dogs. This is a world where people have to talk about everything using quotes from a little red book. This is a world where riddles and contradiction are accepted at face value and the normal emotions of basic human relationships are drastically perverted.
>
> —Ben Xu

The "Great Proletarian Cultural Revolution" was officially launched by Chairman Mao Zedong in 1966. It was intended that the Revolution would re-imbue China's masses with revolutionary fervor, and overturn "old", traditional, feudal or "bourgeois" ideologies, practices and power structures. It attacked the "Four Olds": old culture, old ideas, old customs and old habits. During the ten years that followed before Mao's death in 1976, the Cultural Revolution escalated, causing unprecedented upheaval, political terror and violence, poverty, famine and hardship across China. Human rights were violated on a massive scale. Author Nien Cheng describes this period as a "dark penumbra which overshadows China's present and future" (*Mao and China: A Legacy of Turmoil*, xi). In their 2005 study of Mao, Jung Chang and Jon Halliday estimate the death toll during the Cultural Revolution in the region of three million people.[1] As Harriet Evans and Stephanie Donald also note, this was a time when "artistic endeavor, whatever its form, was subjected to perilously exacting standards of political and cultural purity" ("Introducing Posters of the Cultural Revolution", p. 4). Mao famously emphasized the imperative for literature—as with all aesthetic production—to have political furtherment at its core.[2] Libricide— the state-sponsored destruction of unpalatable books—was also widespread during this period. Narratives memorializing, exploring and re-examining this harrowing period of history were unsurprisingly slow to appear within China, and as I later discuss, only began to appear in significant numbers in the 1980s.[3] The same has been true of expatriate perspectives. When Jung Chang published *Wild Swans: Three Daughters of China* in 1991, it received widespread critical acclaim, as well as commercial success, including winning the 1992 NCR Book Award. Much of this critical attention focussed upon the text's novelty, as a unique personal memoir and history of China during the period after the Communist Party gained control and of the Cultural Revolution, 1966–1976. This chapter will contextualise Jung Chang's high-profile work within a wider history of writing about Communist China, with specific emphasis upon the period of the Cultural Revolution, when Mao escalated China's emerging communist agenda, and in so doing, I want to advance three separate arguments. Firstly, I will suggest that despite initial responses, Chang's work is not in fact a new form of writing, but instead can be located within a long—and continuing— tradition of Chinese expatriate—American and British—writing. Chang's book did however usher in a renewed literary interest in Communist China, as can be seen in the plethora of texts which 'write Red China', which have appeared since 1991.[4] These include writing by women from mainland China, who were born into early generation Communist families: Anchee Min's *Red Azalea* (1993), Hong Ying's (1998) memoir, *Daughter of the River*, Meihong Xu's *Daughter of China* (also 1998), Anhua Gao's *To the Edge of the Sky* (2000), Aiping Mu's *Vermilion Gate* (2000), Ting-xing Ye's *A Leaf in the Bitter Wind* (2000), Liu Hong's fictionalised *Startling Moon* (2001), Rae Yang's *Spider Eaters* (1997), Ji-Li Jiang's *Red Scarf Girl* (1997), Nanchu's *Red Sorrow* (2001), Sun Shuyin's *Ten Thousand Miles Without a Cloud* (2003), Guo Sheng's *Tears of the Moon* (2003), Chun Yu's poetic *Little Green: Growing Up During the Chinese Cultural Revolution* (2005), and Moying Li's *Snow Falling in Spring: Coming of Age in China During the Cultural Revolution* (2008), as well as texts by women born outside of the mainland such as Jan Wong's *Red China Blues* (1996; Wong was born in Canada), Pang-Mei Natasha Chang's *Bound Feet and Western Dress* (1996; Chang is Chinese American), and Adeline Yen-Mah's *Falling Leaves: The True Story of an Unwanted Chinese Daughter* (1997; Mah was born and brought up in Hong Kong).[5] These narratives provide a unique range of inside perspectives—especially of women's experiences—on a country which has not only undergone radical political changes throughout the twentieth century, but which has also largely been closed to the West, and in this sense, I will argue that an important new sub-genre of women's life writing is emerging. For one reason or another, it has fallen to a group of expatriate women to be spokespersons for their country's history of the emergence of Communism.[6] Finally, I will ask whether the critical reception of these recent books about Communist China may be symptomatic of a cultural resurgence of Saidean orientalism, what one might term a "neo-orientalism".

## CRITICAL HISTORIES

The critical reception of and reaction to Jung Chang's *Wild Swans* in 1991 in the West betrayed a certain confusion about how to characterise her work, an uncertainty which is obvious in relation to later works, too. This was partly engendered by the title itself, in particular the subtitle, 'Three Daughters of China', which suggested that the text was at once a personal history/biography/memoir, and an example of Chinese American women's writing about matrilineality, a genre which had garnered increasing popularity in recent years with the success of Maxine Hong Kingston's and Amy Tan's work. In fact, the critical confusion over the generic status of Chang's work is very reminiscent of a similar uncertainty surrounding Maxine Hong Kingston's *The Woman Warrior* nearly twenty years earlier. This textual dual-identity was also partly created by Jung Chang herself, who said in an interview that whilst the text was primarily a personal history of the Cultural Revolution, "'on a smaller scale [ . . . ] it is the process of understanding my mother".[7] Of the many reviews of the book when it first appeared, several located it within very different generic traditions. Lucy Hughes-Hallet, writing in *The Independent*, read it as "'popular history at its most compelling", illustrating the "pleasures of good historical fiction".[8] Richard Heller also read it as "living history", whilst Martin Amis located it as both "family memoir" and as "social history". Several other reviews found similarities between *Wild Swans* and more popular fiction: Caroline Moorehead declared it "a loving family saga", whilst Edward Behr went even further, labelling it "real-life saga", and compared it with the soap opera *Dynasty*. An even more bizarre interpretation, by Carolyn See, announced it as several different things at once: "a mad adventure story, a fairy tale of courage—calm and measured history". Minette Marrin summed up this divergence of critical perspectives in her interpretation of the text as "an unusual masterpiece—not only a popular bestseller [ . . . ] it has also received serious critical attention". *Wild Swans* was thus received in very different ways by a reading public who have continued to enjoy stories of Communist China in contemporary times, yet by dint of the assumptions which accompany the generic label attached to the text (which clearly differ widely), these differences emerge as crucial in explaining the cultural reception of *Wild Swans* and later similar texts. The critical reception of *Wild Swans* and other texts which 'write Red China', has not differentiated adequately between different genres of writing about Communist China, resulting in the confusion that I have outlined over just exactly how to characterise these narratives. This is partly due to the marketing of these books by publishers eager to commercially exploit a cultural moment that has seen Communist China become an increasingly profitable fad for Western readers. Hence, each subsequently published text is declared to be in the same vein as the last, a claim that in fact often masks very real differences in style, tone, location, social circumstances, intended audience and focus between books.[9] There are crucial differences too, in the temporal distance between each author and her story: Jung Chang took many years to articulate her experiences; while Anhua Gao's narrative appeared barely six years after her arrival in Britain.

Reviewing *Wild Swans* in the *New York Review of Books*, Jonathan Mirsky read the text alongside Feng Jicai's *Voices from the Whirlwind: An Oral History of the Chinese Cultural Revolution*, published in the same year. In an attempt to link Chang's very extensive and detailed memoir of her family's experiences during the Cultural Revolution with the necessarily shorter and more episodic reminiscences to be found in *Voices from the Whirlwind*, Mirsky usefully proposed a common unifying category: "literature of the wounded".[10] In yet another attempt to generically fix Chang's text, Mirsky argues that what these texts have in common is that they are "intimate studies in persecution". While Mirsky's claim may have some basis in the many dreadful incidents that Chang relates, we must nevertheless be cautious in overtly linking this writing to a currently fashionable (but in some ways highly problematic) critical discourse on the 'literatures of trauma', in a move that effectively obscures the cultural and historical specificities of the period 1909–1976 in China. Extending Mirsky's description to other texts illustrates further problems with adopting this phrase. Certainly, all the texts discussed here take as their central focus and organising rubric the central character's/author's suffering and pain as the victim of a totalitarian regime. Yet although all of these texts deal to varying degrees with the negative aspects of life in Mao's China, and especially during the Cultural Revolution, including torture, persecution, execution and famine, several also address other forms of trauma as well. This is often a specific form of gender trauma. Adeline Yen Mah's *Falling Leaves*, for example, also extensively describes the mistreatment and neglect that she suffered at the hands of her family as an unwanted daughter, and in fact this preoccupation at times obscures the narrative of the Cultural Revolution with which it is juxtaposed. Anhua

Gao's story in *To the Edge of the Sky* is partly her story of abuse at the hands of a vicious husband. Similarly, Hong Ying's *Daughter of the River* develops a dual narrative: the narrator's attempts to uncover the mysterious familial secrets which seem to cause her family to resent her (and that as it turns out, relate to her identity as an illegitimate daughter), which are related alongside the events of the Cultural Revolution. It is difficult to see how Mirsky's label, "literature of the wounded", can adequately describe the content of all of these narratives without either reducing the different kinds and levels of suffering to one, or ignoring the gender aspects of many of these accounts. Despite this, Mirsky's nomenclature does offer useful analogies to the ways in which testimonial literature of the Holocaust and other traumatic experiences have been characterised, by critics like Kalí Tal, Cathy Caruth, and others. Tal has argued that any literature which "bears witness" on one level is aggressively political, emotionally charged and culturally sensitive, and furthermore that it is the politically sensitive aspects of a narrative that come to dominate the text, to be privileged over other thematic concerns or dimensions, and in this sense at least, Mirsky's phrase arguably does possess some validity.[11] Schematically and thematically, there are commonalities between many of the memoirs. It is common, for instance, for the personal story of the individual woman to feature against the backdrop of key moments in the period leading up to, and the years of, the Cultural Revolution, such as The Great Leap Forward, the Rustification campaign, or Move to the Country campaign, or the later "criticize Lin Biao" campaign. In this respect, the woman's individual suffering is figured as a direct result of political changes, and the eventual move to escape and then to reflect back on the events of the past in China from the security of the American present, forms the structure of most of the life narratives. This enables the Cultural Revolution narrative to intertwine with a more personal sub-plot—a lesbian relationship in *Red Azalea*, childhood abuse in *Falling Leaves*, the struggle for education in *Red Scarf Girl*. Yet, as Wendy Somerson has pointed out, the personal subplot is also subordinated to the public narrative of political struggle:

> In official socialist discourse, the public/private relationship was one of absolute hierarchy. [ . . . ] The space of the private sphere was literally diminished in the cities where houses were subdivided to accommodate several families who shared cooking and toilet facilities, as well as in the labor camps where large groups of workers [ . . . ] shared all facilities. [ . . . ] private relations literally had no space in the Cultural Revolution, official rhetoric sublimated all desires into desire to work for the revolution. ("Under the Mosquito Net", p. 4)

As many theoretical debates have demonstrated, the problems of representing the past—writing a history—are myriad, and they are especially exaggerated when that history is subject to all forms of government censorship and overt manipulation.

## WRITING THE CULTURAL REVOLUTION

> Now as part of a Diaspora in the liberal and neo-capitalist world, some Mainland Chinese immigrants experience both the necessity and the possibility of narrating their past as a history of painfully entangled complicity with terror. They are adopting a vocabulary that allows them to understand and speak of their involvement in the Cultural Revolution and making use of a reading public who can redeem their "inhumanity".
>
> —Wenying Xu

Xiaomei Chen asks:

> How is the Cultural Revolution remembered? More to the point, is it remembered in a way that accords with its all-important role in modern Chinese political and cultural history? The official culture of the People's Republic of China (PRC) would erase it as an unprecedented "ten-year disaster," the darkest period in history. ("Growing Up with Posters in the Maoist Era", p. 101)

Efforts within China since 1976 to re-evaluate the Cultural Revolution have been described as "inconsistent" and periodic (for instance marking major anniversaries such as the death of Mao or Zhou Enlai); and have predictably proceeded along lines of "political expediency", according to China scholars William A. Joseph, Christine P. W. Wong and David Zweig in their study *New Perspectives on the Cultural Revolution* (p. 20). In *The Chinese Cultural Revolution as History* we find a similar evaluation. The Cultural Revolution

> became a thriving sub-topic that focused particularly on the upheavals of 1966–68, and especially on the most visible protagonists: student red guards, worker rebels, and the mass organizations engaged in factional struggles. A major theme of this work—which appeared with greatest frequency from the mid-1970s to the early-1980s—was that the political struggles of the late 1960s expressed the conflicting interests of identifiable groups in Chinese society. (*The Chinese Cultural Revolution as History*, p. 3)

Despite this history of internal struggle, some commentators have likened the collective experience of the Cultural Revolution to that of the Holocaust (ibid), and later Chinese perspectives on the Cultural Revolution are largely critical: "If publicity praising the CR dominated Chinese airwaves and print media for ten years (1966–1976), publicity damning the experience has now prevailed for an even longer period" (*New Perspectives on the Cultural Revolution*, p. 38).[12] This mood shift reflects Deng Xiaoping's designation of the Cultural Revolution in 1981 as "a tragedy for the entire state, nation and people of China".[13] Furthermore, as Joseph Esherwick, Paul Pickowicz and Andrew Walder observe, in contemporary Chinese historiography of the Cultural Revolution

> the passage of time has permitted fresh perspectives and allowed us to see how the dynamics of political and social conflict have played out as an ongoing historical process. The accumulation of published and archival, official and unofficial sources, together with the availability of extensive oral history accounts permits a new level of detail and nuance that was impossible in the earlier generation of Cultural Revolution scholarship. (*The Chinese Cultural Revolution as History,* p. 26)

Significantly, the major impetus for this renewed scholarship was the emergence of life writing accounts of the Cultural Revolution, both within China and beyond its geographical borders, as well as novels penned by those who had first-hand experience of the Cultural Revolution, such as the 1980s "sent down youth" novels by Liang Xiaosheng (*Snowstorm Tonight*) and Wang Xiaobo *(Golden Age)* (These Chinese language novels are discussed by Henry Zhao in "The River Fans Out: Chinese fiction since the late 1970's", *European Review* (2008) 11, pp. 193-208.), who, as Liyan Qin tells us "lamented their past sufferings and miseries, which formed the main motifs of the literary movement loosely referred to as 'scar literature'". ("The Sublime and the Profane", p. 260)

Liyan Qin outlines the conditions necessary for an individual to produce a critically revisionist account of the Cultural Revolution:

> First, the writer must come from a "bad" family background, but not so bad as to lead to alienation from the Cultural Revolution experience entirely [ . . . ] The writer's parents must be intellectuals, so that a private collection of books to read will be at hand in addition to the meager "official" selections. The writer must be quite young at the outset of the Cultural Revolution, otherwise he or she would be too old to escape the Cultural Revolution rhetoric. The writer must not be too successful during the Cultural Revolution, lest he or she develop a too strong identification with its alleged cause. The writer must enter university, preferably after 1977, since the worker-peasant-soldier university students in the Cultural Revolution only got an impoverished education. The writer must go overseas [ . . . ] to see an alternative way of life and a different culture. ("The Sublime and the Profane", pp. 264–5)

Although this description refers to Chinese language writers, it also accurately describes the circumstances of many of the expatriate writers of concern here, notably Jung Chang, Moying Li, Ji-Li Jiang, Nanchu, as well as Anchee Min.[14] Just as the (pre)conditions for writing must be right, so narratives within China about the Cultural Revolution have also tended to be somewhat formulaic—or as filmmaker Joan Chen terms it, "generic" (p. 3). As she outlines, there are several commonalities of feeling and perception to be found in these Chinese CR narratives:

1. Ambivalence towards Mao and the Cultural Revolution;
2. A sense of both collective identity and a shared history;
3. A sense of alienation and detachment from today's society;
4. Criticism of reform *and* the Chinese Communist Party (Joan Chen, pp. 3–4)[15]

This description also accurately describes the general narrative pattern to be found in expatriate memoirs as well.

*Red Azalea* by Anchee Min, was published just two years after *Wild Swans*, and also betrayed its publisher's eagerness to capitalise upon the success of Chang's text, as well as upon Amy Tan's *The Kitchen God's Wife*, which had appeared the year before, and which is also a personal story set against a background of China in the twentieth century (notably the 1930s). Min's story was particularly sensational, as she became a film star in Mao's China, and led a high-flying and quite racy life. *Red Azalea* was reviewed by Amy Tan for the dust jacket, where she confesses that she found Min's memoir "riveting [ . . . ] this is not just another book on the cultural revolution". Like *Wild Swans*, a wider survey of the reviews of Min's memoir also reveals a wide spectrum of generic interpretations. Min's story has received wider critical attention than many other texts, possibly due to its transgressive blend of Cultural Revolution narrative and lesbian love story. Certainly, critics see it as a significant text. According to Wendy Somerson,

> her text works particularly well as both transnational and feminist because she is writing from the space of the U.S. about gendered sexuality in China. Through her translation of the Chinese Cultural Revolution into a story told in English for the "West," Min negotiates a space of resistance where, in Homi Bhabha's terms, cultural difference is "inscribed in the 'in-between' in the temporal break-up that weaves the global text" [ . . . ] Crossing "West" and "East," Min's story refuses classification as purely "Chinese" or "American," but instead articulates a specific interstitial space on the borderland of discourse between the two countries. ("Under the Mosquito Net", p. 2)

Later narratives, such as *Bound Feet and Western Dress*, by Pang-Mei Natasha Chang and *Red China Blues* by Jan Wong, published in the same year (1996), by the same press, Bantam, actually share little in common, although the *New York Times* also described both as part of the "family memoir genre". *Bound Feet and Western Dress* was actually written by a first-generation Chinese American woman, who related the story of her great-aunt after undertaking many hours of taped interviewing. Yu-i, Chang's aunt, lived through the Cultural Revolution, and *Bound Feet* described these years, alongside Yu-i's own story of female resistance and bravery (the title refers to her childhood refusal to have her feet bound).[16] It covered the period from 1900, when Yu-i was born, until her death in 1989. Like *Wild Swans*, it included a chronology of events that juxtaposes Yu-i's story with the events of the Cultural Revolution. In contrast, Jan Wong's *Red China Blues* was a personal memoir about the author's experience of travelling from her home in Canada to China in order to become involved in the Cultural Revolution in the 1980s. Wong's narrative thus only covered a short period and had a quite different, externalized—and certainly more limited—perspective on Communist China. Yet Bantam quite obviously marketed the two books together: *Red China Blues* was advertised within the pages of *Bound Feet*.

Adeline Yen Mah's *Falling Leaves: The True Story of an Unwanted Chinese Daughter*, was arguably one of the most commercially successful of these books (it spent more than thirty weeks on the *Times* bestseller list, and to date has sold almost half a million copies in Britain alone). Possibly owing to its subtitle, which again suggested a connection with Chinese American writing about mothers and daughters, it was reviewed by Amy Tan for the dust jacket, who described it as "riveting [ . . . ] I am still haunted by Mah's memoir. A marvel of memory". Apart from the fact that Amy Tan only seems to have one thing to say about these texts, that they are "riveting", it is, I think, significant that she is repeatedly asked to review them, not just as a well-known Chinese American writer, but also because of the publishers' attempts to connect these texts about Communist China with the commercially successful subject of Chinese experience and Chinese American mothers and daughters. This can also be seen in another story, by the Chinese expatriate and poet, Hong Ying. Her partly fictionalised memoir *Daughter of the River*, was published in 1997. Despite its title, this book is not substantially about matrilineality: 'daughter of the river' refers to the Yangtze River, on the banks of which Hong Ying grew up, in a slum. Yet the review that was printed on the back cover, originally published in the *Times*, connects Hong Ying's narrative with both *Wild Swans* and Tan's *The Joy Luck Club*: "Dealing as it does with the nightmare of Mao's China, comparisons with Jung Chang's *Wild Swans* will be inevitable, but Ying's book more closely resembles Amy Tan's *The Joy Luck Club*".

All of this critical confusion about gender, genre, domestic and national forms can be summed up in the one of the more recent texts to be published, *Daughter of China: The True Story of Forbidden Love in Modern China*, by Meihong Xu. Reviewed for the dust jacket by Anchee Min, author of *Red Azalea*, the blurb announced it "as dramatic as *Wild Swans*, as moving as *Falling Leaves* and as revealing as *Memoirs of a Geisha*, *Daughter of China* tells how a nation's troubled history shaped the destiny of one remarkable young woman".

## 'WRITING RED CHINA': MID-CENTURY PRECURSORS, 1950–1990

Although these contemporary texts share commercial as well as critical success, they have not yet received substantial critical analysis.[17] While they have been accepted as a new body of writing, they do in fact have important precursors in Chinese expatriate literature. In her ground breaking study *Between Worlds: Women Writers of Chinese Ancestry*, Amy Ling discussed a range of texts by Chinese American women that focussed upon China after the Communist Party gained control, and that according to Ling, took a "critical and negative stance" towards this period in China's history. In a section entitled "Life in the People's Republic of China: The Critical Stance", Ling discussed a series of key auto/biographical texts about Communist China. These include the autobiography by Maria Yen (1954) *The Umbrella Garden*, which related Yen's experiences as a student of the National Beijing University in the late 1940s; Sansan's memoir *Eighth Moon* (1964), the story of a child who grew up separated from her parents in the People's Republic; Yuan-tsung Chen's autobiographical novel *The Dragon's Village* (1980), charting Chen's experiences as a land reformer in the 1950s and 1960s; and a more recent precursor to the texts that I have discussed, Nien Cheng's *Life and Death in Shanghai* (1987), the story of an upper-class wife of an ambassador, who became a political prisoner, which was published in 1987. As with the more contemporary writers under discussion here, these women "found publishers and a ready audience for expressions of discontent".[18] As Ling made clear, because America regarded China as a dangerous enemy in the 1950s (this was after all the period when the House UnAmerican Activities Committee was active under Senator Joseph McCarthy), the political climate was perhaps even riper for books critical of Communist China than it is today.

Ling also discussed the novels of Eileen Chang, which were published in the 1950s and 1960s. Chang's novels are particularly interesting, both as fictionalised documents of the Cultural Revolution era, and in the light of the critical acclaim that they have subsequently received.[19] Eileen Chang was a Chinese woman writer of upper-class and educated background who emigrated to the United States as a young adult. She was born and raised in China's old society, although her perspective on the Communist Party has much in common with later writers. She was the author of several novels, including *The Rice Sprout Song* (1955), *The Naked Earth* (1956) and *Rouge of the North* (1967). She was also the author of the acclaimed novella, *The Golden Cangue* (1943), which draws heavily upon her experience of her father's opium habit and the familial destruction this caused. This piece was later to be expanded into her novel, *The Rouge of the North*.[20] Chang's work is also currently enjoying a significant revival in the West in the wake of Ang Lee's controversially sexually explicit production of her novel, *Lust, Caution* which was released in 2007.

Chang's critical reputation largely rests upon her 1955 novel, *The Rice Sprout Song*, which, like *The Naked Earth*, was originally written in Chinese, but was later translated into English by the writer herself. Like *The Naked Earth*, *The Rice Sprout Song* deals with the period of Chinese history that Chang experienced: Communist China, and the failure of the government during this time. Significantly, both novels were commissioned by the United States Information Agency, for barely-concealed propaganda purposes. The initial inspiration for *The Rice Sprout Song* was an article written by a Communist Party cadre who had been involved in quelling a peasant attack upon a granary store during a period of particular hardship. The party member asked in his article how the ideals of the Communist Party could have gone so wrong, so much so that the party was pitted against the people it sought to help. He subsequently published a retraction of these earlier views, and it is these two viewpoints that were expressed by the party member that Chang explores in her novel. *The Rice Sprout Song* was more successful than *The Naked Earth* in transcending the narrow contractual brief within which Chang was forced to work, as she herself has admitted. The novel offered a subtle but sophisticated critique of the values spawned by Communist China through the dual lenses of both the peasant hardship created by the Revolution and subsequent government, and the party itself. So the novel opens with a peasant village wedding and then proceeds through the lives of party members such as Ku, the party intellectual prone to petty deceptions. The contact between Ku and peasant hardship poignantly illustrates the distance between the ideals and the realities of Communist China. Juxtaposed with these two, is the situation of the higher-ranking party member, Comrade Wong, whose demands upon the peasants culminates in a riot that he is forced to viciously quell. These individuals provide the means for Chang to demonstrate the impossible demands and conditions of survival in Communist China, as well as the fracture of both party ideas and ideals, as Wong finally notes: "We have failed". The eponymous rice sprout song, or *yanko*, is the dance of the revolution that ultimately provides a powerful and ironic symbol in Chang's novel.

Chang's critical reputation predominantly rests upon *The Golden Cangue* and *The Rice Sprout Song*. Although one critic has described Chang as "the only novelist of real competence who has deserted Red China and written of life in that country from this side of the Bamboo curtain",[21] her work may be fruitfully compared with Nien Cheng's autobiographical *Life and Death in Shanghai* (1987), another account of the period of the Cultural Revolution and its aftermath grounded in the personal experience of the author.[22] Chang's work has also been compared by Amy Ling with other Chinese women writers who have made America their home, including Han Suyin, Helena Kuo, Hazel Lin and Yuan-tsung Chen. As the renowned Chinese literary expert C. T. Hsia has noted, *The Rice Sprout Song*'s position at the forefront of Chinese writing in English extends beyond its linguistic boundaries, so that it may also be considered to be "among the classics of Chinese fiction".[23] Partly the novel's importance may be attributed to the unusually critical and ruthlessly unsentimental account that it offers of life in Communist China, in which respect it may be placed alongside Maria Yen's *The Umbrella Garden: A Picture of Student Life in Red China* (1954) and Yuan-tsung Chen's *The Dragon's Village* (1980). However, *The Rice Sprout Song*'s reputation is equally explained by Chang's literary skill. As Amy Ling has noted, Chang's sparse but effective descriptions and striking images also contribute much to the success of this novel.

## NEW ORIENTALISMS? AGENCY, RECEPTION AND READING

The conditions that governed the marketing and reception of many of these narratives about Communist China may be partly indicative of the advent of a new orientalism, as Harriet Evans also observed in the epigraphal quotation to this chapter. In Edward Said's definition, 'orientalism' was a perspective on world relations in which the West produced a particular representation of the 'Orient' that then served to justify its subjugation as culturally, morally and politically inferior to the West.[24] Many life-writing narratives about the atrocities that occurred in Communist China have been key in retrospectively confirming China in the minds of Western readers as a politically and socially draconian state. As Wendy Somerson observes, the "U.S. becomes the spectator of oppression in China" (p. 3). In some cases there has been a very blatant anti-China propaganda campaign, such as in Eileen Chang's case where the United States actually sponsored her anti-Communist narratives.[25] This is clearly a deliberate strategy of vilification, since with the collapse of Communist Russia, China has become the new cultural, political and economic target, especially in recent years, in the light of the events which took place in Tiananmen Square on June 4, 1989, and the current global spotlight upon China's poor record of human rights, both within China, and in Tibet in the shadow of the Beijing Olympic Games.[26] As Asian states have become increasingly prominent rivals to the West in the global economy, neo-orientalist discourses have escalated the definition of Asians as culturally and racially other.[27] In her memorial essay, "Growing Up with Posters in the Maoist Era", expatriate scholar Xiaomei Chen recalls:

> popular China-bashing memoirs, were useful during the post-Cold War era to enhance the nationalism of an America—and a West—whose hegemonic position was beginning to be challenged. In this manner the United States could uphold its role as "international policeman" by constantly replaying the record of the suffering other who needed to be rescued from the socialist camp. ("Growing Up with Posters in the Maoist Era", p. 103)

Cultural Revolution narratives are convenient in other ways too. In her article, "Agency via Guilt in Anchee Min's *Red Azalea*", another Chinese expatriate scholar, Wenying Xu, points out the repeatedly convenient omission of individual agency and guilt in Cultural Revolution memoirs. It is both politically and individually expedient to ignore that these memoirists bear some responsibility, if not complicity, for their participation in the many horrors of the era. She writes:

> As someone who lived through ten years of the political turmoil and personal agony of China's "Cultural Revolution," I find these autobiographies unsatisfactory because of their high moral tone, which exonerates them from any responsibility for the horrors. Some, like Nien Cheng's *Life and Death in Shanghai*, portray solely the authors' courage in surviving immense physical and psychological torture. Many of them strive to portray their own moral superiority to those Chinese who betrayed, persecuted, or brutalized others for their own political security or advancement. Such is the tone of Jung Chang's *Wild Swans* and Liu Binyan's *A Higher Kind of Loyalty*. Almost all of these writers are silent about any personal complicity in the horrors of these events. ("Agency via Guilt in Anchee Min's *Red Azalea*", p. 2)

Xu connects this awkwardness of omission with the individual author's vantage point writing within the secure and uncritical environment of the West, where the author is ensured approval of her struggle for freedom, survival and individuality. Of Anchee Min, for instance, she notes:

> Min needed the West in order to write this book even as she needed to write this book in order to reconstitute her identity in the West [ . . . ] She needed the luxury of having many Western liberal readers who feel that she is being too hard on herself in her confessions. ("Agency via Guilt in Anchee Min's *Red Azalea*", p. 5)

In short, Xu argues, Cultural Revolution memoirists escape any sense of political or social responsibility or even reprehension for their past actions by appealing to a Western readership, and by unproblematically assuming a perspective of victimhood, which goes unchallenged. When I first wrote about Cultural Revolution memoirists in 2002, I put this point in a letter to Anhua Gao, who had recently published *To the Edge of the Sky*. Her response, perhaps to be expected, was an offended rebuttal.[28]

It should be noted, however, that the failings of these perspectives are not limited to Chinese expatriate accounts of the Cultural Revolution. In an exploration of Chinese language Cultural Revolution literature of the 1980s, Liyan Qin posits:

reflections on the Cultural Revolution crafted in the 1980s had great limitations. Both the former rightist writers and the sent-down youth writers saw themselves as victims of the Cultural Revolution [ . . . ] Believing themselves cheated and victimized, they emerged morally intact from the Cultural Revolution. Thus, they failed to explore the psychological and social foundations of the Cultural Revolution's mass mobilization in addition to its legacy of persecution. ("The Sublime and the Profane", pp. 260–1)

As Xiaomei Chen has similarly observed, this phenomenon is also characteristic of a certain kind of convenient and selective amnesia identified in Chinese historical accounts of the Cultural Revolution. The period is remembered "as a chaotic event, one without agency and in which no subjects were to be held responsible", and warns that "these views expunge the connection between earth-shaking events as they occur in history and the mystified participants and collaborators, who cede their authority as witnesses to, and owners of, that history" ("Growing Up", p. 101). There is an additional drawback to be found in the expatriate accounts discussed here. As Joan Chen cautions in relation to expatriate memoirs

> Such polished accounts, written by expatriates and clearly prepared for a non-Chinese public, represent only one part of a much larger story. [ . . . ] Invariably, these memoirs tell how the various authors both played an active role in the Cultural Revolution *and* were victimized by it. Written and edited for Western readers, it is hardly surprising that they rarely challenge dominant western (and, often, Chinese) perceptions of the Cultural Revolution as one of "ten lost years." Moreover, because the authors of such books left China nearly twenty years ago, they have little or nothing to say about Deng Xiaoping's economic reform or its consequences. (Joan Chen, p.xii; p .3)

The point that expatriate perspectives are rarely complete and do not take into account post-CR events in China is an important one, although this is now beginning to change.[29] That so many authors–Jung Chang, Anhua Gao, Ji-Li Jiang to name but three—figure their personal recuperation as both enabled by and located in the West is a troublesome conclusion to the narrative, since the political narrative is thereby left incomplete.

The perils of homogenising texts that to varying degrees 'write Red China', can perhaps best be illustrated by a recent article in the British broadsheet newspaper *The Guardian*'s supplement 'The Editor', which presented "five novels about women in China, to save you the burden of reading them".[30] These 'Five of a Kind' included Kingston's *The Woman Warrior*, Tan's *The Kitchen God's Wife*, Chang's *Bound Feet*, Mah's *Falling Leaves* and Chang's *Wild Swans*. The item reduces Chinese American writing to its lowest common denominator, and the final section of each brief review gives the 'best Chinese proverb cited'. In another case, an article by Vanessa Thorpe in *The Observer* commented upon the manner in which 'the East is Read: How the Orient captivated the West'. She noted:

> First came *Wild Swans*, then *Falling Leaves*. Now an equally authentic story about rural China [ . . . ] is expected to surpass both those bestsellers. [ . . . ] The book business is still prepared to bank on the British reader's obsession with all things oriental. With Arthur Golden's semi-factual study of Japan, *Memoirs of a Geisha*, still selling well, hunger for detailed chronicles of lives lived out in far flung places grows unabated.[31]

*The Observer* article cites a fiction editor at a prominent publishing house, who notes that "there is still an interest in story-telling that is exotic and yet fairly familiar. *Memoirs of a Geisha*, for instance, was an extraordinary story, with no Westerners in it, yet somehow readers here are able to relate to it".[32] It seems that, as these comments indicate, publishers are currently engaged in selling a reading public an 'orientalism' that continues to be extremely profitable, one that continues to fetishise Asia and Asians. Indeed, it is precisely the *absence* of 'Westerners', along with the *presence* of the 'exotic' East, that is attractive, alluring, and open to commodification. Ultimately, that publishers seem to have happened upon a highly successful (if unspoken) narrative formula may have more to do with the content of these texts (and the experiences related within, that are all conflated as 'Asian'), than with artistic merit or political integrity.

Central to the conditions of reception of these texts, are issues of representation and reading. For these writers, although representation is to some extent under their authorial control, reading is not. Yet, as John McLeod warns, and as the critical reception of many of these texts illustrates, "the act of reading in postcolonial contexts is by no means a neutral activity. *How* we read is just as important as *what* we read".[33] It is clear that several of these narratives were intended by their authors to be exposés of China's hypocrisy and the severity of elements of the Communist regime during the twentieth century, often from a gendered perspective. If we recognise that these texts (like all texts) are sites of multiaccentuality or sites of pluralistic meaning, one can account for their potential derailment. By this, I mean that there is the possibility that these texts may be construed or consumed as appealing to the stereotypical assumptions about China's "cultural difference" (for this substitute "cultural inferiority"). In this respect, the texts may inadvertently fall prey to a "neo-orientalist" impetus in the West. So whilst their authors produce them as critiques of Maoist China, they are consumed by a readership that is fixated upon a "neo-orientalist" exoticism and voyeurism. This is especially the case if we consider the gender politics at stake within this literature. The uniqueness of several narratives—notably *Wild Swans*, *Bound Feet and Western Dress*, *Falling Leaves*, *Red*

*Azalea* and *Red Scarf Girl* stems from the portrait of women's lives that each text provides. However, precisely because many stereotypical images of Asian women have emerged from the very same experiences that these texts describe, such as foot-binding and prostitution, these narratives may (albeit inadvertently) ultimately invite a voyeuristic fascination.

The critical responses that I have adumbrated are, of course, characteristic responses to texts that slide across generic divides. We should be cautious, too, of taking as representative so many reviews of these texts (tempting though this is) since little substantial critical work has yet been written, in the vein of Amy Ling's extensive analysis of early writing about Communist China. Nevertheless, reviews do function as a *de facto* index of the prevailing cultural zeitgeist. I would also not wish to ignore the complexity of such memoirs, which after all, appeal to a variety of different readerships, from popular consumers of literary exotica, to interested observers of China, to students of Asian American literature. However, what we desperately need is sustained, specific and generically-sensitive analysis of these texts and the ways in which they 'write Red China' from differing social and cultural perspectives, and we need to sensitise our readings to both neo-colonial dynamics and class and gender axes. In the rest of this chapter, therefore, I offer readings of several narratives, each of which is representative of a noteworthy aspect of this literature.

## JUNG CHANG, WILD SWANS (1991)

Published to extraordinary popular acclaim, Jung Chang's style in *Wild Swans* is informal yet compelling, and so it is not surprising that this autobiographical text has been hailed by critics as a masterpiece of popular historical writing. Chang's skill is evident in her masterful blending of personal testimony and popular history in the vein of historian Howard Zinn.[34] Accompanied by many pictures, the memoir traces Chang's family life against the backdrop of China's changing fortunes. Included in the autobiography is a chronology that charts the rise and fall of the Kuomintang, and the rise of the Communist party, alongside corresponding events in the lives of the Chang family. Chang's family was not only extensively affected by the Japanese occupation, the fall of the Kuomintang and the Cultural Revolution, but was also actively involved in these changes. For instance, her grandmother became the concubine of the chief warlord General Xue, her father was governor of the province of Yibin, her mother a head of public affairs in Yibin, and Jung Chang herself a member of the Red Guard. The pictures that accompany the text are particularly important in documenting the tandem histories of the Changs along with that of China more generally. Many of the photographs show the Changs in their official capacities: Jung's grandfather, General Xue Zhi-heng, in his official uniform; Jung's parents in Communist Party uniforms; Jung as a Red

Guard; and Jung's father's funeral in 1975, that depicts an official reading the Communist Party's valedictory. The many photographs are, in fact, one of the most remarkable features of the text, marking its distinction from several other 'Red China' life writings. They offer an intensely personal perspective upon this turbulent period of Chinese history.

Something of a contemporary publishing phenomenon the world over, *Wild Swans* is still banned in China, Chang's native country and the subject of the narrative.³⁵ In response to this censorship, Chang has said that "I feel very angry and frustrated. I would love mainland Chinese to read my book. There is a Chinese translation which I worked on myself, published in Hong Kong and Taiwan".³⁶ The fact that *Wild Swans* is banned in China is not entirely surprising though. The subject of the book is the social and political upheaval of twentieth-century China, which is told through the lives and perspectives of three generations of women: Jung Chang, her mother and her grandmother. Chang's grandmother, Yu-fang, was born into the feudal society of China in 1909, just two years before the Manchu Empire was overthrown, precipitating one of the bloodiest periods in China's past, when regional warlords reigned. Yu-fang's life was typical of Chinese women's lives at the turn of the century: she endured foot-binding and had a very restricted existence as a result. In 1924, three years before Chiang-Kai-shek and the Kuomintang took control of China, Yu-fang became the concubine of General Xue Zhi-heng, a powerful chief of police in Peking. She bore him a daughter, Chang's mother, Bao Qin (or De-hong/'wild swan'), in 1931. After General Xue's death two years later, Yu-Fang escaped from Peking with her infant daughter, and subsequently met and married a respectable middle-class doctor, Dr. Xia, who was almost forty years her senior. This period coincided with the growth and consolidation of the Communist Party, against the backdrop of Japanese aggression in Manchuria, and eventually across China, culminating in the proclamation of the People's Republic in 1949. It was also during this period after the overthrow of the Kuomintang, that Chang's mother, now a young adult, joined the Communist Party, first becoming a student leader, then a member of the Communist Youth League. She also met and married Chang's father, Wang Yu, who became a Maoist guerilla soldier. As a civil servant herself, and as the wife of a party official, Bao Qin gained certain privileges, and Jung and her four siblings enjoyed a relatively secure upbringing until the first years of the 1960s. Jung Chang herself became a Red Guard briefly in 1966. Eventually, however, the ritual party purgings and human rights atrocities occurring at the time invaded the young girl's world when the tide turned against her parents in the early 1960s. Both parents became scapegoats and were punished as enemies of the people, and Jung was banished to the countryside to be re-educated as a peasant in Deyang. As part of her punishment and humiliation, Jung's mother was forced to kneel on broken glass. Jung herself was forced to become a 'barefoot doctor', serving the Communist Party as a medic, despite her lack of training. Jung's father died in 1975, barely three years after his release from a detainment camp. In 1978, the same year as Deng Xiaoping returned to power, Jung, now an educated twenty-six year old, won a scholarship to Britain, which then became her home. It was not until after her mother's visit in 1988, though, that Jung made the decision to commit her story to paper:

> in 1988 my mother came to England to visit me. For the first time, she told me the story of her life and that of my grandmother. When she returned to Chengdu, I sat down and let my memory surge out and the unshed tears flood my mind. I decided to write *Wild Swans*. The past was no longer too painful to recall because I had found love and fulfillment and therefore tranquility. (*Wild Swans*, p. 673)

Censorship of Chang's story was thus not just official and public, it also existed on a private psychological level. Chang seems to have suffered from an almost intentional amnesia about her past. Yet, as with many traumatic histories, Chang found writing *Wild Swans* simultaneously both difficult and yet cathartic. She has said:

> The process of writing was perhaps more painful, but afterwards it became cathartic because I no longer have the terrible nightmares that I used to have when I first came to Britain. I came over in 1978, Mao had just died in 1976, and China began to open up. For the first time scholarships to go the West to study were awarded on academic merit. If my mother had spoken out against the Communists to me when I was a child, I would not have been allowed to come. (*Wild Swans*, p. 673)

In fact, it was Chang's mother who instigated the writing process. As Chang observes:

> Inevitably when you write a book you have to be selective editorially, but there was nothing I left out because it was too painful. In fact before my mother told me the story in 1988, I tried to write something about my past, but I couldn't dig deep into my memory. Then my mother told me her story and she struck me as being so honest, she really let herself go, and felt I was drawing strength from her so I was really able to open myself up to face the most painful parts. (*Wild Swans*, p. 673)

As an invaluable personalised testament especially to the horrors of the Cultural Revolution era, and as a useful historical perspective on Mao's impact upon China in the last century, *Wild Swans* is still unparalleled. Although it offers insights into the brutality and deep corruption that existed within Mao's China, it is most interesting in its depiction of Chinese women's lives through the century. Chang's grandmother's experience, with her 'three inch golden lilies', or bound feet, was exceptionally burdensome to her, and limited, in comparison with her daughter's life as a revolutionary. Yet this was disempowering in its own way, as was Jung's life before leaving China in 1978. The text also functions as a tribute to Chang's female forebears, especially by foregrounding their personal stories against the epic sweep of China's history. *Wild Swans* thus successfully combines family history and personal testimony with other documentary forms (Chang includes a family tree, a chronology, and an extensive list of illustrations).

## ANHUA GAO, TO THE EDGE OF THE SKY (2000)

Like Jung Chang, Anhua Gao felt the need to bear testimony to the horrors that she both witnessed and endured during her life in China. She has said: "I wanted the world to know the truth about China. People living outside didn't really understand what happened". Like Chang, too, Gao also wanted to pay homage to her parents, who were unable to tell their own story: 'Because my parents died a long time ago I could not do my duty and look after them, I was too young. So I have written a book for them' (book jacket). Although Gao's narrative starts slightly later than Chang's (in 1926), it covers roughly the same period of Chinese history, ending with Gao's escape to the West in 1994. As with *Wild Swans* she also makes use of the paraphernalia of documentary and testimony, such as many illustrations, as well as a map of China.

Gao's perspective on the story of the Cultural Revolution is, like Jung Chang's, that of an insider-observer. Gao's parents, both People's Liberation Army officials, were hailed as revolutionary martyrs by Mao, and this label served to protect Anhua and her siblings from the harsh reality of advancing Communism in China for many years. However, both died prematurely (of a combination of poor nutrition and inadequate medical care), leaving Anhua, her brother, and two sisters, orphans at the mercy of disinterested and uncaring relatives, who separated the vulnerable children, thus initiating their induction into life in the new China. From this point onwards, Gao's life proved increasingly difficult. She was zealous both in her academic studies, and her desire to serve Mao. She became a Young Pioneer, then a Red Guard, and studied Mao's teachings so hard that she collapsed with exhaustion. Like Jung Chang, she relates this period of her life in a curiously detached manner, and although she stresses her revolutionary fervor at this point, her narrative misses no opportunity to highlight the hypocrisy and hardship permeating the lives of Chinese people at this time. A notable instance of this occurs in the chapter dealing with the so-called 'Great Leap Forward', in 1958. This was Mao's attempt to accelerate the development of China into a modern industrialised economy to rival the most advanced Western countries. It was also an effort to reverse the stirrings of discontent that had begun in the wake of Mao's last campaign, the so-called 'Anti-Rightist Campaign'. This was a virtual witch hunt, in which 5 per cent of every work unit in China was 'outed' by their peers as rightists, and persecuted. Gao writes:

> After the Anti-rightist campaign, the Chinese people had been silenced. Their enthusiasm for socialist reconstruction waned to almost nothing, causing consternation in Beijing. In the spring of 1958 Mao decided to launch yet another campaign in an attempt to save his face and to revive interest in Communism. He called it the Great Leap Forward. He wanted to prove to the world how clever he was by building the Chinese economy many times faster than any capitalist country in the West. (*To the Edge of the Sky*, p. 64)

The Great Leap Forward consisted of two strategies. The first was to "eliminate the four pests, flies, bedbugs, mice and sparrows" (*To the Edge of the Sky*, p. 65). In a section typical of Gao's narrative style, she dispassionately describes the Chinese people's attempts to implement this policy, despite its ludicrousness. Typically, though, she does not miss the chance to offer her own view of this incident, and not without an element of wry irony:

> Of course, you will think, How stupid! What about all the insects that the birds eat? But when Chairman Mao said we should kill the birds, we did it without question. He was always right. We, the people, followed him blindly, as we followed the emperor's instructions in the old days. Mao was our inspiration and our leader. We worshipped him as a god. The Chinese people were not allowed to belong to any religious group, so Mao became the focus of our spiritual needs. He wished it to be so, and it was. (*To the Edge of the Sky*, p. 65)

The second strategy of the Great Leap Forward was to exponentially increase iron and steel production across China. This involved the mass surrender of implements fashioned from these materials, including vast numbers of cooking items, and farming equipment. As a result, the Great Leap Forward precipitated one of the worst famines in China's history. As Gao bitterly observes, "The 'Great Leap Forward' catapulted China back at least twenty years" (*To the Edge of the Sky*, p. 67)

Like millions of other Chinese, Anhua Gao was intimidated into silence and acquiescence against her better judgement during the Cultural Revolution, as she watched countless friends, relatives and teachers denounced as counter-revolutionaries, and tortured. Although she relates her growing misgivings and disillusionment with Mao's China, she does not dare to speak critically in the open until much later. At one point, she notes:

> By this time I had lost all interest in taking part in the Cultural Revolution. All the people I loved and respected most were dead or in disgrace—my teachers, uncles, aunties, and friends. None, as far as I knew, had done anything against China, or the Communist Party, or Chairman Mao. (*To the Edge of the Sky*, p. 166)

"The Escape from Asia Tradition"   31

Meanwhile, Gao's troubles continued. She joined the army in an effort to escape deployment to the countryside, only to find herself denounced by her own sister as a bourgeois decadent and expelled. She was then banished to work as an assembly worker in the Nanjing Radio Factory, where she was diagnosed as suffering from Meniere's disease, a debilitating condition that plagued her for many years.

Like Adeline Yen Mah and Hong Ying, Gao's story is noticeably marked by gender oppression. Her marriage to a young family friend, Zhao Lin, proved disastrous, as he began to abuse her, and she suffered extreme emotional and physical abuse at his hands. Shortly after they had a child, Little Yan, Lin died in a freak accident, leaving Anhua a vulnerable penniless widow and single mother. Then came her harshest test. In 1985 Anhua was arrested and accused of being an "enemy agent and a foreign-paid spy" (p. 311), dragged away from her home by force and thrown into the Wawaqiao, a Communist prison, torture and interrogation centre. Gao was imprisoned for two months, with little idea of what crime she was accused of committing, before being released when the State Security Bureau failed to prove any charges against her. Despite this, Gao left prison to find her life in tatters: she had no job, no income, and a tarnished political record that meant that everyone, from former friends to family, shunned her. It was at this point that Gao decided to rebel, by speaking out against the injustices that she had endured in Mao's new China. Gao finally succeeded in exonerating herself, and finding work (the narrative thus concludes in a manner very reminiscent of Meihong Xu's *Daughter of China*). Anhua resolves to find a way to leave China, and she does this by corresponding with, and finally falling in love with, a British man. She marries him, and eventually, in 1994, moves to England to begin a new life, leaving the persecution so endemic in China behind:

> At two p.m. on 15 December 1994, I climbed the steps to board the Air China Boeing 747 bound for the United Kingdom, soon to be my second Motherland. I was flying to a land where there was no State Security Bureau, no 'unseen eyes' ever ready to betray the unwary, a land where I would no longer be frightened of political victimization or of what I might say, or even of what I might think. (*To the Edge of the Sky*, p. 398)

## HONG YING, DAUGHTER OF THE RIVER (1998)

In some ways, *Daughter of the River* is the most remarkable of these books that deal with twentieth-century Chinese history. Unlike all of the other texts discussed here, Hong Ying's memoir tells the story of a particularly disenfranchised young woman, and therefore adds a unique class dimension to this corpus of writing.[37] This is less a book written from the inside, than a book written from below. Whereas Jung Chang, Adeline

Yen Mah, Anhua Gao, Anchee Min, Nien Cheng and Meihong Xu occupied fairly comfortable positions in China's social hierarchy (in the case of Anchee Min as a Chinese film star, Adeline Yen Mah as the daughter of an affluent Shanghai family, and for Nien Cheng as the upper-class wife of an ambassador), Hong Ying was the daughter of peasants, and grew up in a slum on the Yangtze river, in Chongqing, in Sichuan province. Her perspective is thus of the underside of Chinese society, of a raw existence without food, income, and in unhygienic conditions. The very fact that Hong Ying has been able to write her memoir is in itself remarkable.

Unlike *Wild Swans* or *To the Edge of the Sky*, *Daughter of the River* does not have the epic sweep of a century's history; but only deals with the period of the 1980s. Thus it is one of the most contemporary texts in terms of its portrait of Chinese life. This is partly because of Ying's youthful age (she was born in 1962, at the height of the Cultural Revolution, and only embarks upon her story as she turns eighteen), and partly due to Ying's emphasis upon her own personal story, and that of her immediate family, rather than upon China's history in general. Her story also graphically illustrates the myriad ways in which the effects of the Cultural Revolution were felt by China's peasants for decades after its official end. Her perspective is likewise limited by her social circumstances. As a member of an uneducated peasant family, Hong Ying simply did not have an intellectualised, or even broad perspective on Mao's machinations and China's political and economic changes, except where they directly infringed upon the circumstances of her immediate community. When she does refer to an incident or a moment in China's history, or an action taken by Mao, it is invariably filtered through her community, and is often reported as unsubstantiated hearsay. Her narrative thus deals with the experience of ordinary, poor, Chinese people and the manner in which they were affected by the turbulent years of the Cultural Revolution and its aftermath.

Like most of the other narratives, this is a first-person account, but it is also one that is characterised by a remarkable intensity of feeling, and a sparse narrative style. Partly this is due to her adolescent perspective. But Hong Ying is also a poet, and this is very apparent in her striking prose style, which lends an almost surreal quality to the text. This sparseness is also underscored by the extreme, almost unbelievable poverty that Ying describes:

> The hills in South Bank teem with simple wooden thatched sheds made of asphalt felt and asbestos board. Rickety and darkened by weather, they have something sinister about them. When you enter the dark, misshapen courtyards off twisting little lanes, it is all but impossible to find your way back out; these are home to millions of people engaged in coolie labour. Along the meandering lines of South Bank there are hardly any sewers or garbage-collecting facilities, so the accumulated

filth spills out into roadside ditches and runs down the hills. (*Daughter of the River,* pp. 3–4)

In Hong Ying's words, the river and the lives that it supports take on a quasi-magical, if horrific, quality:

> The other side of the river is as different as night from day. The centre of the city might as well be in another world, with red flags everywhere you look and rousing political songs filling the air [ . . . ] South Bank [ . . . ] is the city's garbage dump, an unsalvageable slum; a curtain of mist above the river hides this dark corner, this rotting urban appendix, from sight. (*Daughter of the River,* p. 5)

Hong Ying lived with her family of five siblings and her parents in an unheated two-room slum by the river, where they shared a communal kitchen and yard with several other families. Washing took place in the river and sewage was poured into the street. Both of her parents worked as coolie laborers, on wages of just two *yuan* a day. It was this employment that prevented the family from starving during the great famine that swept across China in the late 1950s. Ying's mother's life was especially hard. She became the sole wage-earner after Ying's father was forced to retire on disability benefit, due to failing sight. She was fired from her job when she offended the head of her residents' committee and lost her work permit. With her job went her ability to contribute to the family income, and the Hong's life deteriorated as a result. She also suffered from poor health. Ying writes:

> Decades of coolie labour had left Mother with heart problems, anaemia that eventually developed into high blood pressure, rheumatism, a damaged hip, and aches and pains all over. It wasn't until I entered middle school that she managed to find different work: stoking a boiler in the shipyard. (*Daughter of the River,* p. 11)

Ying's own life was equally impoverished. She was born in the midst of the famine, and grew up rarely having enough to eat: "Hunger was my embryonic education. Mother and daughter survived the ordeal, but only after the spectre of hunger was indelibly stamped in my mind" (p. 41). Peasant hardship became a condition of her childhood existence. As she grew up, she spent long hours helping out with domestic chores, in addition to her schoolwork. During this period, Ying had a very problematic relationship with her mother, who often seemed angered by the young girl. This puzzled Ying, as it hinted at some forgotten crime, and part of the thrust of the narrative is Ying's attempt to discover what exactly causes the inexplicable guilt by which she feels constantly burdened. Eventually, Ying persuades her elder sister to tell her the story of their parents' life, and this is what forms the central section of the narrative. At the same time, Ying struggled to continue with her studies, and to prepare for the local college entrance examination, although this was against her mother's wishes (as well as beyond her parents' pocket). She is increasingly forced into subterfuge to maintain her learning, including surreptitiously borrowing books from her neighbour, Auntie Zhang, and eventually embarking upon a sexual relationship with her history tutor. This proved disastrous as Ying became pregnant and was forced to have an abortion without anaesthetic. It is this particular predicament that highlights Ying's trying and limited circumstances as a young, poor Chinese woman. Lacking either political connections or financial security, Ying is in an especially precarious position when she discovers her pregnancy, as she observes: "'Pre-marital pregnancy!' I'd learned in school, even as a little girl, that this was the most shameless [sic] sin of all, scarier than death itself [ . . . ] My life would be ruined, and all because of this child" (*Daughter of the River*, pp. 251–2).

Finally, towards the end of the narrative, Ying's mother reveals the reason why Ying has always felt unwelcome in the family: she was the illegitimate offspring of an affair Ying's mother had with a young visiting bookkeeper. Ying's mother wanted to have an abortion, but was prevented from doing so by Ying's father, who compassionately insisted that the sins of the parents should not affect the child, and thus, Ying was born, but grew up in the shadow of her mother's guilt and animosity, as well as the resentment of her siblings. She was not only vilified as the "daughter of a slut" (p. 208), but was also held responsible for the food shortage that the family endured during the famine. Disillusioned, Ying left home, and became an impoverished underground poet. Eventually, she was able to study at the Lu Xun Literature Academy for Writers in Beijing, and this marked Ying's moment of escape from the poverty and uncertainty of her childhood.

Hong Ying's story is thus primarily that of her own adolescence and her accompanying dawning sexual and emotional awareness, set against the backdrop of China in the 1980s. As such, it provides a uniquely personalised, as well as sensitive and lyrical, account of life in China at the end of the twentieth century. It forms a useful contemporary counterpart to the story of Adeline Yen Mah, which is equally individual, but focuses upon the period up to the 1980s (as well as from a different class perspective). Ying's story is also closely juxtaposed with that of her mother. The fate of both women was determined by their gender: in each case, a pregnancy outside of wedlock is shown to irrevocably alter the lives of both, in an intolerant China.

## CHILDHOOD PERSPECTIVES I: ADELINE YEN MAH, FALLING LEAVES: THE TRUE STORY OF AN UNWANTED CHINESE DAUGHTER (1997)

*Falling Leaves* has followed closely in the footsteps of *Wild Swans*. Like Chang's book, Mah's book has sold exceptionally well: the most recent figures are more than three hundred and fifty thousand copies in the UK alone. Adeline Yen Mah was actually encouraged to write *Falling Leaves* by her friend Jung Chang, the historian Jon Halliday (who also aided Jung Chang), and also by her agent Toby Eady (also Chang's agent, and agent to Hong Ying, and who married the Chinese expatriate author Xinran Xue in 2002).[38] Like many of the other writers discussed here, this was no easy feat, as Mah asserts in her author's note:

> This is a true story. Much of it was painful and difficult to write but I felt compelled to do so. I continue to have deep feelings towards many members of my family and harbour no wish to hurt anyone unnecessarily. I have therefore disguised the Christian names of all my living siblings, their spouses and their children. However, my parents' names are real, so are all the events described. (*Falling Leaves* n.p.)

Born 'Jun-ling' in the 1930s in Shanghai, Adeline Yen Mah did not write her memoir until the 1980s, when she was in her fifties. Her narrative is cyclical, starting with a family gathering in Hong Kong in 1988, on the occasion of Mah's father's death, before travelling back in time to the late nineteenth century. Like Jung Chang's story, Mah's is distinctive in its emphasis upon female experience, here predominantly that of Adeline herself, but also of her grand-aunt, grandmother, aunt, mother and stepmother. Therefore, like *Wild Swans* (and perhaps even more so), it offers a detailed account of the shifting social and political circumstances of Chinese women's lives throughout the twentieth century.[39] In fact, the narrative is defined by the presence of a series of strong female influences in Adeline's life, not all of them positive. Her stepmother, Jeanne (called 'Niang' by Adeline), in particular, is a vitriolic and pernicious influence upon Adeline, and in many ways, Jeanne's persecution of her step-daughter defines Adeline's traumatic story.

The narrative starts with the issue of foot-binding, a defining as well as ultimately debilitating experience for Chinese women at the turn of the twentieth century. Adeline's grand-aunt refused to have her feet bound and thus started her life as a relatively emancipated woman of her time. This experience also introduces the narrative's perennial oscillation between the themes of women's subordination and their rebellion. Adeline's grand-aunt learned to horse-ride, was educated, never married, and generally cut an imposing, striking and somewhat unusual figure. Adeline recalls:

> I remember Grand Aunt as a tall, imposing figure, treated with great esteem by every member of our family. Even Ye Ye and Father deferred to her every wish, which was remarkable in a society where women were disdained. Out of respect, we children were instructed to call her [ . . . ] "Gong Gong", which meant Great Uncle. It was common practice for high-achieving women within the clan to assume the male equivalent of their female titles. [ . . . ] Erect, dignified, her feet unbound, she had

a striking presence, in contrast to the obsequious demeanour befitting women of her time. (*Falling Leaves*, p. 8)

In 1924 Adeline's aunt founded her own bank in Shanghai, the Shanghai Women's Bank, which became a highly successful venture. Adeline's aunt was thus a powerful and influential female role model in the young girl's life, as something of a pioneer. As Adeline notes, "It is impossible to overestimate the scale of her achievement. In a feudal society where the very idea of a woman being capable of simple everyday decisions, let alone important business negotiations, was scoffed at, Grand Aunt's courage was extraordinary" (p. 9). These events occurred long before Mah's birth, and the narrative goes on to describe Mah's grandmother's marriage, her giving birth to seven children, the life of Mah's aunt Baba, the marriage of Adeline's parents, and her mother's death during childbirth. Of these events, Mah's grandmother's and mother's lives stand in stark contrast to the liberated existence enjoyed by Mah's Grand Aunt. Mah's grandmother, although not much younger than Grand Aunt, had bound feet, and this affected her ability to lead a normal life. Mah is careful to emphasise this for the reader:

> At the age of three, Grandmother's feet had been wrapped tightly with a long, narrow cloth bandage, forcing the four lateral toes under the soles so that only the big toe protruded. The bandage was tightened daily for a number of years, squeezing the toes painfully inwards and permanently arresting the foot's growth in order to achieve the tiny feet so prized by Chinese men. Women were in effect crippled and their inability to walk with ease was a symbol both of their subservience and of their family's wealth. Grandmother's feet caused her pain throughout her life. Later, she braved social ridicule rather than inflict this suffering on her own daughter. (*Falling Leaves*, p. 11)

Adeline's mother, Miss Ren, also had a troubled life. Although Adeline's parents were happy and had four children, Adeline's mother experienced tremendous difficulties in childbirth, and finally died after giving birth to Adeline. In its own way, this event was catastrophic for Adeline, as she was subsequently thought to carry bad luck by her family, and was virtually ostracised as a result. Like Hong Ying, she became an 'unwanted Chinese daughter'. After her father remarried, Adeline's life became a misery. Adeline's stepmother Jeanne had expensive tastes and a vindictive, spiteful nature. She re-named all of her step-children (Jun-ling became Adeline) and banished them below-stairs, blatantly favoring her own children; she belittled her husband's surviving relatives, and she established a quasi-dictatorship in her husband's house. Yet it was Adeline who was singled out for the harshest treatment. Eventually, in 1948, barely a teenager, Adeline was placed as a boarder in a convent named St. Joseph's, in Tianjin, many miles north of her home, where she was forbidden to communicate with the rest of her family. Finally rescued by her aunt, as all residents of Tianjin were fleeing from the Communists, Adeline was taken to Hong Kong to be briefly reunited with her family, before being re-enrolled in a convent in Hong Kong, and then in England. In a paradigmatic statement, Adeline ponders her possible fate with trepidation:

> Girls were a cheap commodity in China. Unwanted daughters were peddled as virtual slaves, sometimes by brokers, to unknown families. Once sold, a child's destiny was at the whim of her buyer. She had no papers and no rights. A few lucky ones became legally adopted by their owners. Many more were subjected to beatings and other abuses. Prostitution or even death were the fate of some child slaves. [ . . . ] I did not know what Niang's intentions were but my future was in her hands. (*Falling Leaves*, p. 100)

Adeline eventually transcends her family's treatment, and becomes a successful doctor, married to a Chinese American, with a son, and based in New York City. Her siblings likewise find a semblance of happiness away from Niang and her machinations. Yet Niang continued to influence and harass her step-children, culminating in her manouevres to disinherit them following Adeline's father's death in 1988.

Throughout the narrative, Mah intersperses her own tragic story with the turbulent events shaping China at the time. In a curious manner, the personal incidents affecting Adeline at particular moments seem to be reflected in the wider political and social changes occurring in China simultaneouly. When Adeline is sent away to school, the family rupture that this engenders is mirrored in the political turmoil of the Communist victory over the Kuomintang, and the end of Japanese occupation. Similarly, at the moment in 1976 when Mao Zedong dies, and Deng Xiaoping begins to reform China, China becomes accessible to Adeline again, not just as a tourist, but members of her family welcome her home as well. Finally, too, it is suggested that Niang's death in 1990 was hastened by the impending return of Hong Kong to Chinese control, symbolising Adeline's release from a lifetime of repressive familial as well as political influence upon her. Unlike several other memoirs, though, Adeline's story does not become the subplot to China's history; instead, events in China are related as a backdrop to the more heart-rending tale of the child Adeline's abuse at the hands of her stepmother. In 1999, Adeline Yen Mah recrafted her story in *Falling Leaves* into a narrative for children. *Chinese Cinderella* relates the same events as in *Falling Leaves*, but here she explicitly addresses a juvenile readership, and she even more resolutely subordinates Chinese history to her own story (she provides an appendix outlining a chronology of Chinese history). In her study of Asian North American autobiographies of childhood, *Begin Here*, Rocío Davis observes that the decision to rewrite the narrative for a youth readership attests to the socially significant role that such memoirs play in educating the Western reader:

These literary decisions were, I believe, enacted precisely because of the authors' consciousness of the effective cultural work that children's texts execute. [ . . . ] Precisely because these texts were successful among adult audiences and became part of the network of cultural narratives that aided the creation of a historically and socially conscious readership, the imperative to offer these narratives to young readers existed. (*Begin Here*, p.158)

Other texts are exclusively written for a juvenile readership. Notable amongst these is Ange Zhang's 2004 pictorial memoir, *Red Land, Yellow River*. As with the transracial adoption stories for children, discussed elsewhere in this book, Zhang has made a significant effort to package what is unavoidably a distressing story in a manner apposite to an immature consciousness. Unlike *Wild Swans* where the pictures serve to underscore the suffering described between the pages, Ange Zhang's elegant illustrations dilute the traumatic impact of his story, whilst undoubtedly also enriching the book. Chun Yu's poetic reminiscences in *Little Green* (2005) are another case in point, in which the lyrical poems recited in the voice of a young girl are strikingly and disjunctively at odds with the horrific events that are remembered. As Maxine Hong Kingston said of the book, "*Little Green* is a miracle—such beauty emerging from the chaos of the Cultural Revolution. A clear-eyed child is born into a surrealistic China, and tells her story." (jacket blurb)

## CHILDHOOD PERSPECTIVES II: RAE YANG'S SPIDER EATERS, MOYING LI'S SNOW FALLING IN SPRING, NANCHU'S RED SORROW AND JI-LI JIANG'S RED SCARF GIRL

> Childhood accounts, importantly, offer the reading public access to versions of the history of Asian countries that correspond to private stories, unofficial records, microhistories. We cannot underestimate the discursive potential of these texts.
> 
> —Rocío G. Davis

The device of the 'clear-eyed child' appears elsewhere too. Ben Xu writes of Anchee Min that she "is a Cultural Revolution child without childhood" ("A Face that Grows into a Mask", p. 3). Some Cultural Revolution memoirs recall the experiences of children only in order to figure that childhood as abruptly halted. Rae Yang's *Spider Eaters*, Moying Li's *Snow Falling in Spring: Coming of Age in China During the Cultural Revolution*, Nanchu's *Red Sorrow* and Ji-Li Jiang's *Red Scarf Girl* are four such cases. Moying Li writes:

> Most people cannot remember when their childhood ended. I, on the other hand, have a crystal-clear memory of that moment. It happened

one night in the summer of 1966, when my elementary school headmaster hanged himself. (*Snow Falling in Spring*, jacket blurb)

Li was twelve years old. In her memoir of a Cultural Revolution childhood—with its telling subtitle "Coming of Age in China During the Cultural Revolution"—Li stresses the personal impact that living through such a period of turmoil had upon her: "Thirty years have passed since the end of the Cultural Revolution, but that dramatic time, and the many historical events leading up to it, still feel so close, so personal" (*Snow Falling in Spring*, p. xi). A common textual strategy in the telling of children's stories during periods of upheaval is the emphasis upon the child's sense that they are a lone figure of calm, rationality or sense in a world that seems to have become chaotic and beyond comprehension. Time and again, these narratives stress this. In his memoir *Blood Red Sunset* (1994), Ma Bo asks:

> What sort of age were we living in, when all loyalties were abolished except devotion to one man? Constantly encouraged to turn against our own, we were caught up in a frenzy of betrayal. Not even our own parents were to be trusted. (*Blood Red Sunset*, p. 131)

Likewise, Moying Li recalls that

> All of life's principles so carefully instilled in me by my parents and reinforced by school and society seemed to have been suddenly turned upside down. Friends became enemies, love turned into hatred. Heaven and hell seemed to have switched places. Now I felt confused, vulnerable, and deeply saddened. (*Snow Falling in Spring*, pp. 74–5)

As she later evaluates: "The Cultural Revolution, allegedly initiated to break the old order, had shattered *all* order on its long march" (p. 142). The child's individual, often problematic, always conflicted, maturation, is figured against the backdrop of national history. Here Moying Li describes the end of the Cultural Revolution in 1976:

> The year 1976 began and ended like a long, tragic saga, when the historical curtain finally shut, it closed on the lives of the most dramatic players on the stage of twentieth-century China–Chairman Mao Zedong, Premier Zhou Enlai, and Marshall Zhu De. For almost a century, these powerful figures had dominated the Chinese scene, changing the country's history forever. This fateful year stayed in my memory as a series of shock waves. By the end of it, I felt as if I had lived through several lifetimes packed with unexpected events—all of them earthshaking, and all of them very sad. (*Snow Falling in Spring*, p. 140)

The perspective of the child in Cultural Revolution history is both unique and potent. Traumatic historical or life stories always carry additional poignancy when told (and experienced) by a child. As John Hodgson observes:

> The twentieth century has witnessed the publication of a number of significant accounts of childhood moulded by oppressive totalitarian political regimes [ . . . ] Such accounts tell us much about the workings of the regimes and the effects of prejudice upon life chances. In this respect they should be accepted as significant historical documents. They also suggest ways in which revolutionary consciousness is developed. (*The Search for the Self: Childhood in Autobiography and Fiction since 1940*, p. 87)

The particularly unique position of children as actors within the history of the Cultural Revolution is also a noteworthy factor. When Mao decided to escalate the revolution in 1966, it was to China's children he turned. The Red Guard comprised zealous youths across China, and it was this force that Mao unleashed. In *Mao and China: A Legacy of Turmoil*, Stanley Karnow calls the Red Guards' mobilization "The Children's Revolt", in a designation reminiscent of the children's role in *The Lord of the Flies*. Much revisionist history of the Cultural Revolution period has sought to explain the particular and peculiar consequences and dynamics of placing the Red Guard—as children an inexperienced and unstable group at best—at the vanguard of the Cultural Revolution, including close scrutiny of Red Guard testimonies.[40] The Cultural Revolution memoirs discussed here, whether penned by former Red Guards or not, also consider this question. They attempt to reproduce the child's fresh vantage point as she encounters the complexities of the adult world, one that in mid-to-late-twentieth century China was itself in chaos. Again, the version we receive as readers is therefore from below, as the adult memoirist attempts to recall her sense of revolutionary turmoil as she experienced it as a child. In so doing, of course, the child's viewpoint both unwittingly and knowingly comments, often critically or ironically, upon the adult context of those memories (such as questioning the prevailing ideological assumptions of the time). There is no doubt, too, that these experiences are both formative (we might recall Wordsworth's statement that the child is the father of the man) and deformative. Time and again, these authors refer longingly to the potentially recuperative power of recollection and storytelling. Take, for example, Nanchu's memoir *Red Sorrow* (2001). As its title suggests, this is a burdensome memoir of Nanchu's childhood suffering during the Cultural Revolution. In her acknowledgements she paradigmatically says this:

> I started writing this book in August 1998. Memories, like a turbulent torrent, raged out of my heart and flew down vigorously on the page.

Often my face was bathed in tears. But I dared not slow down. Our past cannot be forgotten; those who do forget must relive it. This mission has already been long delayed. [ . . . ] With its publication, I, as a living witness, victim, participant, and survivor of the immense human tragedy, can relieve some of the burden that has long weighed down on me. (*Red Sorrow*, np.)

One of the most startling aspects of Nanchu's memoir is its stark portrait of the cruelty of children, especially child-to-child persecution. Nanchu's childhood suffering occurs in tandem with the Red Guards' persecution of other children—she repeatedly tells us that "As the Revolution continued, the children intensified their abuse" (*Red Sorrow*, p. 35), and that "Although I was only thirteen in 1966, I felt I had to participate in the great revolution" (*Red Sorrow*, p. 43). Like so many other memoirists, she also recognizes the perilously reckless behaviour of the Red Guards:

Like unbridled horses running wild on the vast plain, like the swift torrents rushing down a mountain, we in our youthful vigor and feverish adulation of Mao had gotten out of control. (*Red Sorrow*, p. 56)

She acts with equally remarkable viciousness towards her own parents, condemning their politics and disowning them. She recalls that her father "wondered aloud how the interrogations had come to the dinner table in his own home and why the interrogator was his little girl" (*Red Sorrow*, p. 25), and his careful warning to her "don't let yourself be used by others as a gun to shoot me" (*Red Sorrow*, p. 28).

Like *Red Sorrow*, Ji-Li Jiang's *Red Scarf Girl* focuses upon the period of Ji-Li's adolescence, which coincided with the advent of the Cultural Revolution (she was twelve in 1966). Her optimistic youth as a Young Pioneer adorned with the emblematic red scarf of the memoir's title dissolves into disillusionment and tragedy as Ji-Li finds herself denounced as rightist by dint of her father's former class status as a landlord, a 'black' category. Along the way, she witnesses relatives commit suicide, her father incarcerated as a political prisoner, and she is personally pressured to denounce her family by local party cadres. Her adolescent narrative eventually terminates abruptly, along with the remnants of her childhood innocence, with the illness of her mother. Ji-Li Jiang is fourteen. Like Nanchu, in her epilogue, the adult Ji-Li Jiang evaluates her childhood suffering and expresses her hope for the healing power of her writing:

Thirty years have passed since I was the little girl with the red scarf who believed she would always succeed at everything. I grew up and moved to the United States, but still, whatever I did, wherever I went, vivid memories of my childhood kept coming back to me. After thinking so much about that time, I wanted to do something for the little girl

I had been, and for all the children who lost their childhoods as I did. This book is the result. (*Red Scarf Girl*, p. 266)

If the personal and political imperatives to write coincide across the genre, then it is also the case that structurally, these childhood memoirs are all very similar. The reconstructed childhood or adolescence (which always coincides with the period of the Cultural Revolution) is buttressed by a preface that establishes the terms and tones of reading, and a reflective epilogue—like Ji-Li Jiang's above—that mourns lost youth, expresses regret on both personal and national scales, and establishes a degree of rehabilitation in the author's outlook. Here is Rae Yang's:

> As for the memory of the Cultural Revolution, the dreams and nightmares, I carry them too. I don't think I will ever forget them as long as I live. I don't think I should forget them either, despite the pain and shame they constantly cause me. [ . . . ] And I believe that as a human being, Chinese or American, I have responsibilities beyond ones to make a living for my son and myself. Part of these is to make the lessons we learned with such tremendous sacrifice known and remembered by people in the world, including the younger generation in China. (*Spider Eaters*, pp. 284–5)

There is often also an effort to distinguish between the youthful and adult voices of the memoir. For instance, in *Spider Eaters*, Rae Yang oscillates between an italicized voice and plain text: "In this book the italicized parts are meant to show what I thought and how I felt when the events were unfolding, in contrast with my understanding of such events afterwards" (*Spider Eaters*, p. xi).

The enduring popularity of such juvenile accounts can also be seen in some recent, translated texts. Xinran Xue's smash hit *The Good Women of China: Hidden Voices* (2003) is probably the best known. Based upon her Chinese radio programme, "Words on the Night Breeze" that aired throughout the 1980s, Xinran's book combined personal memoir with the testimonies of myriad women, including young girls, who struggled with personal issues alongside and against the difficulties of speaking in a politically restrictive environment. The success of her book is such that she now writes a column about her experiences for *The Guardian* newspaper, which was recently collated and published as *What the Chinese Don't Eat* (2006). As this book went to press, Xinran's forthcoming book was also advertised. *China Witness: Voices from a Silent Generation* will be a collection of oral histories of twentieth-century China from many different Chinese perspectives. *The Diary of Ma Yan: The Life of a Chinese Schoolgirl* (2002), is a heart-rending and intimate document of the harsh life of China's contemporary rural poor, penned by a thirteen-year-old girl with a yearning to learn and a determination to succeed. What is striking about

Ma Yan's story is that like Hong Ying's memoir, *Daughter of the River*, and like the stories told by Xinran, life is not so very different from the portraits of childhood under Mao.[41]

## REMEMBERING THE 'OTHER': AGENCY AND RESPONSIBILITY

If nation states are underwritten by history, then they can also by undermined by it. In 'writing Red China', the women discussed in this chapter, from Eileen Chang to Anhua Gao, are inserting a range of expatriate female voices into the cultural discourse revisiting China's twentieth-century history. At the same time, although it may be strategically and politically productive to foreground female history, and thus to gain access to previously obscured or suppressed perspectives, it is important that readers recognise the differences between these representations of Chinese women. It remains to be seen whether the mounting popular interest in Asia that I have charted, contributes to the efforts of Asian Americanists and other parties in furthering a multicultural agenda, and increasing inter-ethnic and inter-cultural awareness and understanding.

# 3 Contemporary Transracial Adoption Narratives
## Prospects and Perspectives

> As reflected in child abandonment, the price of birth planning in China has indeed been high in recent years.
> —Kay Johnson

> China's birth control program has earned a worldwide reputation as the most draconian since King Herod's slaughter of the innocents.
> —John S. Aird

> [T]his is a new ethnic family form . . . it is a story about the making of individual families through international adoption, of the building of cultural bridges between the United States and the People's Republic of China, and of the need to change public attitudes so that persons of Chinese ancestry are recognized as full Americans. [These are] families whose personal biographies intersect with social history.
> —Richard Tessler, Gail Gamache and Liming Liu

> [T]heir presence in domestic America demands a reckoning with liminality, especially at the busy intersections where internal relations of race and capital meet trans-Pacific practices of exchange.
> —Sara K. Dorow, *Transnational Adoption: A Cultural Economy of Race, Gender and Kinship* (p. 8)

This chapter explores the connected phenomena of the increase in international, transracial adoption in the 1990s and beyond, and the proliferation of US narratives addressing the experience of transracial adoption and associated issues. I argue that adoption in China in particular is an especially gendered phenomenon, since it is a direct consequence of China's one-child population policy, which has led to an epidemic of abandonment of female babies in China. This in turn has created a gender-specific group of adoptees in the United States, who are confronted with a unique and unprecedented range of cross-cultural, but gender-specific concerns and hurdles. Ultimately, I suggest, the increase in transracial adoption and the appearance of a genre of transracial adoption narratives represents a new perspective upon transglobal relations, and the meeting and connecting of cultures.

The practice of adopting children from overseas is increasingly a burgeoning one in the United States, and especially since the 1980s. Between 1985 and 2003 there were 40,496 adoptions of children from China into the United States. In 1997 alone, 13,620 children were adopted internationally by US families; of these, 3,318 were from China. By 2003, this figure had reached 6,859 adoptions from China (these figures are taken from the Families With Children From China website and the US State Department statistics on inter-country adoptions; see the Works Cited).[1] In the wake of this increasing phenomenon, life and fictional narratives addressing the complexities and emotional turbulence of the process of transracial, international adoption have started to appear with increasing frequency. It is clear from reading these accounts that several cross-cultural issues are at stake. Since the majority of parents who adopt across racial lines are white, concerns about differences between white perceptions of the world and the experiences and world views of children of color become particularly acute. Amongst others, issues of identity are thrown into especially sharp focus: visible differences in appearance between adoptees and their parents; the question of how to cope with racial stereotyping and racial slur; the chasm between an Anglo-American family heritage and an alternative ethnic ancestral heritage and cultural background. Together, these narratives document a unique perspective upon transglobal relations, and the meeting and connecting of cultures. As Karin Evans, author of the memoir *The Lost Daughters of China*, and an adopting mother, observes: "It's a phenomenon that spans the gaps of distance, culture, race, language, economics, and heritage. It is a tale of twentieth-century cultures mixing with each other in an unprecedented way" (*The Lost Daughters of China*, p. 3).

The phenomenon of Chinese-American adoption in particular has an additional dimension. The story of Chinese adoption to US parents is also a tale of gender woe, as almost all Chinese children adopted by overseas parents are abandoned little girls. Ninety per cent of the children in China's orphanages are female (the rest are mainly disabled children). This is not mere coincidence, but the tragic consequence of China's one-child policy, which has been in operation since the late 1970s, in combination with China's traditional cultural preference for male offspring. As adoption expert, sociologist, and adopting mother Kay Johnson puts it:

> girls occupy a structurally marginal place in a patrilineal kinship and family system that puts them at far greater risk than boys of being abandoned. Conversely, the central importance and cultural value placed on the role of sons in family and kinship makes it highly unlikely that a

boy would be abandoned except under dire circumstances. ("The Politics of the Revival of Infant Abandonment in China" p. 79)

Jing-Bao Nie also reminds us that "giving birth to a boy is not merely culturally preferred in China for the sake of the family bloodline, but in the countryside a son is essential for the well-being of the aged because of the lack of basic social security".[2] Chinese women are not even allowed to give birth without the all-important *shengyu zheng* document, which officially permits a woman to give birth. Without this, a woman could be forced to submit to a termination, (which have even occurred at full-term), and subsequently to a sterilisation or the enforced use of an IUD (this is known as *jihua shengyu*, or the planned birth policy). It is well-documented that excess force has sometimes been used in the implementation of these policies by population officials and cadres. Jing-Bao Nie writes that "Since the 1980s thousands upon thousands of Chinese women have been pressured and coerced to terminate their pregnancies in accordance with national population policies" (*Behind the Silence*, p.189), and his book *Behind the Silence* records myriad such testimonies. A 1995 report by the group Human Rights in China, "Unfair Burdens: The Impact of the Population Control Policies on the Human Rights of Women and Girls" found for instance that "Persons acting in an official capacity[ . . . ]took away and detained women for abortion, sterilization or IUD insertion; beat up those who resisted; confiscated property and demolished houses."[3] Tessler, Gamache and Liu note:

> The agents of the one-child policy go far beyond propaganda: the policy is linked to techniques of campaign mobilization at every level of organizational structure in which citizens of China are involved. Women are empowered through women's associations to monitor other women's menstruation cycles, pregnancies and birth control usage, and to administer rewards and incentives. Intense social pressure is used to persuade women to abort unscheduled pregnancies. Intense persuasion often turns to coercion when cadres get carried away with their missions. (*West Meets East*, p. 86)

Testimonial evidence by both ex-population officials and violated women confirms this. One population official confessed:

> we go out at night[ . . . ]we take the woman away[ . . . ]she is sent[ . . . ] to get sterilized in the middle of the night by half-asleep nurses and doctors. The woman usually screams and kicks, and our men hold her down for anesthesia. (HRIC 1995 report, no page number)

An account by a Chinese gynaecologist, who worked in Beijing between 1983 and 1993, tells a similar story:

> Women who are seven, eight, or nine months pregnant with their second or third baby are taken to the hospital by regional population control officials for induced abortion[ . . . ]her baby should not be let out alive. (ibid., no page number)

One woman from Xi'an, who was forced to submit to a termination at eight and a half months, described her experience:

> I was held down[ . . . ]One doctor injected through my belly formaldehyde liquid[ . . . ]I knew my child was to die in a few minutes[ . . . ]48 hours later, after being induced into labour, in front of a room full of people, I gave birth to a lively boy[ . . . ]the doctors immediately killed him. (ibid., no page number)

Although these quite graphic accounts offer anecdotal and even slightly sensationalized testimonial to the existence of these practices during the period from 1995 onwards, more recent socio-historical research on China's population policies does continue to support this evidence.[4] For instance, sociologist Kay Johnson's chapter, "Chinese Orphanages Today, 2003" in her expansive 2004 study *Wanting a Daughter, Needing a Son: Abandonment, Adoption, and Orphanage Care in China*, notes that although "in recent years there have been some indications of change. The style and method of implementing the one-child policy [is] becoming less punitive" (*Wanting a Daughter*, p. 206) and that "fines and threats of sterilization have been replaced in some areas with fees" (ibid), nevertheless

> the continuing practice in many areas of sterilization after two children, or after the first overquota child, means that if a couple gets caught too soon after the birth of a second or third girl, they may lose forever the chance to try again for a son (ibid)[5]

and that furthermore "intense monitoring of all fertile women, accompanied by severe penalties for failure to comply, increased in many rural areas at the end of the 1990s and 2000" (*Wanting a Daughter*, p. 207).

Despite the apparent success of the one-child policy—Nie asserts that "the population growth rate in China has been reduced to below 2% within two decades" (*Behind the Silence*, p. 200)—the extremely late-term enforced abortions described above, effectively amount to state-sanctioned infanticide. It is also well-documented that families in China sometimes commit female infanticide at birth in order to avoid detection after having an unplanned baby girl (although exact numbers are obviously unknown). This policy has led to startling statistics: as many as 1.7 million female babies go "missing" every year (*The Lost Daughters of China*, p. 118).[6] This figure was thrown into stark relief when a census in China in November 2000 revealed an alarmingly skewed gender ratio: that there were

116 boys for every 100 girls in China today, compared with a biologically normal ratio of 105:100 ("Lost Babies, Found Babies", p. 25).[7] Jing-Bao Nie writes that "it is inconceivable to deny any connection between female infanticide and family planning policies [ . . . ] the continuation of female infanticide as well as the severely unbalanced birth ratio were never intended by policy makers. But any social policy has the potential to yield unintended negative consequences as well as intended benefits" (*The Lost Daughters of China*, p. 50).

The abandonment of female babies, of course, is also only one example in a long list of codified gender violence and discrimination against Chinese women, which also includes the historical practice of footbinding, and the trade in female slaves, as Human Rights Watch and other observers have made clear (see *www.hrw.org*).[8] Jing-Bao Nie ironically comments that it is no "surprise that a deep feeling of powerlessness prevails in Chinese women" (*Behind the Silence*, p. 161). The forsaking of female babies has been called an "epidemic of abandonment" by Human Rights Watch/Asia, despite the fact that "forsaking" baby girls is illegal in China, as it is specifically forbidden by the 1992 Law on the Protection of Women's Rights and Interests.[9] As the group Human Rights in China observes: "the pursuit of demographic goals have overridden the needs and interests of women and girls, and have led to the use of physical violence and other coercive measures."[10] In recent years, the implementation of the one-child policy and its consequences for women's individual human rights has attracted increasing international attention, not just by human rights groups and non-governmental organizations, but by governments as well. For instance, Jing-Bao Nie writes:

> In 1995 and 1998, two hearings on forced abortion and coercive population control in China were held before the Subcommittee on International Relations and Human Rights of the Committee on International Relations in the U.S. House of Representatives. A resolution by the subcommittee condemned forced abortion as a crime against humanity[ . . . ] "a double insult to humanity". (*Behind the Silence*, p. 15)

More recently, the American press has published in-depth reports of the issue, such as those that appeared in *The Washington Post* and *Time* magazine at the time of the Chinese President Hu Jintao's visit to the United States, where he addressed the United Nations, in 2005.[11] Hu Jintao subsequently faced human rights protests during this visit, and at the time, it was widely reported that this would force President George W. Bush to put the "right to life" issue on his agenda when he visited China in November 2005.[12] However, China has vehemently rejected such criticisms, suggesting as Nie puts it, that such Western critics as the United States are "imposing their own values on China" (p. 39), and China's sensitivity to international discussion of the issue has not diminished. Individual Chinese perspectives also support this view: Nie cites one doctor remarking that "I do not think that abortion in China should be debated in the American way, that is, dominated by the language of human rights" (*Behind the Silence*, p. 237). In his provocative and controversial study, *Slaughter of the Innocents: Coercive Birth Control in China* (1990), John S. Aird goes further. A former senior research specialist on China for the U.S. Bureau for the Census, Aird is well placed to discuss the issue, one which he condemns without reservation, noting that although "the published record [on coercion] is fragmentary, sometimes contradictory, and not very accessible except to China scholars", ... "From the founding of the People's Republic of China (PRC) in October, 1949, its leaders have seldom allowed human rights to stand in the way of their policies and programs".[13] Aird also points out that the violations of human rights are a systematic violation first and foremost of women's rights: birth mothers and baby daughters. The history of these female children is also crucially one that has been obscured, both by active official Chinese government suppression of the reality of the abandonment situation, and by a more general cultural reluctance in China to acknowledge a problem that is seen as shameful. Official statistics relating to the numbers of abandoned babies are extremely difficult to obtain and any that are released are widely regarded to be very conservative estimates. Consequently, narratives that describe the experience of adopting from China take on an added significance, as they provide an important, if necessarily mediated, perspective upon a story of gender persecution hitherto untold.[14]

This chapter seeks to explore specifically the dynamics of transracial adoption in relation to the emerging genre of transracial adoption narratives, and in so doing, to make several claims: that issues of identity are negotiated by adoptive mothers in interesting and self-reflexive ways within these narratives; that the crossing of racial lines that occurs with frequency in the process of transracial, international adoption documents a unique instance of intercultural interaction; that the phenomenon of Chinese-American adoption is specifically gendered; that this is a story that has been obscured; and that these narratives partly redress this suppression. I will look at a series of texts published during the period 1997–2005. These include two memoirs by adoptive mothers, Karin Evans' *The Lost Daughters of China* (2000), Emily Prager's *Wuhu Diary* (2001), and also extracts from Amy Klatzin's edited collection, *A Passage to the Heart: Writings from Families with Children from China* (1999); six children's memoirs/stories: Ying Ying Fry's *Kids Like Me in China* (2001), Carol Antoinette Peacock's *Mommy Far, Mommy Near* (2000), Sara Dorow's *When You Were Born in China* (1997), Jean McLeod's *At Home in this World: A China Adoption Story* (2003), Jacqueline Kolosov's *Grace from China* and Rose Lewis' *I Love You Like Crazy Cakes* (2000); and an adoption guide manual for adopting parents, *Inside Transracial Adoption*, by Gail Steinberg and Beth Hall (2000).[15]

Three quite different perspectives prevail in this literature, from narratives written by adoptive parents for adoptive parents, by parents for children (adoptees) and by children (adoptees) for children (adoptees). In the final category, of narratives written by, as well as for, children, there is only one, and as the sole example of a child's voice this is the only narrative that can be said to truly express the perspective and experience of a child adoptee's negotiation of identity.[16] As I later discuss, the exploration of identity in this lone narrative is quite unique, and has radically different implications for reading and interpreting this body of work, from the parent-authored books that attempt to negotiate their child's identity. In fact, to a certain degree, whilst these parent-authored narratives purport to stake out and resolve identity issues and problems faced by the child adoptee, it is actually *parental* identity that is being negotiated to a large degree through these efforts. Thus, parent-authored books actually tell us as much about the identity problems of being an adopted mother in a transracial adoption, and of living in a race-conscious (and racist) society that privileges biological mothering over adoptive mothering.[17]

## PARENTAL VOICES

> it is important to note the impossible contradictions of narrating adoption to the satisfaction of all whom it affects. As not only a transnational political economy but also a very personal experience, it invites intense debate.
> —Sara Dorow, *Transnational Adoption: A Cultural Economy of Race, Gender and Kinship* (p. 28)

### Adult Adoption Memoirs: The Lost Daughters of China and Wuhu Diary

In a sense, Karin Evans' and Emily Prager's narrative memoirs complement each other, since Evans' memoir focuses upon the period leading up to her daughter's adoption and the experience itself, and *Wuhu Diary* deals more thoroughly with the post-adoption period of adjustment undergone by both mother and adopted daughter. It is also worth noting that both these adult memoirs are authored by women who become adoptive mothers; in fact the fathers—and the perspective of the fathers—are noticeably absent from the whole genre, as they neither author a single text, nor appear with any significance in any of the narrative accounts explored here.

*Wuhu Diary* describes Emily Prager's journey to China with her five-year-old adopted daughter LuLu, when they went back to Wuhu City in Anhui Province, on the Yangtze in eastern China, where LuLu had been found abandoned as an infant. The primary impetus for this visit was to enable LuLu to make some sort of connection with her ancestral country and culture, and also to see the places where she was found and cared for, as part of the child's on-going project to reconcile herself with her traumatic early history of separation. The narrative describes this journey, as well as the obstacles encountered by Prager. These include the diplomatic crisis that followed NATO's inadvertent bombing of the Chinese embassy in Belgrade, which not only created an atmosphere of hostility and tension towards visitors like Prager and her daughter, but also ultimately sabotaged any chance that the two may have had to see inside LuLu's orphanage, or to meet her first caretakers. Nevertheless, the trip proved cathartic for both mother and daughter, as Prager charts in detail. Both learned to re-negotiate the relationship that they had with each other, as well as with China and the imagined birth parents, as this extract shows:

> It was as if a big black ball of confusion had been pushed out of LuLu's head. She came back from China[ . . . ]having reclaimed, I think, some essential part of herself . . . One night last month[ . . . ]she had a momentary resurfacing of longing for her Chinese mother, the first in two years, and we wept together again. But there is a location for this grief now, and it now longer sweeps over her being, an incomprehensible maelstrom that threatens her very identity and her attachments. (*Wuhu Diary*, p. 236)

*Wuhu Diary* is narrated in the form of a retrospective episodic diary of events that took place on the Pragers' trip in April, May and June, 1999. Through the memories of both mother and daughter, we travel back to learn about the time between LuLu's adoption in 1994 and the present day of the narrative. This lends an emotional immediacy to the narrative, that is not so prevalent in Karin Evans' *The Lost Daughters of China*. Evans' narrative oscillates between relating the story of her own adoption of a baby girl named Kelly Xiao Yu in October, 1997, in the Pearl River Delta in southern China, and a wider study of the socio-political circumstances in China that have given rise to the Chinese→American transracial adoption phenomenon. As such, chapters deal with all aspects of the adoption procedure and China's population policy, and bear titles such as "The One-Child, Maybe-One-More Policy" and "Through the Chinese Looking Glass," as well as "From China with Love" and "East-West Lives." By way of this dual focus, Evans manages to provide a thorough contextual exploration of both China's devastating population policy and its far-reaching effects across cultural and geographical boundaries. The difference between the narratives can be summed up by their authors' respective stated reasons for writing. Karin Evans muses:

> Someday, I knew, I would need to tell my daughter what I could about life in China in the time she was born. I had a duty to understand what I'd been part of, but I approached the subject cautiously, aware that I

> was no China scholar, nor even a neutral observer. [ . . . ] I wanted to know what had happened in the lives of the mothers in that country that had led them to such desperate acts. What cultural, political, and social forces had made China a uniquely difficult place for this generation of female infants? This book began as an inquiry into those questions, an exploration of this particular intersection between American and Chinese history. (*The Lost Daughters of China*, p. 5)

Prager is less explicit about her reasons for writing, although she does say this:

> At different times over the last six years[ . . . ]I have asked myself in utter exasperation: "Why are you doing this? Is this really necessary? Couldn't you just raise her as a total American, playing down the birth parents, and have done with it?" [ . . . ] to my surprise, I already [know] the answers to those questions. (*Wuhu Diary*, p. 237)

Thus, whereas Evans writes predominantly about her *own* journey of education and discovery, Prager ostensibly writes mainly of her *daughter's*, albeit by proxy. In this sense, Prager's memoir is closer to the anthology of short narratives by adopting parents edited by Amy Klatzin, entitled *A Passage to the Heart*.

## A PARENT'S GUIDE BOOK: A PASSAGE TO THE HEART

This multi-genre collection comprises a variety of different kinds of personal writing emerging out of the local US chapters of the Families with Children from China organization (FCC), and is arranged so that it tracks the adoption process from beginning to end, with additional sections dealing with associated pertinent issues such as returning to China, race, culture, language and identity.[18] Many of the articles are of the "how to" type, in so far as they offer practical advice and guidance for prospective adoptive parents. Many, though, also offer more personalized accounts of individual experience, along the lines of the longer narratives by Evans and Prager. Not all are prose accounts: the collection also comprises poems, fictional letters to imaginary children, and diaries written by siblings. Like Evans' text, many of these narratives express the desire to learn more about the adopted child's past, not simply as a matter of curiosity, but as an essential element in building the child's self-esteem. As Katherine Cobb puts it in her piece, "Emily's Life Did Not Begin When She Joined Our Family":

> we knew there would be limits to what we could learn about our daughter's early life, but we wanted to try to find out as much as possible. We viewed the requirement that we travel to Emily's birthplace

as a wonderful opportunity to learn about the country where she was born. [ . . . ] We knew how much our older daughter, now eight, loves to hear stories about her own birth and early infancy, and we wanted to be able to have stories to share with Emily about her life before we adopted her. (*A Passage to the Heart*, p. 38)

Many of the authors in the collection observe that the importance of discovering as much as possible of the adopted baby's history is that they move to a new life, new family and new country with nothing, only that, as Laura Cowan observes of her daughter, "Emily's story belongs to her" (*A Passage to the Heart*, p. 95). This is a responsibility that all the adoptive parents writing about their experiences seem to recognise. As Jane Brown, in "The Importance of Cultural Education," writes:

Our children will, as they grow to adolescence and then to adulthood, need to explain first to *themselves* and then to their peers and to strangers who they are and how they came to be who they are. If their adoptive parents are not Chinese, they will need to understand, accept, and explain their racial identity. They will need to explain why they are not growing up with the parents they were born to. They will need to explain why they could not grow up in China. They will need to feel pride in the land of their birth and in their personal history in order to feel pride in themselves and to give these explanations to others. Thus, teaching them about their cultural origins is a very, very important parenting task. (Klatzin 1999, p. 239)

## BOOKS FOR CHILDREN: I LOVE YOU LIKE CRAZY CAKES, MOMMY FAR, MOMMY NEAR AND WHEN YOU WERE BORN IN CHINA

This parenting task is one that the six books authored for a child readership are attempting to fulfil. The six children's texts: Ying Ying Fry's *Kids Like Me in China* (2001, discussed in the next section), Carol Antoinette Peacock's *Mommy Far, Mommy Near* (2000), Sara Dorow's *When You Were Born in China* (1997), Jean McLeod's *At Home in this World: A China Adoption Story* (2003), Jacqueline Kolosov's *Grace from China* (2004) and Rose Lewis' *I Love You Like Crazy Cakes* (2000), are all written for young children who are faced for the first time, with the difficulties of transracial adoption, be it from direct experience, or more tangentially experienced as an older sibling, or acquaintance.[19]

Of these books, only *I Love You Like Crazy Cakes* is suitable for a very young, pre-school child. It is also the book most explicitly aimed at newly adopted children, addressing the child in the second-person, in the style of a bed-time story. It was written by the author, Rose Lewis, for her adopted daughter Alexandra Mei-Ming Lewis, and is beautifully illustrated and produced. The story charts one young child's journey from an orphanage (which is depicted as clean, modern and well-equipped), through her meeting with her adoptive mother, her journey on an airplane back to the United States, and her period of settling in with her new mother in a house filled with toys, friends and family. The narrative deals sensitively with the issue of abandonment, in language that a young child would understand ("I held you tightly, kissed you softly, and cried. The tears were for your Chinese mother, who could not keep you. I wanted her to know that we would always remember her.") As befits a book intended for toddlers, the narrative accompaniment to the illustrations is relatively brief and simple, and pictures dominate each page.

*Mommy Far, Mommy Near* is written from the perspective of a slightly older child who has been adopted. The organizing rubric is the simple concept of a "mommy near" (the adoptive mother) and a "mommy far" (the birth mother), which works well in explaining the distinction to a young child. The narrative is considerably more detailed about the adoption experience than *I Love You Like Crazy Cakes*. The distinction between birth mothers and adoptive mothers is explored: "She said I had two mommies. I had a mother in China who grew me in her tummy. And I had *her*, the mother who adopted me." Having two mothers is represented positively as a bonus: "Two mommies! I had two mommies! I felt dizzy, like when I do too many somersaults." The story does not shy away from the subject of abandonment either, and explains this at some length:

> Mommy said that China had many people—millions and trillions of people. Too many people for one country. So the China people made up a rule. Each family could only have one child. [ . . . ] One family, one child. Your mother couldn't keep you because she already had a baby. [ . . . ] She did the best thing she could—she bundled you up snugly and left you where she knew someone could find you and take care of you. (*Mommy Far, Mommy Near*, no page number)

The reasons for the desire of "mommy near" to adopt the child are also confronted: "Mommy and Daddy wanted a baby so much. But we couldn't have one"; as well as far more complex issues such as visible differences in appearance between mother and daughter:

> Mommy said, "Are our eyes different or the same?" Different, I told her. Mommy's were two circles, the outside one green, the inside one blue. Mine were one large circle, very black. "Yes, and your eyes are almond and mine are oval," Mommy said. (*Mommy Far, Mommy Near*, no page number)[20]

The overall tone is one of affirmation and of shared affection, which works to offset the potentially emotionally distressing impact of the subject matter.

Like *I Love You Like Crazy Cakes*, the illustrations also vividly depict a sense of connectedness between mother and adopted daughter, intended, no doubt, to be as identity-affirming as possible.

The final book written for children by an adult, Sara Dorow's *When You Were Born in China*, actually blends photographs charting the adoption process with personal reminiscences, to the extent that it could almost be described as a photo essay. *When You Were Born in China* juxtaposes photographs and textual explanation in order to chart the adoption process from beginning to end. It relies more heavily than *Kids Like Me in China* (discussed next) upon pictures to tell the adoption story, and the accompanying text is relatively brief. However, Dorow's narrative endeavours to explain the reasons for transracial adoption clearly, but at the same time, without evading the central issues:

> When you were born in China you may have been born to parents who did not have a son. Your birthparents so much wanted to care for you *and* try to give birth to a son. But having another child would break the government's rule about the number of children they could have in their family, and they would be punished. They would have to pay a very big sum of money, more money than they had. Your birthparents couldn't find a way to keep a daughter in their family and still have a son to take care of them later in life. (*When You Were Born in China*, p. 16)

The book is simultaneously both general and particular: it covers all of the possible situations encountered by the adoptive child, as well as stressing the individuality of each child's story: "No one else has a story exactly like yours, but many other children share part of your story." (*When You Were Born in China*, p. 2)

## A CHILD'S DISTINCTIVE VOICE: KIDS LIKE ME IN CHINA

Ying-Ying Fry is actually the daughter of adoption expert Amy Klatzin (editor of *A Passage to the Heart*), and this is evident in the informed and well-organised narrative that the eight-year-old has produced. Like Emily Prager's *Wuhu Diary*, *Kids Like Me in China* describes a journey undertaken by the five-year-old Ying Ying with her mother back to Changsha, Hunan, in China, where she was adopted by Amy Klatzin a few years earlier. Ying Ying's story is her own, although it is evident that much thought has gone into offering sensitive explanations to the young girl for the reasons as to why she was adopted. Like *Mommy Far, Mommy Near*, there is an attractive simplicity in the way that Ying Ying describes her situation. For instance, of her own, bi-cultural, bi-racial identity—no simple matter, even for an adult—Ying Ying says this: "Like lots of kids in my city, I'm Chinese American. But I wasn't born that way. When I was really small, I was just Chinese. Then my American parents came and adopted me, and that's how I got the American part" (Fry 2000, p. 1). Similarly, although Ying Ying goes into great detail when she discusses the socio-political situation that led to her adoption, the explanation is also straightforward:

> I know why there are so many babies in Chinese orphanages. The government of China is worried that there are too many people. [ . . . ] To get people to have small families, the government made some rules, and they're really strict about them. Parents don't get to choose how many children they have. Usually they're allowed to have one if they live in the city, one or two if they live in the countryside. If they're caught having more, the government can make them pay huge fines and might also take away their jobs or their house, or force them to get an operation that makes it impossible to have another baby. Many parents are afraid of punishments like that. And that's why a lot of babies end up in orphanages in China. (*Kids Like Me in China*, pp. 13–15)

She also acknowledges, with quite startling maturity, the complexity of the gender questions at stake in transracial adoption:

> I think I know why most of them are girls. But it's not easy to explain[ . . . ]Sometimes the [parents] decide they can't raise another baby girl, no matter how much they love her, because they need to try again for a boy. (*Kids Like Me in China*, p. 17)

Ying Ying ends her story with some reminiscences and observations about her life, which suggest her complete ease with her circumstances:

> China isn't my home anymore, but it's where I was born. Even though that was a long time ago, it's a really important part of my life. If I hadn't been born in China, I wouldn't be me. (*Kids Like Me in China*, p. 40)[21]

Ultimately, this book is a fine and mature accomplishment, which does not shy away from the difficult questions at stake, as Anita McClellan notes, such as "lost and found [ . . . ] culture and identity [ . . . ] connecting and disconnecting" ("Bridging the Ocean", p. 9).[22]

In the remainder of this chapter, I address six preoccupations recurrent in these transracial adoption narratives, in order to explore the manner in which conflicts of identity—especially of racialized identity—are managed and resolved. Each of these issues are also shown to be of critical concern especially to mothers adopting transracially, and serve to illustrate the extent to which transracial adoption is imbricated in questions of inter-, bi-, and cross-cultural exchange. I also ask what the future might bring, as these Chinese American adoptees mature, and adult literary and life writing perspectives emerge. To explore this, I turn briefly to the more substantial canon of Korean American adoption literatures.

## THE PROBLEMS OF BIRTH HERITAGE

It becomes clear from reading transracial adoption narratives that a central issue encountered by adopting mothers is the problem of birth heritage. Since the very process of adoption itself is predicated upon the transition from birth family to adoptive family, this is possibly the most pressing—and problematic—aspect of transracial adoption. As Anita D. McClellan observes, the family dynamic at work here is not a simple, two-way parent–child one, but instead must encompass "all sides of the adoption triad: birth parents, child, adoptive parents" ("Bridging the Ocean", p. 7). These narratives all recognise the centrality of birth heritage in the rapidly changing and developing relationship between adoptee and his/her new parents, as well as its importance in the young child's evolving selfhood.

In the adult memoirs by adoptive mothers, by Evans and Prager in particular, there is also an attempt to counter the primacy of birth experience and heritage with assertions of the equal importance of cultural "birth experiences." For instance, it seems a common practice for mothers waiting to adopt to refer to themselves as pregnant (see Evans 2001, p. 42). Similarly, the preparations that adoptive mothers make for meeting their daughters, and the actual moment of meeting are both often described as giving birth (see Evans 2001, pp. 54; 66). Karin Evans, for instance, says this in a letter to her adoptive daughter:

> We humans tend to place much importance upon our particular threads of genetic inheritance. The urge for family continuity and inherited ties is a fine desire, of course, but I know that just as much love and devotion is possible among strangers who choose each other. [ ... ] I ... believe that we each come with a common human heritage, and that this inheritance is every bit as full when the facts of birth are a mystery. (*The Lost Daughters of China*, p. 20)

Another recurrent practice is the re-enactment of a birth "ritual," in which mother and adopted child establish a narrative of sorts to explain how they came together. In *Mommy Far, Mommy Near*, for instance, the mother and child enact an adoption ritual:

> I would say "Show me how you adopted me. Adopt me mommy." So
>     my mommy would hug me and say,
> You are my child.
> You are my own.
> I love you forever.
> I adopt you now. (*Mommy Far, Mommy Near*, no page number)

The most interesting instance of these birth/adoption rituals is described in Emily Prager's *Wuhu Diary*: "we would reenact the 'birth' scene of the adoption ... she wanted me to give birth to her, and I would pretend to, and she would lie on her back between my legs with her head on my stomach and wiggle out and cry. Then I would pretend to suckle her at my breast for a bit" (*Wuhu Diary*, p. 27). This ritual is clearly part of Prager's daughter's ongoing attempt to come to terms with her past, as well, perhaps, as Prager's attempt to replicate a biological birth experience for herself. The pair sometimes enact alternative scenarios, such as this one, imagined by LuLu, and expanded upon by Prager:

> she made me the birth mother and she was the baby. She tried to give me money so that I could keep her. I tried to explain that poverty was not cured with one payment. Then, as the birth mother, I took the opportunity to try to explain in simple terms the reasons behind the Chinese government's one-child policy. (*Wuhu Diary*, p. 29)

LuLu's working out of her history continues when she and Prager travel to China. Here, Prager describes a complex process of readjustment—almost of mourning—through which LuLu passes: "her surety of me in the role of "mother" has gotten rocky now that we are in China, surrounded by Chinese women and all manner of questions about her origins. [ . . . ] I am, it seems, moving from above her in the kinship chart to by her side" (*Wuhu Diary*, p. 45).

The need to counteract the primacy of birth in the process of rearing children, leads both of these authors to explore natural versus cultural notions of belonging and connectedness in some depth. However, whereas Evans' *The Lost Daughters of China* deals mainly with its author's own experiences of transracial adoption, and the early bonding period between mother and daughter, Prager's *Wuhu Diary* traces more resolutely the subsequent period of adjustment undergone by both. Parents like Evans and Prager often try very hard to give their daughters some sense of their birth heritage, such as photos of the place where they were found, or a photocopy of the note that was found with the baby. Yet it is also common for parents to change their daughter's given birth name, or to anglicise it, upon adoption. There seems to be a contradictory impulse at work here. Although the adopting parents recognise the value of retaining what little there is of the child's beginnings, since this will become crucial to the child's future sense of herself, at the same time, there is a desire to impose a new identity upon the child, through naming. Many parents compromise by keeping the child's Chinese name, but adding an Anglo name as the name by which the child will be known, as Karin Evans does, naming her child "Kelly Xiao Yu." The exception to this is Emily Prager, who chooses to keep her daughter's given name, as she says: "I kept the name LuLu because it was, besides the clothes she was wearing, the only thing my child came with that was hers, and like the birth dates in her first mother's note, it placed her nicely in the East *and* the West, which was where we both, evidently, wanted her to be" (*Wuhu Diary*, p. 10). It is also worth noting that LuLu is also an Anglo name as well, so perhaps Prager just did not feel the need to alter it.

Another outcome of the impulse to equip the adopted daughter with some sense of her birth heritage is the decision to take the young child back to her ancestral country, in order for her to connect in some ways with Chinese culture. It is this trip that forms the central subject of Emily Prager's *Wuhu Diary*. Through this endeavor, Prager is clearly also unconsciously attempting to stake out a role for herself, by becoming acquainted with her daughter's ancestral culture. In fact, Prager's encounter when in China with the complexities of her own as well as her daughter's racial identities, sums up the confrontation with racial issues at stake in this literature:

> I don't know what to call myself, really. Am I a Westerner or a Caucasian or an American or what? I hate this race thing, but I have to deal with it so I try. In Chinatown, I'm an American or white, and a Chinese person seems to always be Chinese even if she or he has immigrated and become a U.S. citizen. To me, LuLu is a Chinese-American; but to the Chinese, I think, a Chinese-American is someone who was born and raised in the United States and perhaps doesn't even speak Chinese. (*Wuhu Diary*, p. 18)

This is then complicated further by the issue of visible racial identity:

> I don't like to define myself as "white" and my child as "non-white," although I know a number of Chinese people who do quite freely and refer to this skin as yellow. The whole thing of typing by skin color makes me uncomfortable. (ibid)

LuLu, it appears, is also wrestling with these questions, as her mother observes: "I see her sometimes look back at me, surreptitiously, over her shoulder, wondering who I really am to her and what it means to have me, the Caucasian foreigner, as her mother" (*Wuhu Diary*, p. 129).

There is also a danger that in the effort to transmit a sense of birth heritage to the adoptee, adopting parents of Anglo ancestry might actually over-accentuate this aspect of their cultural experience, as Karin Evans wryly observes:

> Chinese children raised in America by parents conscientious about including Chinese culture in their upbringing may end up more conversant in some of those traditions than will children growing up today in Chinese urban areas. (*The Lost Daughters of China*, p. 186)

The sense of inherited ethnicity is always of critical concern in bi-cultural and bi-racial upbringing; yet it seems that it may become even more acute when complicated by the added experience of adoption. These narratives often explore what is known in ethnicity theory as the issue of "symbolic ethnicity." This is when an individual chooses to emphasise a particular ethnic identity through dress, language and other cultural practices. In these narratives, we witness the phenomenon of symbolic ethnicity by proxy, whereby the adoptive parents actually offer up ethnic experiences such as Chinese meals, or the celebration of Chinese festivals such as lunar New Year or the festival of the Moon Lady as an ethnic "identikit" for their children. In this sense, the adoptive parents become the custodians of Chinese culture as well as American culture. Some parents are all too aware, though, of the difficulties inherent in this, and remain uncomfortable in this role. Karin Evans writes that "to impart Chinese culture to our daughter is to impart a culture in translation—with the pitfalls attendant to any translation" (*The Lost Daughters of China*, p. 181), although she later more pragmatically concludes that "Potstickers or pizza? Mulan or Pokemon? Mandarin opera or punk rock? Ultimately, it is the children themselves who will decide" (*The Lost Daughters of China*, p. 185).

## OVERCOMING THE DIFFICULTIES OF INTERNATIONAL ADOPTION PROCEDURE AND STRATEGIES FOR COMBATING NEGATIVE RACIAL IDENTITIES

Clearly, although some childless couples do adopt children, it is not enough to cope with the large numbers of abandoned girls. Instead, the only chance for these children is often international adoption, which has been allowed in increasing numbers from the early 1990s onwards (China is highly unusual in appearing to prefer international over domestic adoption). However, transracial adoption brings its own problems, and is considerably more complicated than same-country, same-race adoption. Domestic adoptions in China may either involve a direct handover between the birth and adopting parents, or this occurs via orphanages and state welfare centres. International adoption always involves an orphanage or welfare centre, and it is a lengthy and highly regulated procedure.[23] The decision to adopt usually arises out of some sort of life-decision or life-crisis (the inability to have children, or the decision not to have them), and that brings its own dilemmas and problems, to be faced by the adopting parents before they even encounter the intricacies of transracial adoption law and procedure. These are lengthy and complex. The process from start to finish takes upwards of eighteen months, and costs up to $20,000. It is evident that parents who do adopt are both highly motivated and committed to having a transracially-adopted child.

The complexity—or as some would say, difficulty—inherent in successful transracial adoption is not the process itself, but as these narratives that I have analyzed demonstrate, is instead negotiating multiple racial/ethnic/national identities in a manner that will foster and promote self-esteem in the young child. The question of how to promote racial self-esteem is one with which each of the adult memoirs struggles at length. This often requires extensive re-thinking of culturally normalized assumptions about race and ethnicity, and thus becomes as much an issue for the adopting mothers themselves as for their children. As Gail Steinberg and Beth Hall note:

> For children adopted across racial lines, race and adoption often become inextricably connected. Racial differences may serve both appropriately, and at other times inappropriately, as the universal explanation of issues of "not belonging". (*Inside Transracial Adoption*, p. 11)

Steinberg and Hall continue to observe that since race is the most obvious marker of difference between a transracially adopted child and her parents, then it inevitably comes to symbolise the child's unique status, so that race actually becomes a signifier of adoption. Clearly, then, the way in which the child perceives and negotiates her ethnic/racial identity is central to her overall sense of esteem, as well as her acceptance and ease with her adopted status. The parent's role is thus to equip the child with a secure sense of self, and this starts with a feeling of belonging within the family. It could be argued that the children's books discussed here were written for precisely this purpose; similarly, the adult memoirs all devote many pages to the discussion of how they have tried to implement such a challenging role. This often seems to involve difficult decisions, such as when Emily Prager watches her daughter participate in activities while in China or even in Chinatown, while she herself remains an outsider, and has to choose not to intervene. A notable instance of this takes place at LuLu's Chinese pre-school, when at a multicultural Thanksgiving celebration, her daughter tells Prager that she is embarrassed that Prager is not Chinese. Prager endures this because, as she says:

> Her world, as she calls it, is the white, urban, middle-class world of New York City, America. There are Asians, Arabs, African-Americans, and Hispanics in it, to be sure, but for the most part, in her immediate world, in her family, she remains a racial minority. It is for this reason that I sent her to an all-Chinese, Mandarin-speaking preschool in Chinatown, so that in those early years of evolving identity, at least, I would be in the minority someplace, not always she. (*Wuhu Diary*, pp. 6–7)

As Steinberg and Hall sum up: "your child needs to belong to groups you cannot belong to" (*Inside Transracial Adoption*, p. 17).

The effort to promote positive racial self-esteem becomes more challenging in the face of some external pressures, most notably racist reactions from people beyond the family unit. People of color struggle with racism and prejudice on a regular basis; for a young child of transracial background, who is inevitably vulnerable to a precarious self-esteem, this can be especially debilitating.[24] The danger of the cumulative effect of racist encounters will be that the child internalizes this negative view of herself. The challenge for adoptive parents then becomes to acknowledge difference, at the same time as affirming similarity. This ranges from expressing and recognizing visible difference (such as the difference between Asian and Causasian eyes, as we saw discussed in *Mommy Far, Mommy Near*), to re-thinking racialized identities (such as recognising whiteness as a racial identity too, and remaining aware, as Prager and Evans do, that they themselves have not encountered racial challenge and prejudice). At some point too, the issue of race needs to be separated from that of adoption. Steinberg and Hall note that it is common for transracially-adopted toddlers to assume that all Chinese American children are adopted, or that white families do not have adopted children. Part of understanding the complexity of racial identity will inevitably derive from beginning to understand the difference between race and adoption.

An associated issue is the negotiation of gender bias and sexism, since like race, gender comes with birth and cannot be chosen. Thus gender likewise becomes a marker of difference and identity, which can be both positively and negatively expressed. Furthermore, since the entire life course of a transracially-adopted child has often been determined by gender bias from the outset, this is an especially critical issue for young Chinese American adoptees. Gender bias against female babies has actually precipitated the transracial adoption phenomenon, and since this is the place where all the adoption stories start, it is an acutely sensitive area. All of the adoption stories try to emphasize that it is due to an old-fashioned inherited tradition in China that boys are preferred over girls, rather than a contemporary socio-cultural pressure. Of course, this oversimplifies the issue, but it does both make the circumstances leading to transracial adoption easier to understand and accept, and offers a more positive spin on the ramifications of China's population policy.

However, whilst all of the adult female authors discussed here attempt to explore and illuminate the associated issues of gender discrimination in China and the ramifications of the one-child policy, the narratives themselves generally downplay these concerns. For the most part, in fact, the narratives avoid overt criticism of Chinese government and Chinese socio-cultural prejudices, and instead seem to try to focus upon positive elements of Chinese culture rather than on politics. Clearly, these authors are in something of a double bind, since the very logic that led to the one-child policy and its catastrophic social consequences for young girls, has also engendered the transracial adoption phenomenon, thereby enabling childless women such as these to become parents. The authors of these narratives often seem to present the circumstances that lead to abandonment in a way which justifies them (the need for a son in a country without an adequate social welfare system is presented as understandable, for instance). Furthermore, these authors' only link with China is an artificially constructed one that results from transracial adoption, and so the cultural connections with China that are developed seem contrived, however well intentioned. After all, these parents are faced with the quite formidable task of educating their children in a culture that they do not themselves share.

## PROSPECTS FOR THE FUTURE: CHINA AND HUMAN RIGHTS

Is the current situation in China changing? Adoption expert Kay Johnson thinks that in the 2000s there have been limited improvements, notably in the conditions of Chinese orphanages. Yet at the same time, numbers of abandoned children have not dropped, and domestic adoption continues to be under-utilized despite an increase in the numbers of domestic adoptions nationally; and as Kay Johnson observes, there is no "convincing evidence to suggest that the one-child policy has been replaced as the primary cause of the abandonment of healthy children" (*Wanting a Daughter, Needing a Son*, p. 206). Pressure continues to make the birth-planning policy appear successful. Where the problem of abandonment is acknowledged, the solutions proposed by the Chinese authorities simply involve greater surveillance of women and even stricter enforcement of birth-planning policy (which often only serves to increase the incidence of abandonment), rather than the implementation of a child- and woman-centred welfare policy.

Yet, it is also the case that increasing attention paid to the issue of abandonment and the one-child policy, in America and elsewhere, via narratives like those of interest here, is successfully drawing attention to the problems attendant upon China's population policy and its consequences for individual human rights. At the same time, many interested parties face a dilemma: the very conditions that have given rise to the epidemic of female abandonment in China have also enabled many childless couples in America to adopt. International adoption also brings much-needed funds to orphanages, which receive the majority of the high fee for adoption paid by adopting parents. There is also a direct inverse relationship between international publicity about China's foundlings and orphanages, and the ease with which prospective adoptive parents are able to adopt. In the period after 1995, for instance, and the airing of the sensational British documentary, "The Dying Rooms: China's Darkest Secret," adoption in China became much more difficult. Clearly, international criticism of China's population policy and its many ramifications is still not welcomed by the Chinese government, and it seems that both the success of international adoption and the effort to improve China's social welfare system will remain subject to the vagaries of China's political climate. In the light of this, transracial adoption narratives like those discussed in this chapter do perform a vital role in drawing international attention to one aspect of China's currently abysmal human rights record.

## PROSPECTS FOR THE FUTURE: THE KOREAN EXAMPLE

In contrast to the voluminous literature written by young adult and adult Korean adoptees, Chinese adulthood adoptee literature is virtually non-existent at this point due to the young age of the adoptees. Thus, most of what we know about the outcomes of Asian–American adoptions thus far comes from Korean experiences spanning the last twenty-five years. Korean adoption has a much longer history. Since the mid-1950s, an estimated 150,000–200,000 Korean children have been internationally adopted, although this has tailed off since the 1980s.[25] Mostly this was due to American military presence in Korea during the Korean War and its aftermath.[26] Such mature accounts by Korean adult adoptees tend to be noticeably negative. Korean American Jane Jeong Trenka, the author of a compelling memoir, *The Language of Blood*, clearly and succinctly expresses her ambivalence and pain about her experiences of transracial adoption, asking, for instance: "How can an adoptee weigh her terrible loss against the burden of gratitude she feels for her adoptive country and parents?" (*The Language of Blood*, p. 201). Sara Dorow remarks upon this "cautionary tone" in Korean adult adoptee literature as well (*Transracial Adoption*, p. 164). She also notes that even in the best examples within the Korean adult adoptee memoir genre—Trenka's *The Language of Blood, Passing Through, Searching for Go-hyang, First Person Plural*, "nothing is finally resolved; rather, new, more complex layers and possibilities for narrating their stories are created."[27] The trajectories of their identities turn out to be circuitous, referring to geographically separated mothers and nations, racial and kinship divides, institutional and state impositions, discursive chasms, historical happenstance" (*Transracial Adoption*, p. 263). My own reading of Korean adoptee literature confirms this. Two recent narratives stand out in particular. Marie Myung-Ok Lee's fictional *Somebody's Daughter* (2005) is a bleak exploration of the transracial adoption scenario from the twin imaginative perspectives of the Korean American adoptee Sarah, and her Korean mother, Kyung-sook. As with many of the Korean American narratives that I discuss in Chapter 5, this novel exposes the flip side and the seedy underside of the long-standing American involvement in Korea, from the unwanted and discarded mixed-race children of American GI soldiers, to the prostitute-laden "America towns' scattered across Korea, as well as Korean cultural revulsion towards mixed-race offspring and the cultural shame attached to transracial adoption in Korea. Both an overwhelming sense of helplessness and rootlessness pervade this novel. Sarah paradigmatically observes that she is

Sarah the misfit, even in her native country. How had it come to this, I wondered, that in the space of a single generation, I had become some kind of Darwinian reject, a fish with lungs, a duck-billed platypus. I wasn't Korean-hyphen-anything, for what was Korean in me had become vestigial, useless. But at the same time, ching-chong eyes prevented me from claiming any race solidarity with [ . . . ] my so-called family, back in Minnesota. (*Somebody's Daughter*, p. 20)

Sarah's life trajectory is ultimately figured as dictated by nothing more significant or meaningful than the vagaries of fate and the whims of adoption officials. Katy Robinson's 2002 memoir, *A Single Square Picture: A Korean Adoptee's Search for Her Roots*, expresses a similarly ambivalent, sometimes tortured perspective, in a narrative deeply imbued with personal bitterness and regret. Katy Robinson—formerly Kim Ji-yun, travels back to Korea in search of her birth family. She fails to find her mother, and her family's story is only excavated in confusing, seemingly disparate, fragments. Katy closes her story with the regret-filled observation

> I once thought the past was like a puzzle that would lock neatly together once I found all of the missing pieces. But even then, the picture constantly shifts, one piece connecting while another is discarded. (*A Single Square Picture*, p. 296)

The yearning for the genealogical neatness of the "single square picture" of Robinson's title is expressed in almost all Korean adoptee 'going back' narratives.[28] As the Chinese adoptee population matures, it remains to be seen whether a similar perspective will emerge. The Korean adoptee cases provide a model for Chinese adoption too, though, as Sara Dorow notes:

> In particular, the stories of Korean adoptees [ . . . ] and the struggle to reckon with the life that might have been and the unknown people with whom it might have been spent—have become a resource from which adoption agencies and parents of Chinese children draw. (*Transracial Adoption*, p. 257)

This is not really surprising, since within the world of transracial adoption, there is a distinct sense of community—of people talking, and writing, to and for each other. Likewise, interested parties in the transracial adoption scenario—whether parents, professionals or children—energetically seek new sources of advice, information, and affirmation. This chapter, for instance, has been cited as forthcoming in an adoption memoir, and it appears as a forthcoming resource on the website of the specialist adoption press, Yeong and Yeong Book Company.[29]

Perhaps more surprisingly, parental perspectives also express a degree of negativity. Cheri Register, the author of the seminal adoption work *Are*

*Those Kids Yours? American Families with Children Adopted from Other Countries*, offers a reflective and at times cautionary evaluation of her experience of adopting from Korea in her 2005 narrative memoir, *Beyond Good Intentions: A Mother Reflects on Raising Internationally Adopted Children*. Structured by listing ten pitfalls likely to occur in the transracial adoption experience, Register dwells upon such vexed issues as "Believing Race Doesn't Matter", "Keeping Our Children Exotic", "Judging Our Country Superior", "Believing Adoption Saves Souls" and "Appropriating Our Children's Heritage", and finally cautions us all that

> We eager globalists need to remember that *our* multicultural dream is our children's daily reality. They take the measure of global harmony every day in the comments they hear, the glances they catch, the questions they're expected to answer. They may not want to be harbingers or symbols of anything [ . . . ] Our kids didn't volunteer for our plan to transform the world. We should be satisfied if they simply figure out how to live comfortably in it. (*Beyond Good Intentions*, pp.175–6)

# 4   A Secret History
## American Representations of Geisha Society

> Geisha ... At the slightest evocation of this little Japanese word there appears instantly before the eyes of Westerners a succession of images swaying idly between languorous voluptousness and erotic fantasy.
> —Bérénice Geoffroy-Schneiter, *Geishas*

> Fetishized as a super-feminized exotic object in whom the soul of the geisha resides, the Japanese woman is configured as ontologically mysterious, sexually available and hungry for contact with the West—via the white western male.
> —Traise Yamamoto, *Masking Selves, Making Subjects: Japanese American Women, Identity, and the Body*

> The West has a continual appetite for the image of sweet, gentle Japanese child-women ... a century-old tradition of Western men writing fiction about Japanese women.
> —Sheridan Prasso, *The Asian Mystique: Dragon Ladies, Geisha Girls and the Fantasies of the Exotic Orient*

> Throughout its history, Hollywood has had a romantic fascination with the geisha.
> —Gina Marchetti, *Romance and the "Yellow Peril"*

> The commodification of Otherness has been so successful because it is offered as a new delight, more intense, more satisfying than normal ways of doing and feeling.
> —bell hooks, *Black Looks: Race and Representation*

Geisha society has traditionally been shrouded in secrecy, which partly accounts for the many myths and mysteries that surround it. Whilst there have only been a few early- and mid-twentieth century examinations of geisha culture, including Akiyama Aizaburo's *Geisha Girl* (1926), P. D. Perkins' *Geisha of Pontocho* (1954), Adolphe Scott's *The Flower and Willow*

*World: The Story of the Geisha* (1960), and Sara Harris' *House of 10,000 Pleasures: A Modern Study of the Geisha and of the Streetwalker in Japan* (1962), interest in geisha culture has proliferated in the period since the 1990s. Only in recent years has the real, obscured history of the geisha been explored extensively, as well as the contemporary life of Japan's remaining geishas. Significantly, many of these explorations have been largely spearheaded by American anthropologists interested in Japan and other scholars of Japan.[1] The traditionally highly regulated and very secret world of Geishahood has also recently been penetrated by a series of Western observers, including two American women who have been trained in the arts of Geishahood, and their subsequent narratives describing this experience are also explored here. Contemporary American books about the history of geisha culture include Liza Dalby's reprinted *Geisha* (1998), Lesley Downer's *Geisha* (2000) and *Women of the Pleasure Quarters: The Secret History of the Geisha* (2001), Kyoko Aihara's *Geisha* (2000), the translation of Sayo Masuda's *Autobiography of a Geisha* (2003) and Mineko Iwasaki's *Geisha of Gion* (2002). Western fascination with the closed world of the Japanese geishas continues, as seen by the enduring popularity of cultural representations (from Pierre Loti's *Madame Crysanthème* in the 1870s and John Luther Long's "Madame Butterfly" in 1899, to Giacomo Puccini's 1904 opera *Madama Butterfly*, and David Henry Hwang's 1988 postmodern version *M. Butterfly* onwards), to later fictional representations. As I discussed at some length in my 2002 monograph, *Negotiating Identities*, the publishing industry's current predilection for texts about an exotic 'orient' is directly traceable to the recent success of Arthur Golden's depiction of geisha life in Japan from the 1920s to the 1960s in his novel *Memoirs of the Geisha* as well as the subsequent film version, also entitled *Memoirs of a Geisha*. Both book (1997) and film (2005) served up a mixture of tantalising eroticism and exoticism, culminating in the account of the apprentice geisha Sayuri's *mizuage*, or ritual deflowering, by one of her patrons. *Memoirs of a Geisha* has been phenomenally successful and extensively instrumental in reviving interest in geishahood. Coterminously, the world of geishahood in Japan's 'hanamachi' or geisha quarters, whilst still defined by silence and mystery, has in recent years increasingly granted a degree of limited access to outsiders, both within Japan and beyond; and in the United States this has spawned a new literary genre charting the history and practices of geisha culture, and the role of geisha women in contemporary Japanese society, one which is tantalisingly at once anachronistic yet modern.

## THE KARY-KAI: "FLOWER AND WILLOW WORLD" IN CONTEXT

Geisha society, known in Japan as *kary-kai* or the 'flower and willow world', has always been a somewhat closed society, accessible only to those with power and privilege. Geisha districts, or *hanamachi*, are mainly found in two cities: Tokyo, where there are two principal *hanamachi*: Shimbashi and Akasaka, and Kyoto, where there are five main geisha districts: Gion, Gion Higashi (East Gion), Pontocho, Kamishichiken and Miyagawa-cho. There is also another category of geisha, called *onsen* geisha (literally, 'hot spring' geisha), who are to be found in the many sulphurous spa resorts throughout Japan. Geisha trace their history back several centuries in the various *hanamachi*, although their numbers—and fortunes—have fluctuated in line with the fortunes of the country itself. For instance, the geisha districts were closed down entirely by government decree during World War II between 1944 and 1945; and the occupants of the *hanamachi okiya* (geisha houses) were forced to find work elsewhere. Likewise, flourishing times in the geisha quarters have tended to coincide with periods of special economic prosperity: the 1920s, 1960s and 1980s, in particular. Geisha numbers mirror this trend. Although estimates vary, in the heyday of the geisha during the 1920s (when Arthur Golden's *Memoirs of a Geisha* is set) there were 80,000 geisha throughout the country. By the mid-1970s this number had shrunk to 17,000 geisha across Japan; but by 1999 there were less than 200 geisha left.[2]

Although thus clearly a dwindling group, geisha continue to be a source of mystery, debate and discussion, both within Japan and beyond. Many commentators observe that although most Japanese people have never encountered a geisha, in the popular imagination they are still held to be supreme custodians of Japanese tradition, especially art, music, poetry, calligraphy, flower arrangement, the codes and customs of kimono attire, tea ceremony and cultural rituals accompanying significant events such as the death of a notable individual.[3] Liza Dalby refers to geisha as "curators" (p. 98). 'Geisha' literally means 'artist'—*gei* is the word for art. Its synonym is 'geigi' or in Kyoto, 'geiko'. Liza Dalby describes the "chosen function" of geishahood as "upholding Japanese tradition" and adds that this is "the defining mode of the profession" (*Geisha*, p. xx). Schooled as they are in elements of Japan's traditions, and attired as they are in traditional Japanese dress, geisha are deliberately as well as functionally anachronistic figures. They are also deliberately as well as practically elusive, as Lesley Downer observes: "The essence of the flower and the willow world was its secrecy. It was open only to a few well-heeled initiates" (*Women of the Pleasure Quarters*, p. 80), and explains:

> Far from seeking publicity, the geisha shun it. Their whole profession depends upon their ability to keep secrets. Many have been the friends of the nation's most powerful men, often for a lifetime. Such men choose to entertain at geisha houses because they can trust these women to keep their lips sealed, no matter what they see or hear. (*Geisha*, p. 8)

The former geisha Mineko Iwasaki describes the force of this pressure to maintain discretion:

> No woman in the three-hundred-year history of the karyukai has ever come forward in public to tell her story. We have been constrained by unwritten rules not to do so, by the robes of tradition, and by the sanctity of our exclusive calling. (*Geisha: A Life*, p. 1)

This 'sanctity' extends to the role that geisha have historically played in political manouevers. Geisha have been present as some of Japan's most important deals were made, both in business and politics, although this role has been occluded, as Lesley Downer observes:

> It is a secret history. In the standard histories of Japan, geisha are never mentioned; yet when I probed a little deeper, I found them there, playing a role in the great events of their day and consorting with the most powerful men of the country as friends, confidantes, mistresses, and sometimes wives. But they are always in the shadows, the women behind the decision makers. (*Women of the Pleasure Quarters*, p. 21)

If the role geisha have played in public affairs has historically been obscured, then the sexual identity of geisha has also been historically extensively misunderstood. Geisha are not prostitutes and do not sleep with men for money. Their role is rather as the hostess of a party, called the *zashiki*, which is rather like a cocktail party or banquet. They provide companionship and entertainment, which takes the form of elegant and sometimes coquettish, even slightly risqué, conversation, traditional song and dance, playing the shamisen, and pouring saké. For this the *okiya* or geisha houses are paid exorbitant fees, known as *hanadai* or 'flower money'. Apprentice geisha, known as *maiko*, undergo a rigorous and quite extensive period of training in order to master the various arts in the geisha's repertoire. Due to the exclusivity and cost of such parties, only the very wealthiest and most influential members of Japanese society could ever hope to afford to hold a *zashiki* event; similarly, access to such events is strictly by invitation or introduction only. Company presidents and politicians therefore tend to be the geishas' main customers. One source of the misunderstanding of geisha sexuality is the role of patrons, or *danna*, in the flower and willow world. The process by which a geisha takes a *danna* is both formal and ritualised, and is a serious commitment on the part of the patron, not least in financial terms. This process has become confused in the popular Western imagination with the ceremony of *mizuage*, or ritual deflowering, which used to mark the young, apprentice maiko's (geisha's) initiation into both sexual maturity and full-blown geishahood. In fact, as with some other elements of the geisha lifestyle, this practice is now anachronistic and superannuated, yet it does partly account for the enduring popular confusions about geisha and sex.

## "MINARAI", LIZA CRIHFIELD DALBY AND LESLEY DOWNER: ETHNOGRAPHIC STUDIES OF GEISHA CULTURE

Apprentice geisha, or *maiko*, learn by observing their older geisha 'sisters', both in the *okiya* (geisha residence) and the *ochaya* (the teahouse where geisha entertain), which is known as *minarai*. In her study, which was the first study of geisha culture to be undertaken by an American woman, Liza Crihfield Dalby evokes the concept of *minarai* in her attempt to explain her own penetration of geisha culture in the mid-1970s:

> All new geisha go through a period of *minarai*, or learning by observation, a Japanese category that I was able to slip into easily. The other geisha thought it perfectly reasonable that I should undertake minarai; in fact, once they recognized that I was serious about understanding their world, they suggested it themselves. (*Geisha*, p. xvi)

Yet, as a practicing anthropologist, she is also at pains to explain the why as well as how of her involvement in the flower and willow world, that is, her own motivations for and biases in writing:

> I have combined two viewpoints in writing this book: that of the outsider seizing upon those things most in need of explanation, and that of the insider, dwelling on things that may not even occur to the outsider to question but that in fact are of central importance in the geishas' view of the world. (*Geisha*, p. xvi)[4]

This emphasis upon the insider/outsider perspective becomes increasingly central to Western explorations of geisha society, as I will discuss later. It is, of course, likewise, an important concern in the discipline of anthropology, where practitioners are required to render explicit the mode of their research methodology. More typically, though, and as Dalby also acknowledges, the anthropological approach involves both the undertaking of fieldwork—of what is known as 'participant observation' and eventually, the comparison and analysis of cultural traits. What is interesting about Dalby's approach is that from the outset of her study, she rejects both of these imperatives and instead makes clear that she has attempted something different. Of participant observation, Dalby asserts:

> The notion of participant observation is also common in anthropological studies, and my joining the geisha ranks in the community of Pontocho in Kyoto has been called that. I myself dislike the term, as it implies a degree of emotional distance that only creates a false sense of objectivity. [ . . . ] I soon found that I had plunged my whole heart

into the endeavor and could not maintain the conventional researcher's separation from the object of study. (*Geisha*, p. xv)

Likewise, although Dalby recognises that "as a student of anthropology, the discipline of cross-cultural studies, I have been under some pressure to consider this question", she does not attempt this since "this study has gone in the opposite direction and attempts to elaborate upon what is culturally unique to geisha" (*Geisha*, p. xvii). Thus, since she rejects participant observation, and *minarai* is not quite right either, Dalby's solution is to undertake what she terms "interpretive ethnography", apposite, she believes, to her attempt to explain the "cultural meaning of persons, objects, and situations in the geisha world" (*Geisha*, p. xvi). Dalby's unease over the terms of her access to geisha society also reflects contemporary shifts in the discipline of cultural anthropology, whereby practitioners have become much more careful about making explicit their own positionality vis-à-vis their ethnographic subject(s).[5]

The implications of this are manifold. As I later show, fictional and fictionalized accounts of geisha life have often adopted an approach akin to the ethnographic and/or anthropological as a means of coating the representation of geishahood in a veneer of authenticity; that Dalby seems anxious to veer in the opposite direction is significant, since it also attests to the oddly emotional politics of engagement with geisha that people seem to experience. She thus underscores that her interaction with geisha society has not been merely that of a cultural amanuensis. It is also significant that Dalby's study, undertaken in the 1970s, published in 1978[6], and thus the first of the contemporary American geisha studies, searched for a new generic mode in which to inscribe her encounter with the flower and willow world, an effort echoed in later works too. Finally, it is also significant that Dalby settles upon the term "interpretive ethnography", one that at once extends both the authenticity of subjective first-hand cultural participation and a certain degree of authoritative detachment—the "objectivity" of the academic researcher, if you like; an accomplished authorial sleight-of-hand that we will see repeated some twenty years later by Arthur Golden in *Memoirs of a Geisha*.

Of course, this manner of hyperconsciousness of straddling the multiple boundaries of genre is not new in academic discourses in cultural anthropology and ethnography. The innovative and noteworthy effort here is the quite skilful manipulation of the representations of the cultural encounter between geisha and interested Western observant in the "contact zone" of the flower and willow world, whether in a genuine effort, like Dalby's, to step carefully across cultural borders or Golden's more deliberately duplicitously in order to muddy the waters of representation (as I discuss later in this study). In both instances, the reader's attention is occasionally explicitly re-directed away from the subject of study—the geisha—to the observant, in order to remind the reader of issues of both authority and authenticity.[7]

Liza Dalby's study, which has become the authoritative classic of the genre of geisha literature, undoubtedly negotiates carefully between Dalby's own experiences living amongst geisha in Pontocho, Kyoto as the geisha Ichigiku, and both her and others' pre-conceptions about the nature of the geishas' lives.[8] For instance, whilst not detracting from her own admitted curiosities about geishahood (she romantically describes imagining herself as the Margaret Mead of the geisha world), and whilst anticipating those of her readers, Dalby nevertheless maintains an insistence upon the importance of reading and interpreting geishahood solely in relation to its own cultural context—Japanese culture itself. She writes:

> This book is, first and last, about geisha. It is intended to speak to anyone whose curiosity has ever been piqued by the geisha's evocative image. It is secondarily a book about Japanese culture. What geisha do and what they represent are intelligible only within their cultural context. [ . . . ] I do not view geisha as constituting a microcosm, a symbol, or a typification of the larger entity: Japanese society. But neither are they a marginal subculture. Geisha are embedded in Japanese culture—Japanese regard them as "more Japanese" than almost any other definable group—but only in showing how they differ from other Japanese does their multifaceted identity become clear. (*Geisha*, p. xiii)

A further marked feature of Dalby's study is her emphasis upon the difficulties of penetrating geisha society. As I have mentioned, geisha society is distinctive in its secrecy and its closed ranks, a feature to which Dalby repeatedly refers:

> The modern world of flowers and willows seems to be an exotic garden, surrounded by a fence of tradition and closed to outsiders. I began my study with no idea what my chances were of being allowed to step behind the fence. (*Geisha*, p. 174)

Clearly this assertion of her ethnographic exclusivity is partly an authorial strategy that enables Dalby to underscore the exclusivity of her own access and her subsequent findings—a recurrent feature of geisha literature—since what follows is some two-hundred pages describing Dalby's life "behind the fence". Dalby's ethnographic exclusivity is an aspect of her work that she has continued to promulgate. On her website biography, for instance, she presents her ethnographic research almost as a collaborative endeavour:

> It quickly became apparent that geisha felt themselves to be misunderstood in the west. After spending six months on interviews and historical research, Liza found the geisha had come to accept her seriousness and seemed to think she might be someone who could

articulate their own point of view to a western audience. It was as if the geisha themselves developed a stake in her gaining an understanding of their world. [ . . . ] When she eventually wrote her book geisha, her experiences as a novice geisha proved invaluable in presenting the insider's view of this world.[9]

The next person to step 'behind the fence' did so in 2000, three years after the publication of Arthur Golden's novel. This was Lesley Downer, who wrote *Geisha: The Secret History of a Vanishing World* (published with slight variations in the United Kingdom as *Women of the Pleasure Quarters: The Secret History of the Geisha*), and her biography of the famous geisha Sada Yakko, *Madame Sadayakko: The Geisha Who Seduced the West* (2003). In many ways, Downer built upon the work of Liza Dalby— in fact, Downer takes a discussion of Dalby's *Geisha* as her starting point. Unlike Dalby, Downer is a freelance reporter and writer who lived in Japan for some years, and who specialises in Japanese history and culture[10], yet she acknowledges the influence of Dalby's study upon her own: "Like everyone who studies the geisha, my first step was to turn to Liza Dalby's brilliant anthropological analysis, *Geisha*, the bible of geisha studies" (xi). Like Dalby, Downer's initial motivation for her study was also a certain inquisitiveness about geishahood:

> I wanted to meet the real women behind the painted faces, the charming chit-chat, and the eternal mysterious smile. The geisha, it seemed to me, were purveyors of dreams. Theirs was a misty world of romance created for the enjoyment and entertainment of men, in which the most browbeaten office worker could be king. It was not my intention to spoil the illusion or dispel the mystery. But as a woman, I wondered out of what past the geisha had come. Who were the women who, in modern Japan, had chosen to live this life? For men it was a dream world; but who were the women whose job it was to create this dream? (*Women of the Pleasure Quarters*, p. 3)

From the outset, though, the differences between Downer's and Dalby's study become apparent. Possibly by dint of the spread of second-wave feminism in the years between Dalby's and Downer's involvement with the geisha, Downer's interest is tipped firmly towards an exploration of geisha as *women*, as *über* icons of Japanese femininity, exoticism and eroticism. As she notes, "Inevitably I find myself looking at what it means to be a woman in Japan. What is the dividing line between geisha and prostitutes and between wives and geisha?" (*Women of the Pleasure Quarters*, p. 22); and as becomes apparent, her concern lies at least equally in dismantling the elements of this image as it is with penetrating the actual world of geishas. She writes of the image of the geisha:

> She was not so much a woman as a walking work of art, a compilation of symbols and markers of eroticism, as far removed from a human being as a bonsai is from a natural tree. Geisha have been described as icons of femininity. If that is the case it is a very stylized image of femininity. (*Women of the Pleasure Quarters*, p. 9)

At the same time as Downer attempts an analysis of the structures of femininity that inform geishahood, as this quotation attests, Downer also tends repeatedly to succumb to a certain enthrallment with her subjects of study. The following is representative:

> She was a vision made for darkness, for an era when geisha used to flit through the gloom of unlit teahouses, glimpsed only by flickering candlelight. Their painted faces transmuted them into shamanesses who could transport men into another world, a world of dreams.
>
> She passed with a rustle of silk, revealing a breathtaking expanse of exquisitely white-painted back. I had not realized that geisha wore their kimono quite so shockingly low. It was like a décolletage in reverse, enormously erotic. At the nape of the neck, which Japanese men find especially sexy, was a titillating fork of naked, unpainted skin, shaped like a serpent's tongue. It was the most mesmerizing of all, a reminder that beneath the alabaster mask, beneath the layers of silk and brocade, was a real flesh and blood woman. (*Women of the Pleasure Quarters*, p. 2)

In fact, this phenomenon in Downer's writing has also been noticed by others, such as in her biography of Sada Yakko, where one reviewer observed that "Downer herself seems dazzled by the same old orientalist aura, gushing and swooning with the best of them" ("Madame Sadayakko", p. 102).[11] The same reviewer criticizes Downer's approach to her subject, suggesting that Downer seems disproportionately interested in revealing "Japanese sexual practices" ("Madame Sadayakko", p. 104) and the like, and comments acerbically that "no doubt prurient details like this help to sell books, but it only goes to prove that orientalism is alive and well" (ibid.). Herein lies the rub. For all of the writers discussed in this chapter, an inquisitiveness due in no small part to the mysteries of the *hanamachi* and the rumoured prurience of geisha practices, provides the initial motivation for study.

Like Dalby, Downer is at pains to emphasize both the closeted nature of geishahood and therefore the exclusivity of her own access. Her opening section is entitled "Breaching a Secret World", and Downer speaks here of her own hope to "breach this closed world" (*Women of the Pleasure Quarters*, p. 8). In another case, Downer firmly reminds her readers that "The essence of the flower and willow world was its secrecy. It was open to only a few well-heeled initiates" (p. 80). In fact, at moments, Downer seems to treat her subjects and the *hanamachi* world as slightly curious, certainly culturally outmodish, and the geisha themselves as cultural artefacts:

> It is a kind of parallel universe coexisting with the world of everyday life but accessible only to those who have the key. Outsiders walk the same streets but see only nondescript houses, shops and passersby. But those in the know can tell which of the anonymous houses are geisha houses and which of the ordinary-looking women blossom into geisha at night. [ . . . ] there are still geisha for those who know where to look. (*Madame Sadayakko*, p. 6)

Thus figured by Downer as mysterious, elusive, and teetering on extinction, one can see why her writing has attracted criticisms of exoticizing the geisha and their world. Yet Downer is equally interested in exploring this history of exoticizing the geisha, both within Japan and from a Western viewpoint. For instance, at one point in *Women of the Pleasure Quarters* she discusses *shunga* prints, which are extremely explicit woodcut prints of the so-called *ukiye-e*, or pictures of the "floating world", as well as the long history of the stereotyping of Japanese women:

> Ever since the West first heard of Japan, even before Commodore Perry's ships arrived in Japanese waters, the myth of the exotic geisha has somehow filtered out of that closed country. The very word carried an erotic frisson. It conjured up a submissive almond-eyed Oriental maiden, the embodiment of all the seductive femininity and sexual freedom of some fanciful exotic East dreamt up in the fevered imaginations of repressed, frustrated Westerners. Everyone wanted a peep beneath the veil. (*Madame Sadayakko*, p. 100)

Downer, of course, included. Yet Downer's books are more than simply historical and cultural explorations of the geisha world and its history, both within Japan and in the Western imagination. Although she is not a formally trained ethnographer, Downer's study adopts and mirrors many of the practices and approaches of ethnographic research in her exploration of geishahood. Like Liza Dalby, for instance, Lesley Downer lives amongst– if not exactly with–the geisha in Kyoto. Downer's own website biography records that she "lived among the geisha and little by little found herself being transformed into one of them".[12] Like Dalby, too, Downer conducts extensive interviews with geisha and both figures in the *hanamachi*, such as *okasan* (geisha house mothers) and geisha hairdressers and other attendants. Unlike Dalby, though, Downer is never granted the same degree of access to the *hanamachi* that would have enabled her, for instance, to attend a *zashiki* as an apprentice. She substitutes such moments of participation with a greater degree of emphasis upon the history of geisha in

Japanese culture; yet despite this, Downer still achieves a comprehensive study of geishahood firmly in the ethnographic vein.

## "THE ASIAN MYSTIQUE": GEISHAHOOD AND NEO-ORIENTALISM

A significant departure in Downer's work that marks the difference of her approach from Dalby's is the exploration of Western stereotypes of geisha. As the epigraphs to this chapter graphically illustrate, the word 'geisha' and the images it conjures in the Western imagination function as a shorthand for a hypersexualized, eroticized and generally mysterious image of the Japanese woman. In her book *Embracing the East*, Mari Yoshihara locates geisha as the zenith of Orientalized iconographic representations of Japanese women.[13] In her study of the stereotyping of Asian women in the West, Sheridan Prasso suggests that the existence of this shorthand is due in no small part to the production of images of Japanese women by Hollywood and other Western art arenas:

> *Madame Butterfly* modernized into the musical *Miss Saigon*; our own fable of Cinderella turned into the oddly unrealistic devotion of a young woman in *Memoirs of a Geisha*; the soft-spoken, servile Mrs. Livingston in *The Courtship of Eddie's Father*, sexually uninhibited Mariko of the TV miniseries and novel *Shogun*; the quietly enigmatic Phuong in *The Quiet American*; the graceful Hana-ogi in *Sayonara*; the pouty prostitute in *The World of Suzie Wong*; the kick-ass dominatrix played by Lucy Liu. These depictions can and sometimes do cause Asian women to be perceived in Western culture as gentle geisha or China dolls—servile, submissive, exotic, sexually available, mysterious, and guiding. (*The Asian Mystique*, p.xii)

Other commentators have explored the manner in which this shorthand becomes a shorthand for Japan itself. In her article, "Innocence to Deviance: The Fetishisation of Japanese Women in Western Fiction, 1890s–1990s", Narrelle Morris observes:

> Since the mid-nineteenth century, there has been an enduring relationship between Western imaginings and the Japanese woman. Dressed in kimono and made up as a geisha, she has often been used in illustrations and cartoons as an archetypical gendered symbol of her country. ("Innocence to Deviance")[14]

This is a phenomenon also explored by Gina Marchetti in her study, *Romance and the "Yellow Peril": Race, Sex, and Discursive Strategies in*

*Hollywood Fiction*, in which she concludes that "Hollywood's fictitious Orient" is

> feminized in the Western imagination, the entire continent becomes an exotic, beckoning woman, who can both satisfy the male Westerner's forbidden desires and ensnare him in an unyielding web of deceit. (*Romance and the "Yellow Peril"*, p. 67)[15]

More specifically, Marchetti analyzes Hollywood's on-going fascination with the image of the geisha, from *Teahouse of the August Moon* (1956); *The Barbarian and the Geisha* (1958); *Cry for Happy* (1961); and *My Geisha* (1962) onwards, and concludes that the enduring appeal of representations of the geisha is due to the ability of geisha stories to appeal to different readers/audiences, by flexibly indulging various needs simultaneously and catering to different tastes. For

> male viewers, these stories promote a fantasy [ . . . ] [of] desire for the exoticism of a nonwhite beauty. [ . . . ] These tales, like all geisha stories, allow for the indulgence of the pleasure of watching female bodies set in a beautiful locale, where Western conceptions of morality do not take precedence over sexual desire. [ . . . ] For men, they offer sexual titillation as well as a core of moral certainty. (*Romance and the "Yellow Peril"*, p. 177)

For women, these stories are

> situated somewhere between women's romance fictions that feature naïve young girls cast adrift in a foreign world of dark strangers and more rugged travel adventures of Americans staking their claims to alien cultural secrets and treasures, these female-centred narratives can appeal in different ways to different viewers. (Ibid.)

The malleability of the geisha tale and image is not just evident in its ability to appeal to different audience/readership needs. Narrelle Morris furthermore suggests that the evolution of these stereotypes and images is in fact cyclical, tracking Japan's economic and political relationship with the West:

> By the mid-to-late 1990s, the bursting of Japan's economic 'bubble' and the general downturn in the economic climate gradually saw a reduction in the 'aggressive' Japan genre [ . . . ] and consequently, a reduction in these types of depictions of Japanese women. ("Innocence to Deviance")

In her historical analysis of American images of the Japanese woman, Yoshi Kuzume argues that between 1860 and 1990, American images of

Japanese femininity have undergone four distinct phases, that correspond to critical moments in Japanese-American involvement: the sensual geisha girl of 19th century representations (1860–1900); the heathen woman waiting to be rescued by white Christianity (1910–1945); the Japanese woman emancipated by the post-war occupation-style democracy (1945–1960); and a more liberated and culturally emancipated Japanese woman, affected by the advent of post-war feminisms (1970–1990).[16] Kuzume importantly notes that these phases are more reflective

> of the changes in American attitudes concerning gender in general, and attitudes to Japanese society, than [ ... ] of historical developments in Japan. The American's images of Japanese women has been limited to an American point of view, including stereotypes that symbolize the image of the Japanese woman based on a combination of general images of women, and of interpretations of Japanese society made by Americans in these periods. ("Images of Japanese Women in U.S. Writings", p. 7)[17]

If, then, the image of the Japanese woman as an ideological construction of the Western (male) imagination has responded to historical change in this way, as Kuzume, Morris and Yamamoto suggest, then it is also the case that Western constructions of and interests in, the figure of the geisha have also fluctuated by dint of cultural and political interactions between America and Japan. For instance, Marchetti traces the transmutation of the figure of the geisha from her pre-war representation in the West as the epitome of Japanese eroticism oriented towards Japanese men, to a figure far more susceptible to the charms of the West:

> For a time, in fact, it appeared as if the geisha was Hollywood's chief emblem of postwar reconciliation. Although on the surface she might appear cool, distant, mysterious, or morally suspect, underneath she was seen as docile, eager to please, malleable, child-like, and vulnerable. Metaphorically, a bellicose Japan, through the figure of the geisha, became a yielding and dependent nation. (*Romance and the "Yellow Peril"*, pp. 178-9)

Marchetti traces the evolution of this image through the 1970s and 1980s, when she asserts, the geisha was presented as a figure who was encoded, difficult to read, yet seductively perilous, in line with American suspicions regarding the economic success Japan was enjoying. Thus the geisha served as a convenient metaphor, as

> another entry into an increasingly paranoid American public discourse that looks at Japanese economic and industrial expansion as a more serious threat than its pre-1945 militarism. By choosing to see Japan

metaphorically as a cloistered teahouse, as the secluded world of the geisha quarters [ . . . ] [this] affirms a conservative American belief that the Japanese really prefer their isolation. (*Romance and the "Yellow Peril"*, pp. 186–7)

Post-1998, the image changed again. As I also noted in 2002 in my book *Negotiating Identities*, Narrelle Morris marks the moment of the revivification of the image of and interest in geishahood and the exoticized Japanese woman as the publication of Golden's *Memoirs*: "The apparent cyclical return of Western interest in the more gentle exoticised side of Japan is perhaps typified best by Arthur Golden's [ . . . ] *Memoirs of a Geisha*" ("Innocence to Deviance"); a more palatable image which proved immensely popular. Sheridan Prasso notes that this image of the "sweet, gentle Japanese child-women", whilst perennially popular, found a specific appeal via Golden's book and Spielberg's subsequent film, which "gave us yet another permutation of a child-like, pining, devoted Japanese woman on screen in the form of that book's heroine geisha, Sayuri" (p. 87).[18] In fact, *Memoirs of a Geisha* was responsible for initiating nothing short of a geisha craze in the West after 1999, as Lesley Downer recalls:

> The West [ . . . ] had been swept by geisha fervor. Inspired by Golden's heroine, Sayuri, the fashion world rediscovered the allure of femininity. The collections of 1999 were full of kimono-like creations which wrapped and concealed the body, hinting at the mysteries beneath rather than revealing them. That summer Madonna appeared at the Grammies in an extraordinary outfit, described as a kimono, with long flapping sleeves and a plastic obi. (*Women of the Pleasure Quarters*, p. 4)

Newspapers and magazines carried numerous articles offering everything from advice on "Going Geisha" (ZNet commentary, 2001)[19], and "Going Geisha Gorgeous" (*San Francisco Chronicle*, 2005), a "Snapshot of Geisha Life" (*The Sunday Times*, 2005), to advice on achieving the "Look of a Geisha" (*The Sunday Times*, 2006), "geisha boot camp" (ibid), to "Geisha Confidential" (*Daily Telegraph*, 2006), to a "date" with the "geisha muse" (*The Sunday Times*, 2006). In 2006 www.fashion-era.com announced the new look to be "Oriental Fusion Fashion": "Call it what you wish, Chinoiserie, Oriental or Geisha; fashion trends this spring summer 2006 will reveal that east meets west or China meets Japan in Oriental Fusion".[20] Collections that season included "Oriental Fushion Fashion"s by Hermès, Dries Van Noten and Lanvin. American shops reported runs on "memoirs of a geisha" themed bath salts, tea and handbags. Back in 2004 the reviewer M. Cody Poulton already felt able to identify "a mass market schooled in geisha chic" ("Madame Sadayakko", p. 103); by 2006, Liza Dalby published a newspaper article in which she noted that *Memoirs* had reignited "everyone's interest in this exotic sisterhood".[21] Golden, who in the wake of

*Memoirs*' success was invited by Bill Clinton to the White House to a state dinner for the Japanese prime minister, was credited with no less than the creation of "geisha lit".²²

Troublingly, though, the West's response to *Memoirs of a Geisha*—both book and film—is more than reminiscent of the kind of orientalist fascination described by Edward W. Said in his influential study *Orientalism* back in 1978. Said's suggestion that the vestiges of Western colonialism endured in a imperialist view of the "orient", in representations of Egypt and the Middle East, which at once indulged Western (male) fantasies and exoticized images about the "feminine" and "submissive" "Orient", finds unfortunate contemporary currency here. More recently, Sheridan Prasso has identified the "orientalization" of Asian women as "the Asian Mystique"²³—a particularly gendered phenomenon—and argues that it impossible for the West to see Asia without what we might term this neo-orientalizing filter, which reminds us of Said's assertion of the sheer impossibility for a Westerner to see Asia unencumbered by an orientalist perspective:

> For if it is true that no production of knowledge in the human sciences can ever ignore or disclaim its author's involvement as a human subject in his own circumstances, then it must also be true that for a European or American studying the Orient [ . . . ] he comes up against the orient as a European or American first, as an individual second. (*Orientalism*, p. 11)

The success of *Memoirs* is just one example of the current neo-orientalist fascination with all things Asian, which has also, for instance, seen the publishing industry's wider current predilection for other texts about the "orient".²⁴ As I suggest in the next section, *Memoirs of a Geisha* serves up a mixture of tantalising eroticism and exoticism, culminating in the quasi-pornographic account of Sayuri's *mizuage*, that probably largely accounts for its phenomenal success. Current estimates vary, but it is thought to have sold in excess of forty million copies in English alone, and it stayed on the *New York Times* bestseller list for 58 weeks.²⁵

The question of whether Arthur Golden's text was orientalist was one that was also pondered by Anne Allison, in her 2001 article on *Memoirs*, literary fandom, and the pleasures of reading, "Memoirs of the Orient". Allison concluded:

> *Memoirs* also struck me as orientalist in the Saidean sense of treating the "Orient" as innately different from the West whose culture homogenizes as well as differentiates "them" from "us". My concern was not that Golden, as an outsider, could not or should not write about geisha, but rather that the outsider is so central in shaping this story as well as its mass appeal in the United States. [ . . . ] This leads to a certain exoticism. The book is written in such a way that it fosters the

impression of taking a trip to an exotic, distant land. ("Memoirs of the Orient", p. 382)

The question that Allison then poses—"What fuels the appeal and the passion?" ("Memoirs of the Orient", p. 383)—is the subject of my next section.

## AN ASIAN CINDERELLA: MEMOIRS OF A GEISHA, READER PLEASURE AND THE "ETHNOGRAPHIC ALIBI"

Although *Memoirs of a Geisha* is fiction, it is presented as a memoir, complete with a false 'translator's' note regarding the sincerity of Sayuri's story. This narrative ruse has been so successful that several reviewers have reported reading it without becoming aware of its fictional status—a mistake I too made when initially reading it in the late 1990s—and a factor in the memoir-as-guided-tour response described by Allison above.[26] From her ethnographic research on readers' responses to *Memoirs*, Allison concludes that it is what one of her interviewees terms the "authentic aura" (p. 386) of the text that provides its attraction. This is an attraction that operates in the realm of an almost irrational, heightened emotional response to the story, a kind of intoxication, as Allison recalls:

> When readers described their experience of *Memoirs* to me, it was often in language befitting a love affair. They would smile and get excited, talk quickly, and move their bodies. Passion, bordering on arousal, was palpable, and what was verbalized was the sensation of being "moved"—by the gripping story, the beautiful writing, the visual magic, the sensual world. ("Memoirs of the Orient", p. 391)

This is a phenomenon that Allison labels "passionate orientalism" (ibid). In her subsequent further exploration of these reader responses, Allison determines that the book provides "exotic escapism [ . . . ] akin to what bell hooks [ . . . ] means by 'getting a bit of the other'": simultaneously an assumed access to the exclusivity and authenticity of geisha society that also serves to confirm the reader's sense of this world as exotic, distant and "other".

The question of genre is clearly central to reader responses to *Memoirs*. Allison intriguingly records many readers' absolute insistence upon the authenticity of Sayuri's story:

> In *Memoirs* [ . . . ] the fictional abuts continually against what readers absolutely insist is the "authentic," "historically accurate" depiction rendered by Golden of geisha Japan: a presentation that many told me allowed them to better understand Japan and Japanese more broadly. ("Memoirs of the Orient", p. 382)

That readers either intentionally or unintentionally perceive *Memoirs* as the authentic and accurate life story of a young geisha in 1930s Japan, rather than the 1990s fictional effort of a white Western man, is due both to Golden's manipulation of genre and to readers' willingness and/or desire to locate Sayuri's story as a cultural "keyhole" through which to gaze at Japan (a process that Allison terms "distant intimacy", as "fantasy collapses into knowledge" ["Memoirs of the Orient", pp. 384–5]. The deliberate slippage between the enjoyment value of the text and its educative potential in these reader responses is redolent of Said's formulation of orientalism as the satisfaction of fantasies of difference, the exotic and the distant. The reader expectations that are created by Golden's explicit direction to read Sayuri's story as a memoir include anticipating a mode of life story in which the central participant—who is also assumed to be the author—will, in first-person mode, locate her experiences in a social, cultural and historical context. That (by dint of Golden's ruse) the ontological "I" (Sayuri) and the narrating "I" (Golden) are, in fact, different, seems hardly to matter to the readers of the text. The assumption of authenticity is also further strengthened by the presence of the fake "translator's note", by one "Jakob Haarhuis, Arnold Rusoff Professor of Japanese History, New York University", in which Golden further (rather cheekily) lays down several more marks of authenticity as red herrings for his reader, variously including such statements as "As a historian, I have always regarded memoirs as source material" (*Memoirs*, p. 1); "Sayuri chose me as her amanuensis" (p. 3); and "Sayuri did hide the identities of several men" (p. 4). It is only on page 433 in Golden's acknowledgements—the final page—that we read that "the character of Sayuri and her story are completely invented". In their study, *Reading Autobiography*, Sidonie Smith and Julia Watson offer the following advice to readers of life narratives:

> We expect particular kinds of stories to be told by those who have a direct and personal knowledge of that experience. We also have notions about whose life is important, whose life might be of interest to a broader public, and what experiences "count" as significant. In these expectations we imply a set of questions to raise about life narratives.
> 
> Does the narrator address the issue of *authority and authenticity*, that is, the "right" to speak this story, directly in the narrative? Does the narrator seem to be troubled by the act of telling the story? How does the narrator assert, or imply, or enact the authority to tell her story? And what about the transgressive aspects of public exposure? How does the narrator normalize or moderate them? Does she have recourse to an authority figure who introduces the text or is prominently cited in the text as a source of authorization? (*Reading Autobiography*, pp. 173–4).

This set of questions takes us to the heart of the knotty issue of genre—and the authority of genre—in *Memoirs*. Anne Allison terms the trick whereby Golden establishes the authenticity of his masquerade (by means of both Haarhuis's framing testimony and his own ventriloquism of Sayuri) and "the insistence of so many fans that the story spun by Golden reflects a world that is historically real" (p. 388) as the "ethnographic alibi" (ibid).[27] Yet what is interesting here is that Golden's creative efforts to fudge the distinction between the real and the fictional, between the ethnographically authentic and the inauthentic, and between the fabulated and the empirical, is in some ways no more nor less than the justificatory efforts we saw in, say, Lesley Downer's portraits of the flower and willow world. Like Golden, she sought to shrink the distance between her and her subject(s); like Golden she adopted an ethnographic guise; like Golden to a degree she sought to speak *for* as well as *of* her subject(s). Is it not then possible to suggest that within the emergent genre of American geisha studies, there is a range of possible ethnographic postures?

## THE MEMOIRS CONTROVERSY: MINEKO IWASAKI AND THE ISSUE OF MIZUAGE

Nowhere is the thorny issue of geisha sexuality more central than in the question of the existence of the ritual of the geisha's *mizuage* or deflowering by an elder male patron. At once the source of prurient speculation on the part of observers and prudish modesty on the part of geisha, the practice of *mizuage* is one of the most controversial aspects of geishahood, and the source of both heated dispute and salacious speculation. Liza Dalby observes that "the question of geisha and prostitution has always been complicated" (*Geisha*, p. 60); and that "sex in the geisha world" is "a topic that geisha are understandably touchy about" (*Geisha*, p. 115). Dalby records a *zashiki* patron and former *danna* describing the process of *mizuage* in lascivious detail for her benefit:

> The man would tell the maiko to lie down; then, breaking [ . . . ] eggs, he swallowed the yolks and rubbed the whites between her thighs. "This is mizu-age. Good night, my dear," he said, and turned out the lights. The next night the room was readied in just the same way and again he cracked the eggs, consumed the yolks, and applied the whites between the girl's legs. "This is mizu-age. Sleep well, my dear." Again the next night, and the next. Each time, however, he wiggled his fingers in a little deeper with the slippery egg whites. By the end of the week the maiko had gotten used to this little ritual and she was very relaxed. And at that point, fortified as he was with all those egg yolks, you see, mizu-age was easily accomplished. (*Geisha*, p. 115)

Geisha listening to this graphic story immediately are at pains to stress the superannuated nature of this practice though, as Dalby also recalls:

> "It's all changed now," said the okasan. "There's no mizu-age ceremony any more, with or without eggs." [ . . . ] I sensed a faint embarrassment in a few of the older geisha [ . . . ] Today geisha and women in general have more control over their sexuality. Older geisha automatically say how wonderful it is that their daughters do not have to submit to mizuage. (*Geisha*, p. 115)

In her study of geisha, *Women of the Pleasure Quarters*, Lesley Downer also located the practice of *mizuage* in its historical context:

> For women who were maiko before prostitution was made illegal in 1958—in other words, anyone aged over about fifty-five, which included many of the older members of the community—compulsory deflowering at an early age was simply a part of life. It made no difference whether they were the spoiled children of generations of geisha and had grown up in a wealthy geisha house. [ . . . ] Like a young man's circumcision, painful but unavoidable, it was an initiation ritual. It marked the transition from maiko to geisha, from girl to woman, and was a prerequisite for changing one's collar, synonymous with growing up. Until you had it, you were not a woman. A virgin geisha would have been as much a contradiction in terms as a virgin wife. (*Women of the Pleasure Quarters*, p. 129)

The existence—and prevalence—of the practice of *mizuage* crystallizes many of the issues at stake in representing the geisha world, and nowhere is this thrown into such stark relief as the *mizuage* furore that following the publication of Golden's *Memoirs of a Geisha*. Golden writes of Sayuri's *mizuage* ceremony at the age of fifteen, at the hands of one Dr. Crab, in unsparing detail. Sayuri's *mizuage* privilege was sold for a record sum and in the text it is figured as a defining moment in the geisha Sayuri's maturation. As I have discussed, Golden stresses the authenticity of Sayuri's story via a series of strategies, not least of which is his acknowledgement of the input from the geisha Mineko Iwasaki. In the acknowledgements to *Memoirs of a Geisha*, Arthur Golden writes:

> In the course of my extensive research I am indebted to one individual above all others. Mineko Iwasaki, one of Gion's top geisha in the 1960s and 1970s, opened her Kyoto home to me during May 1992, and corrected my every misconception about the life of a geisha [ . . . ] she took me on an insider's tour of Gion, and [ . . . ] patiently answered all my questions about the ritual of a geisha's life in intimate detail. She became, and remains, a good friend. (*Memoirs*, p. 433)

Mineko Iwasaki's version of this encounter, though, is somewhat different:

> When he came here, I explained and explained and explained for over two weeks. I almost lost my voice. I thought he could understand. [ . . . ] I explained so much about our life and our world, and yet it became like a confusion. That is why I really feel regret. His words are a fiction. [ . . . ] the problem is the misrepresentation of the geisha world. (*The Asian Mystique*, p. 208)

In her own memoir, which she penned as a direct rebuttal of Golden's novel and what she perceived as its tarnishing of her reputation, Mineko Iwasaki further firmly distances herself and by implication, her profession, from the practice of *mizuage* and its representation and discussion in Western studies:

> A young oiran also underwent a ritual called "mizuage" but hers consisted of being ceremoniously deflowered by a patron who had paid handsomely for the privilege. (This alternative definition of the word "mizuage" has been the source of some confusion about what it means to be a geisha). (*Geisha: A Life*, p. 253)

In an interview with Sheridan Prasso, she further directly expressed her dismay at Golden's promulgation of what she adamantly insisted was a false picture of geisha practice:

> The worst crime in her mind is confounding the practices of prostitutes or lower-class geisha with those of the geisha of High Gion—namely, that the Sayuri girl has her virginity auctioned off in a system of *mizuage*. [ . . . ] A real geisha from this quarter would never have auctioned her virginity, she asserts. Miss Iwasaki herself did not, and nobody she knew or knew of did either. [ . . . ] when she had spoken of her *mizuage* with Golden, she says, she meant that her monthly earnings, the payments by customers to the geisha house in exchange for her presence at parties, were the highest of any geisha in Gion. When she said her *mizuage* was the highest in Gion, it simply meant that she had the most number of requests for her presence, not that a customer had paid for her virginity, she says. (*The Asian Mystique*, p. 209)

The word "mizuage" thus seems to bear different meanings according to context. It also carries connotations of water (it literally means "raising the waters"), which in Japanese is intimately connected with sexual imagery. For instance, prostitution is known as the "water business", *mizu shobai*. Clearly it is largely the practice of *mizuage* that has created the confusion between geisha and prostitutes, and this is also the source of the offence of Western representations of geisha to those who inhabit the flower and willow world. As Prasso concludes after reading the books by Golden, Dalby and Downer:

> I realized that they [ . . . ]mention the auction of virginity of young geisha, the *mizuage*. That is what is common to all three books [ . . . ] and that is what has upset her. [ . . . ] She insists that, because foreigners keep writing about auctioning of virginity and having sex with male patrons it needs clarifiying. Surely it is what sells books back in the West, but it is grossly inaccurate. (*The Asian Mystique*, pp. 212-3)

Yet, as Liza Dalby also notes:

> The common misunderstandings and arguments about the connection between geisha and prostitution spring from an indiscriminate collapsing of a wide variety of categories of geisha. Whereas in one sense we may speak of a Kyoto apprentice and an onsen [hot springs] geisha in the same breath as part of Japan's living geisha tradition, in another sense combining them at all is ludicrous. (*Geisha*, p. 173)

The life of the *onsen* geisha was—and still is—radically different from the artisan high practitioners of Kyoto and Tokyo. Former (initially indentured) *onsen* geisha Sayo Masuda's *Autobiography of a Geisha*, penned in 1956, carries the subtitle "half a lifetime of pain and struggle", and describes a relentless life of toil, in which sex for sale features prominently. In her translator's introduction, to the Columbia University Press 2003 English edition, the Japan scholar G. G. Rowley writes:

> The romanticization of geisha life as dedicated principally to the pursuit of traditional arts ignores the poverty that drove many parents to indenture their daughters to geisha houses. Such romanticization also erases certain geisha from the collective memory and overlooks the bottom line of the whole geisha business. The geisha thus erased are hot-springs-resort geisha, and the bottom line of the geisha business is, of course, sex for money. [ . . . ] One of Masuda Sayo's aims in writing her autobiography was to describe this bottom line. In her sixteenth year, after the party at which she made her debut as a professional geisha, Masuda underwent sexual initiation (*mizuage*) at the hands of her patron (*danna*) who had paid her house handsomely for the privilege. The mother of her geisha house then sold her "virginity" four more times. Masuda's description of this is brisk and completely devoid of self-pity. [ . . . ] In this passage and elsewhere in her memoir, Masuda completely demolishes the notion that geisha do not provide sexual services for payment. (*Autobiography of a Geisha*, p. 7)

The tough lives of *onsen* geisha thus throw into relief the more cushioned existence of the inhabitants of the higher echelons of the flower and willow world. In some ways, Golden's representation is thus more in line with Sayo

Masuda's life than that of geisha like Mineko Iwasaki. As G.G. Rowley also observes:

> In the modern era . . . the art of the geisha, however intimately related to sex it may remain in the workplace of the geisha, tends to be presented to the outside world as "art" performed purely for its own sake and in no way related to sex. The connection between the two has been deliberately obscured, one result of which is that many writers either emphasize unduly the geisha's artistic accomplishments or deny her sexual duties, or both. (*Autobiography of a Geisha*, p. 173)

Anne Allison's analysis of American reader-responses to *Memoirs* was published in 2001 and thus did not include a consideration of Rob Marshall's film version of 2005. The furore over issues of authenticity and representation in the book, which as I have explored centred upon the ritual of *mizuage*, was re-ignited when the film was released, but this time the controversy surrounded the equally sensitive issue of race and representation. As bell hooks reminds us, "the field of representation remains the place of struggle", and "the emphasis on film is central because it, more than any other media experience, determines how [ . . . ] [we] are seen and how others will respond to us based on their relation to these constructed and consumed images" (*Black Looks: Race and Representation*, pp. 3–5). Although the film of *Memoirs* attracted the perhaps to-be-expected criticisms of being too soft-focus in its representation of hardship and poverty in 1930s Japan, and at the same time too hard-core in its coverage of Sayuri's sexual initiation, the loudest protestations concerned the casting of the Chinese actors Zhang Ziyi, Michelle Yeoh and Gong Li in the film's central roles. The film's producer, Rob Marshall, defended this decision, telling reporters that "I have a very simple philosophy about casting, and that is: the best person for the role. [ . . . ] The demands were enormous and Ziyi was the best" (CBC News); as did Arthur Golden who wryly noted that "Hugh Grant is an Englishman who can play an American and Russell Crowe is an Australian who can play an Englishman and nobody gets upset about that" ("Geisha Guy Seeks New Date with the Muse", *The Sunday Times*, January 15, 2006). Golden also wrote to several newspapers in defence of the film's representation of Japanese culture, including *The Washington Post*, to lament that:

> No storyteller or journalist is ever exact enough for an expert. [ . . . ] It's worth bearing in mind that Hamlet makes poor Danish history and Lawrence of Arabia grossly oversimplifies the politics and culture of the Middle East. (*The Washington Post*)

Japan's recurrent sensitivity over its representation in the West also came to the fore once again. CBC News reported that:

> In Japan, critics questioned whether a Hollywood movie can accurately depict the nuanced culture of geishas—the women trained from childhood in music, dance and conversation so as to be elegant companions to wealthy men. In the past, other cultures have portrayed geishas as simply glorified prostitutes. (CBC News, Tuesday, 29 November 2005)

The film's production history starkly illustrates these sensitivities. The film rights were initially bought by Steven Spielberg, and in the late-1990s it was widely reported in the Western media that he intended to make a film version of *Memoirs* himself. Many observers took this as further evidence of the 'geisha fervor' to which I have already alluded, as I did to in my 2002 exploration in *Negotiating Identities*.[28] Spielberg's attraction to the movie was reportedly that it was "a kind of Cinderella story" ("Spielberg Looks to the East", *New York Times*, 11 September 1998).[29] The notion that *Memoirs of a Geisha* functions as a kind of "Asian Cinderella" helps to explain its crossover appeal to a Western audience (Sheridan Prasso describes it as a lovely, Cinderella-like love story" [*The Asian Mystique*, p. 202], and Anne Allison observes that the Cinderella element soldered onto the geisha strand renders the story "more palatable and familiar to Western audiences" ["Memoirs of the Orient", p. 394]).[30] Yet it also explains the source of its offence in some Japanese quarters, since it is this very aspect of fabulation, and the melding of a Western story archetype with an exclusively high-Japanese cultural enclave, that also in some minds denigrates geisha culture. Commenting upon *Memoirs*, one Tokyo geisha named Yachiyoko observed:

> Some Westerners read books which must give them misguided information, but after they see us, they realize. For example, some people have an image of a geisha as girls from poor backgrounds being sold into the entertainment business. Nowadays there's not so much that dark image. Those who like art and culture and come from good backgrounds are geisha. ("The Real Memoirs of Geisha", p. 219)

## THE GEISHA-IZED WOMAN AND THE "GLOBAL IMAGINARY"

The geishas' distaste for what they view as the distorted Western representation of their profession as expressed above by Yachiyoko reminds us once more of the position of geishahood at the extreme end of Western (male) imaginings—fantasies—of the 'oriental', exotic and fetishized Japanese woman. When researching this chapter, time and again I came upon gratuitously lubricious materials, from graphic visual compilations to extraordinary pornographic fantasies.[31] It is not easy to distinguish between 'respectable' texts and the more obviously pornographic. There is a generic slippage between the salaciously titillating pillow book[32] and the fictional and the anthropological in geisha writing which is not simple to explain. Where does spectacle stop and pornography start? In one notable example, "cultural anthropologist" S. Z. Ahmed's *I am a Geisha* masquerades as an anthropological project relating the story of one ex-geisha called Miko. But the text comprises nothing short of a graphic pornographic account of Miko's encounters with a range of Western men, in the manner of sexual memoirs like Catherine Millet's *The Sexual Life of Catherine M*. The front cover blurb reads: "She had no experience with strange western men, She made one big mistake for a geisha". Art historian and journalist Bérénice Geoffroy-Schneiter's *Geishas* provides another example. Ostensibly a study of visual representations of the geisha, the book includes explicit *shunga* prints of men engaged in sex with geisha from original *shunga* pillow books, and the accompanying text underscores the heightened eroticism that is conjured by such images:

> Geisha . . . at the slightest evocation of this little Japanese word there appears instantly before the eyes of Westerners a succession of images swaying gently between languorous voluptuousness and erotic fantasy. And yet, far from being a simple "creature" destined to satisfy carnal pleasures, the "geisha", on her own, sums up the quintessence of Japanese refinement. A source of inspiration for print artists who took the delicate curve of a shoulder, the roundness of a breast and the delicacy of a neck to satiation, she embodies, above all, the ideal "Woman". This intelligent and cultured courtesan is simultaneously musician, poet and dancer. Westerners prefer to celebrate in her the myth of the girl-woman, midway between spouse and doll. (*Geisha*, back cover copy)

At the extreme end of the spectrum is unadorned pornography, such as *Geisha Secrets: A Pillow Book for Lovers* by Miranda Reigns, which again contains a series of explicitly graphic *shunga* illustrations. Even coffee table compilations, such as Eleanor Underwood's classic *The Life of a Geisha* (1999; complete with Foreword by Liza Dalby and jacket blurb by Arthur Golden) and John Gallagher's *Geisha: A Unique World of Tradition, Elegance, and Art* (2003), linger upon some of the more salacious aspects of geishahood. For instance, both Eleanor Underwood and John Gallagher discuss *mizuage*, and describe aspects of the more erotic bodily symbolism of geisha make-up, such as the 'split peach' hairstyle or *wareshinobu* (in the past worn by geisha before they were deflowered, a visual echo of their sexuality).[33] It is precisely this commodification and appropriation of the more erotic aspects of geisha allure to which the practitioners of traditional Japanese arts strenuously object, since in their minds, emphasising these elements at the expense of others devalues the geisha's art. Traise Yamamoto terms this appropriation "the geisha-ized woman", which she views as both metaphorically and metonymically pliable:

She serves as both the sign of willing Japanese capitulation to aggressive acts of military paternalism and the vestibular site through which white Western manhood reassures itself of its coherence and primacy. [ ... ] the "geisha-ized" Japanese woman as both racial and sexual other is not merely a distasteful expression of Western stereotyping but the necessary mechanism of a paradigm in which Japan, femininely infantile and sexually exotic, may be mastered. (*Masking Selves, Making Subjects*, pp. 60–1)

In *Women on the Verge: Japanese Women, Western Dreams* (2002), Karen Kelsky goes further. Kelsky discusses the "transnational signifier" of the Japanese woman, who is only granted agency in Western representations insofar as she offers a service to the Western male. If this is the case, then the apex of this stereotype is the geisha. In fact, Kelsky identifies geisha as the "sexual nexus", a kind of cultural cross-pollination that affects—infects—Japanese views of Japanese femininity as well. Kelsky identifies

> an emergent global Imaginary, derived from the increasingly frenetic circulation of images through media ranging from American products like CNN, MTV, and the tireless output of Hollywood to the more dispersed media of Star TV. [ ... ] This global Imaginary is productive of dispersed and disruptive desires that exceed the possibilities of the nation, or, for that matter, the transnational media itself. (*Women on the Verge*, p. 13)

This transnational or "global Imaginary" has the power to both eroticize and racialize; and the extent to which it might be possible to resist this power is questionable. Geisha like Mineko Iwasaki have proved that they are not merely passive subjects of a transnational cultural script, since the autobiographical act itself is evidence of both a degree of cultural agency and the potential to resist an imposed (trans)cultural narrative. Yet the wrangle to claim the ultimate authority of understanding geishahood is also one that is ongoing, as the tactics to assert authorial and ethnographic authority engaged by Liza Dalby, Lesley Downer and Arthur Golden demonstrate. In *Reading Autobiography*, Sidonie Smith and Julia Watson identify the processes of what they call "new subject formations" in life narrative, and cite Caren Kaplan's notion of emergent "out-law" genres as evidence of this. For Kaplan, out-law genres "mix two conventionally 'unmixable' elements" to create complex and interventionist new forms, in a manner quite reminiscent of the kinds of genre slippage we have seen emerge in geisha literature.[34]

# 5 Korean Expatriate Writing and the History of the Korean Peninsula

> I am speaking of histories that all of us should know.
> —John Kwang, *Native Speaker*

> When the unified life of our country is cut in two . . . our country will be like a nail stuck in the flow of history.
> —Paek Ki-wan

> Korean American writers . . . draw, in their works, upon that background resonance that lurks like an unavoidable indication of cultural memory, that residue of blood, language, custom, and historical trauma.
> —Heinz Insu Fenkl and Walter Lew, *Kŏri*

## THE "EMPTY CUPBOARD" OF KOREAN HISTORY

Renowned historian of Korea Bruce Cumings has written:

> In the South of Korea, one particular decade—that between 1935 and 1945—is an empty cupboard: millions of people used and abused by the Japanese cannot get records on what they know to have happened to them, and thousands of Koreans who worked with the Japanese have simply erased that history as if it had never happened. (*Korea's Place in the Sun*, qtd. Park, p. 193)

The empty cupboard to which Cumings refers—that of the period of Japan's colonial occupation of Korea and its aftermath—is poignantly phrased.[1] If this is true for the millions who suffered under colonial rule, it is also the case that the Korean War, the bifurcation of the Korean peninsula by foreign powers in 1953, and the terrible suffering of the North Korean people under the repressive communist regime of Kim Il Sung in the decades that followed, are similarly shrouded pasts concealing unprecedented hardship, starvation and the loss of political and personal freedom. The dilemma for the personal memoirists, fictionalists and historians who have sought to reverse this omission in the latter part of the twentieth century onwards—to fill the empty cupboard—is the compelling yet vexing question of this chapter; that is to say, how best to achieve this? In her memoir *Home Was the Land of Morning Calm* K. Connie Kang voices this very concern:

> We have the indelible scars on our psyches of the Japanese occupation, the Korean War, the partition that still keeps eleven million Korean families separated [ . . . ] we have many stories to tell, but we have been reticent. Where do we begin? (*Home Was the Land of Morning Calm*, p. xvi)

It is perhaps even more difficult for Korean female voices, whose perspectives have often been delegitimized, and who have traditionally been constrained by the Korean Confucian ethic that discourages any forthrightness of female expression, as well as struggling against a prevailing androcentric discourse of national history in Korea[2], as novelist Mia Yun asserts: "I saw how Korean women, the descendents of the she-bear woman and the son of the king of heaven, lived in the folds of history", and consequently as she laments, the "stories of Korean women—were not there" (*House of the Winds*, p. 56; p. 172). Yet twentieth-century Korean history *is* Korean women's history, as well as a record of external and colonial involvement, from Japan as the century opened to the United States today, as Chungmoo Choi observes in *Dangerous Women: Gender and Korean Nationalism*, when she refers to Korea's "gendered and sexualized international relationship" (p. 15).

Writing against this tradition of silence and omission, most expatriate Korean writers deal in different ways with the effects of the Japanese colonisation of Korea, the period of the Korean War and its aftermath, and the division of Korea into North Korea and South Korea that followed. In fact, Korean American writing in particular is quite distinctive in that it has a noticeable history of political activism, both in its depiction of Korean and Korean American activists and through the political propaganda purposes of the writing itself (which is often to protest colonial intervention in Korean internal affairs or to promote the Korean nationalist case), elements that can be found in well-known fictional works such as Ronyoung Kim's *Clay Walls* (1987), Nora Okja Keller's companion novels *Comfort Woman* (1997) and *Fox Girl* (2002), Mia Yun's *House of the Winds* (1998) and *Translations of Beauty* 2004), and the edited fictional collections *Kŏri* (2001), *Echoes upon Echoes* (2002), *Surfacing Sadness* (2003), and *Yobo* (2003). Life writing examples include Mary Paik Lee's *Quiet Odyssey* (1990), Peter Hyun's *Man Sei! The Making of a Korean American* (1986), Margaret K. Pai's *The Dreams of Two Yi-Min* (1989), Helie Lee's celebrated *Still Life with Rice* (1996) and *In the Absence of Sun* (2002), Linda Sue Park's *When My Name*

*Was Keoko* (2002), the translation of Kang Chol-Hwan's *The Aquariums of Pyongyang* (2001), K. Connie Kang's *Home Was the Land of Morning Calm* (1995), Hyun Sook Han's *Many Lives Intertwined* (2004), Elizabeth Kim's *Ten Thousand Sorrows* (2000), Sook Nyul Choi's autobiographical fictional trilogy, *Year of Impossible Goodbyes* (1991), *Echoes of the White Giraffe* (1993) and *Gathering of Pearls* (1994), and the edited collections *East to America: Korean American Life Stories* (1996) and the bi-lingual *The Letter Never Sent I* and *II* (2004 and 2005).[3] All of these texts depict to varying degrees Korean and Korean American resistance to Japanese colonial rule; the damage wreaked by successive conflicts across the Korean peninsula; protest against the racist treatment of Korean Americans by the American state; as well as promoting both a strong nationalist cause and the movement towards eventual reunification in Korea.

In this chapter, then, I will investigate the example of Korean American writing, both through some of the increasingly well-known texts mentioned above, and also through emerging new voices. In each case, I seek to explore the manner in which twentieth-century Korean history is revisited, memorialised and revised by means of personal testimonies and hitherto unheard fictional and non-fictional voices and perspectives. I will place these explorations against the dual backdrop of the Korean peninsula's turbulent twentieth-century past and the story of twentieth-century Korean immigration to America. My specific and detailed textual analysis has three sub-sections. I have chosen firstly to place two main texts in counterpoint: K. Connie Kang's *Home Was the Land of Morning Calm* (1995), and Kang Chol-Hwan's *The Aquariums of Pyongyang* (2001). Each text is representative of the two strands of the emerging genre of what we might term Korean "protest literature" that I am seeking to identify. Kang's *Home Was the Land of Morning Calm* is a predominantly Seoul-based narrative, which relates the author's family flight from North Korea to the south, then eventually to the United States, and demonstrates the distinct blend of traumatic personal recollection, impeccable historical research and political determination that is the hallmark of this literature. The historical sweep is also epic—1900–1994—the analysis astute and erudite, and the narrative thrust radical.

Kang Chol-Hwan's *The Aquariums of Pyongyang* is illuminating in juxtaposition both by connection and as a point of departure. Published in translation, this is uniquely a *North* Korean memoir of the harsh and harrowing life in the notorious North Korean gulag of Yodok. It is a tale of political persecution, of individual suffering and ultimately of a state in crisis. Framed by both a preface and a politically strident introduction, this is a plea for human rights and political intervention on a grand scale, reminiscent perhaps of anti-slavery or anti-apartheid writing. Kang Chol-Hwan and K. Connie Kang are of the same generation, both born just prior to, or just after, the Korean War, and both write with the advantage of historical hindsight and from the comparative comfort and freedom of the

United States; yet as voices of the north and south of Korea respectively, as male and female respectively, each contribution emerges as quite variable in texture. Reading both in conjunction reveals the manner in which the same history of invasion, war and the division of the country along the 38$^{th}$ Parallel, affected people of different gender, geographical and class backgrounds, as well as starkly illustrating the direct relationship between the degree of trauma experienced by the individual, and the subsequent compulsion to record it. Of Koreans who have lived through war, conflict and the restriction of freedom (that is, virtually everyone), Patrick Dowdey and Wei Hsin Gui write "these people caught in war share a silent unity that bridges the categories of North, South, civilian, soldier and prisoner. They become part of history and memory" ("Introduction", *Living Through the Forgotten War*, p. 7).

My third principal textual focus is Nora Okja Keller's celebrated fictional trilogy about Korea, of which *Comfort Woman* and *Fox Girl* have appeared to date. Nora Okja Keller's historical novels *Comfort Woman* (1997) and *Fox Girl* (2002), the first two installments in a planned trilogy, tell the story of the Korean 'comfort women' and the Korean GI camp-towns that sprang up during the Korean War (and that often became notorious sites of prostitution), and similarly collectively provide a revisionist history of Japanese colonialism, the Korean War, and US involvement in Korea. Comfort women were young girls, usually of school age, sometimes as young as twelve, who were forcibly drafted into prostitution to service the Japanese military, during its occupation of Korea, between the late 1930s and 1945. Keller's protagonists in this novel are Akiko, a refugee who has fled to the U.S., and her daughter by an American missionary, Beccah. Thus by dint of her characterization alone, Keller marks the history of Korean-American entanglement within her narrative. This text charts Akiko's struggle to come to terms with her past as a comfort woman, the story of which she gradually reveals to her daughter. As I go on to describe, critical attention is increasingly being paid to the stories of Korean Military 'comfort women'. Until the early 1990s, the issue had hardly been discussed. Records and documents relating to the practice have been suppressed (the Japanese government 'classified' documents relating to comfort women), and this was coupled with an "intentional amnesia" on the part of many of the victims. It is only recently that oral testimonies, written accounts and academic research have begun to appear on the subject; apart from Keller's fictionalized account, there is now also an edited collection by several former comfort women, entitled *The True Stories of the Korean Comfort Women*. As I will also show, the global controversy over the very existence of the comfort women has been reignited in the recent past, with an American-led drive for compensation on one hand, and the Japanese government's repeated insistence that comfort women were at worst voluntary sex workers, at best, that they did not provide sexual services at all, on the other.

Finally, I discuss these books in conjunction with Helie Lee's life narrative diptych, *Still Life with Rice* and *In the Absence of Sun*, and Sook Nyul Choi's "Korea" trilogy: *Year of Impossible Goodbyes*, *Echoes of the White Giraffe* and *Gathering of Pearls*, in order to demonstrate the range of the contemporary expanding canon of Korean protest literatures. These two authors have produced innovative multi-volume works exploring aspects of the Korean and Korean American experience in unprecedented depth and breadth, and with an unerring emphasis upon issues of human rights and political intervention.

## WOMEN'S NARRATIVES

> By simply telling the stories of the women, I hope I am giving them voices.
>
> —Mia Yun, *House of the Winds*

To date, it is perhaps the writer Theresa Hak Kyung Cha who has explored Korean political issues the most experimentally as well as extensively in the increasingly well-known, experimental and multi-genre text *Dictee*. Cha was born in Korea in 1951 during the Korean War, and emigrated with her family to the United States in 1962, where she lived first in Hawaii and then in San Francisco. She first published *Dictee* in 1982. It weaves together a variety of narrative modes, including poetry, journal entries, letters and excerpts from history books, to document both Korean life under Japanese colonial control and the immigrant experience in America. The text is punctuated by non-textual material, such as photographs, maps and calligraphy. Owing to its complexity, *Dictee* is an intriguing text, that has been read variously as a postmodernist narrative, protest memoir and Korean American autobiography, although it is presented here primarily as a revisionist history. In relation to the concentration upon female experiences in very recent Korean American writing by women, it is also possible to see how Theresa Hak Kyung Cha's work has influenced writers such as Nora Okja Keller and Sook Nyul Choi (discussed later), in terms of an overtly politicized perspective and an unerring emphasis upon the stories of women.

It is also particularly noticeable that it has been women who have sought to undertake significant and substantial multi-volume projects that resolutely memorialise and mark Korea's history. As with Nora Okja Keller's "Korea" trilogy, which spotlights a different aspect of Korean women's sexual subjugation in each book, so Sook Nyul Choi's trilogy: *Year of Impossible Goodbyes* (1991), *Echoes of the White Giraffe* (1993) and *Gathering of Pearls* (1994), presents us with a chronological exploration of Korean history, once again by foregrounding the stories of Korea's women. As Elaine Kim observes, "Choi's characters are women who are able successfully to survive the privations of foreign occupation and the turbulence of war without husbands, fathers, brothers, and sons, from who they are separated by political upheaval and war" ("Korean American Literature", p. 166).

Just as female Korean immigrant writers have refused to tell their national story *sotto voce*, so Korean immigrant women have been at the forefront of other forms of political activity. The emerging prevalence of women's perspectives is additionally reflective of Korean immigrant women's history of political activism. As described by Sucheng Chan in her introduction to Mary Paik Lee's *Quiet Odyssey*, "Korean women who settled in America made crucial contributions not only to the survival of their families, but also to the nationalist struggle. Such responsibilities elevated their position in the immigrant community and transformed their consciousness" (*Quiet Odyssey*, p. xxi). She goes on to detail this remarkable degree of involvement:

> In the wake of the March First Movement [ . . . ] the *Taehan Puin Kujehoe* (Korean Women's Relief Society) was organized, with branches in Hawaii and California, to support the Korean independence movement. [ . . . ] A second organization that grew out of the March First Movement was the *Taehan Yoja Aikuk-dan* (Korean Women's Patriotic Society), with branches in California towns and cities with sizeable Korean populations. (ibid., p. xxxiii)

Yet as Elaine Kim has also cautioned, and as I later discuss, it remains hard to hear some Korean and Korean American women's voices:

> Almost entirely missing [ . . . ] are writings [ . . . ] by the tens of thousands of women who immigrated as wives of U.S. servicemen. Many Korean American viewpoints are represented only through the filtering memories of an English-speaking descendent or the modifying lens of a writer's class privilege. The[se] voices [ . . . ] have thus been faint and mediated. ("Korean American Literature", *An Interethnic Companion to Asian American Literature*, ed. King-kok Cheung, p. 156)

Kim also observes the particularly politicized perspective of Korean American writers:

> Korean American literature [ . . . ] emerges from the didactic interplay between social forces and cultural production, continually altering its boundaries and contours. The resulting shifts and reconfigurations are particularly dramatic currently, because of rapid growth and [ . . . ] shifting sociopolitical circumstances in the United States, Korea, and the world. (Korean American Literature", p. 157)

## "WHEN WHALES FIGHT, SHRIMPS GET THEIR BACKS BROKEN": KOREA'S HISTORY 1910–2008

As Kim notes, Korea's social and political changes have been particularly turbulent in the twentieth century. The above traditional Korean proverb accurately describes Korea's apparent fate to be a pawn in not just East Asian, but global political conflicts throughout the twentieth century. Korea embarked upon the century as a reluctant protectorate of Japan, but by 1910, Japan had formally annexed Korea, and had initiated an aggressive and systematic destruction of Korean language, culture and religious practices, as well as the brutal stripping of Korea's natural resources and the forced conscription of its citizens in support of the war effort. Korea remained under the repressive and often violent colonial control of Japan until 1945, when, with the end of the Second World War, Korea was liberated once more. Yet freedom neither ended Korea's decades of conflict nor brought stability. Following the peninsular split along the 38$^{th}$ Parallel, and the establishment of the separate Republics in the North and South, under Russian and American direction respectively, the Korean War broke out in 1950 initially as a result of northern aggression under Kim Il Sung. Although war ended in 1953, Korea has remained a country divided, the North under the increasingly repressive and isolationist control of the communist Kim dictatorship, and with the more liberal leadership of the South presiding over south Korea's transformation into a successful capitalist— so-called 'tiger'—economy.

All of the texts under the spotlight in this case study cast their eyes across this century-long history, even when, as with *The Aquariums of Pyongyang*, the concentration is upon a single decade (1977–1987), or, as in Linda Sue Park's adolescent novel *When My Name Was Keoko*, a particular moment of history (World War II), or as with Nora Okja Keller's historical novels, the lives of a particular group at the certain moment in time (the existence of 'comfort women' between 1930–1945 and the GI children growing up in Korean camptowns in the 1960s). Other narratives have a noticeable epic historical sweep, regardless of whether we can categorize them as life histories or even historical fiction: Helie Lee's imaginative memoir *Still Life with Rice* spans 1912–1991; Connie Kang's *Home Was the Land of Morning Calm* 1900–1994; and *Quiet Odyssey* 1905–1990. In their edited collection, *Kŏri*, Korean American novelists Heinz Insu Fenkl and Walter K. Lew remark upon this phenomenon of a hyperconsciousness of both politics and history in Korean American writing:

> Epochal shifts in Korea like colonization, division of the country into communist North and capitalist South, war, rapid industrialization, and movements for democratization have been powerful forces within the development of Korean American literary consciousness. (*Kŏri*, p. xv)

They ascribe this tendency not simply to a mere imbrication with Korea's past on the part of Korean American writers, but to a residual trauma that lingers in the very creative consciousness, a wound which like the 38th Parallel that scars Korea, remains unhealed:

> Korean American writers [ . . . ] draw, in their works, upon that background resonance that lurks like an unavoidable indication of cultural memory, that residue of blood, language, custom, and historical trauma. (*Kŏri*, p. xiv)

Indeed, these texts are replete with a sense of loss, the burden of a traumatic past in which the political story of Korea is figured as a *personal* history regardless of genre, a history that cannot be forgotten or suppressed, from Connie Kang:

> Every detail [ . . . ] is etched in my memory, like a video inside my head that never goes away. Even after forty-odd years, I can still taste every piece of food that my resourceful grandmother and mother provided. And the ordeal to survive: I still relive those days as if they happened only yesterday. In an eight-year-old's mind uncluttered by other experiences, responsibilities, or preoccupations, living through a war does not go away. (*Home Was the Land of Morning Calm*, p. 118)

Or from Mia Yun:

> Preserve your memories. Once you start unraveling them, there is no stopping. They become living things. Out of your control. [ . . . ] you see the same simple afternoon light that long ago shone on your mother's hand and give it a ghostly soul. Here and there, you stumble onto secrets [ . . . ] You were a child. You saw but you didn't understand. (*House of the Winds*, p. 1)

Or from Nora Okja Keller:

> It still seems strange to me to think of Korea in terms of north and south, to realize that a line we couldn't see or feel, a line we crossed with two steps, cut the body of my country in two. In dreams I will always see the thousands of people, the living and the dead, forming long queues that spiral out from the head and feet of Korea, not knowing that when they reach the navel they will have to turn back. Not knowing that they will never be able to return home. Not knowing that they are forever lost. (*Comfort Woman*, p. 105)

The very unwieldiness as well as the intractability of historical trauma is thus repeatedly and resonantly expressed in this literature. This is also a history carried by those on the margins of Korean society: the women, the children, the dispossessed. In a haunting passage in Mia Yun's *The House of the Winds*, she writes "Korea seemed [ . . . ] a bloodied Eden full of the voiceless souls of women" (p. 5); "I had seen mother's history", the narrator tells us, "Her very own history, a legacy of a river full of hopes and dreams and despair of women before her" (p. 2). Women and children not only carry the burden of history in these stories, but they are also the very conduits through which the tales are relayed. *House of the Winds*, *Comfort Woman*, *Fox Girl*, *When My Name Was Keoko*, *Still Life with Rice*, *Ten Thousand Sorrows*, *Clay Walls*, *The Aquariums of Pyongyang*, *Year of Impossible Goodbyes*, *Echoes of the White Giraffe* and *Home Was the Land of Morning Calm* are all wholly or partially told from the unique perspective of a child and among these perspectives, it is noticeable too that Kang Chol-Hwan's is one of only a very few male voices. In her recent study, *Begin Here: Reading Asian North American Autobiographies of Childhood*, Rocío G. Davis remarks:

> We can certainly argue that personal trajectories mirror group experiences, while accepting that collective identities are not necessarily the sum of individual experiences. (*Begin Here*, p. 81)

But she also crucially adds that childhood perspectives

> highlight the surprising resilience of children who overcome war and the destruction of families [ . . . ] [and] demonstrate a creative way of dealing with that trauma of childhood, as a gesture toward healing and to connect with a community that shares this history. By articulating strategies for survival—personal resolution and textual inscription—these writers give themselves another chance to begin again. (*Begin Here*, p. 74)

Thus, we may argue that the unique position of childhood perspectives in this literature performs several functions. First, as Davis outlines in relation to her analysis of childhood memoirs of Cambodian survivors of the Khmer Rouge takeover, remembered childhoods that pre-date war experiences enable the connection of the prewar era as a time of nostalgia with the common representation of childhood itself as an Edenic space free from tragedy.[4] An encounter with traumatic experience—war, dispossession, colonial aggression, rape, hunger or imprisonment—abruptly engenders the loss of innocence and propels the child into a period of accelerated maturation. Second, since the perspective of the child in this literature is always necessarily (re)constructed, the typical narrative trajectory that we can roughly identify as childhood innocence—childhood lost/traumatic experiences—recuperation—survival and remembering, must be one of several possible trajectories, so that the performative element of this narrative structure emerges. It can also be assumed that in the case of life writing at least, the narrative vantage point must be that of a survivor perspective. As Davis remarks:

> These texts suggest that the authors have chosen a literary path toward more than just personal recuperation. By engaging traumatic experiences and making readers aware of the silenced histories behind immigration, they promote intercultural understanding and support collective memory. (*Begin Here*, p. 81)

Third, the representation of the trauma of invasion, war, colonial aggression and its aftermath by way of the damage it has wreaked upon the child, a fledgling selfhood, serves to foreground the cathartic potential and recuperative effects of writing. Fourth, the strategic use of the child's voice as testimony underscores Korean expatriate literature's potential to intervene in human rights discourse, since the child is often figured in human rights discourse as deserving of special status (for example in the United Nations 1990 Convention on the Rights of the Child).

It is also true that these personal testimonies carry an additional emotional charge, one that is perhaps not always so obvious in more unproblematically 'dry' historical accounts. This is both deliberate and strategic, in line with many writers' explicit didactic intentions. As Sucheng Chan paradigmatically comments in relation to the educational possibilities of Mary Paik Lee's memoir, "While students learn a great deal from history written in the third person (in the case of Asian immigrants, usually a faceless, nameless 'they'), they become far more engaged in what they read when the information is presented through individual voices" (*Quiet Odyssey*, p. xiii). I suggest that partly by eschewing the blandness of textbook history, this collective body of personalized narratives has at the core of its purpose and consequence the recognition and individualizing of this "faceless, nameless, they".

## KOREAN AMERICAN IMMIGRATION AND THE EMERGENCE OF KOREAN AMERICAN WRITING

Ronald Takaki pinpoints the beginnings of Korean immigration to the United States as 1903.[5] Like the Japanese, many of these pioneer Korean immigrants went to Hawaii, escaping Japanese aggression in Korea at the turn of the century. As the early Korean immigration also included women, the same early appearance of a second-generation occurred as it did with the Japanese. One of the most important early Korean writers was the intellectual Younghill Kang, who arrived in the United States from Korea in 1921, and who was writing at the same time as first-generation Japanese Americans such as the better-known Etsu Sugimoto.[6] However, unlike Sugimoto, Kang did not view himself as a guest in the United States, as Elaine

Kim has observed in *Asian American Literature* (p. 32). Instead, he desired both social integration and to make America his home. Befitting his status as a pioneer new arrival, Kang's perspective is simultaneously that of outsider-observer and immigrant. His novels, *The Grass Roof* (1931) and *East Goes West* (1937) describe both life in Korea and the experience of Korean immigrants in America in the 1920s and 1930s, from a decidedly critical viewpoint.

Surprisingly, since many Korean American women are currently at the vanguard of contemporary Korean American publishing, and given that Korean men and women both emigrated to America early in the twentieth century, Korean American women were comparatively slow to start publishing. Although Elaine Kim discusses the work that Younghill Kang produced between 1931 and 1937 at some length, she mentions no female writers.[7] Korean American female writing really came of age in the 1980s and 1990s, when Margaret K. Pai first published the autobiographical *The Dreams of Two Yi-min* (1989), which recounts the life of her family in Hawaii, and Mary Paik Lee published her story of immigration to California, *Quiet Odyssey: A Pioneer Korean Woman in America* (1990). Both of these autobiographical accounts retrospectively deal with the experience of their subjects as immigrants at the turn of the century through to the 1920s, although they were only written in the latter part of the century.

Nevertheless, a notable early exception to this lack of writing by Korean women is Ronyoung Kim's remarkable novel, *Clay Walls* (1987), published just two years before her death in 1989 at the age of sixty-three. Like *The Dreams of Two Yi-min* and *Quiet Odyssey*, *Clay Walls* tells the story of early Korean immigrants who arrived in Los Angeles in the 1920s. Yet, unlike Pai and Lee, Ronyoung Kim's interest lies specifically in the lives that Korean immigrant women led in America, and, as such, reflects the subsequent direction that Korean American writing has taken. The narrative stresses the story of the central female characters, Haesu, and that of her daughter Faye, thus placing women's perspectives at the centre of their own stories, and also comparing and contrasting the experiences of first- and second-generation women, including the employment opportunities available to them, and their experiences of racism.

Whether authored by men or women though, few Korean American narratives are unencumbered by the burden of a consciousness of Korea's twentieth-century history. As Sucheng Chan observes in her preface to Mary Paik Lee's *Quiet Odyssey*: "homeland politics mattered more to Korean immigrants than did their treatment by American whites" (p. xlix), a phenomenon that has largely continued to this day. One slight exception is South Korean American novelist Chang-Rae Lee's very successful first novel *Native Speaker* (1995), which can, unusually for an Asian American text, be almost characterized as genre fiction. It tells the story of a Korean American spy, Henry Park, who becomes entangled in the corrupt world of a Korean American councilman, John Kwang. It is Park's task to uncover the secrets of Kwang's rise to power, and this endeavour is set against the backdrop of the alienating and turbulent cityscape of New York City. *Native Speaker* has marked something of a new departure for Korean American literature, moving away as it largely does from more traditional narrative preoccupations with ethnic identity, rebutting stereotypes, rehearsing and revising ancestral histories and addressing the processes of Americanization. Yet Lee bears mention here, since he remains true to many of the themes of Korean and Korean American culture, depicting as he does aspects of Korean cuisine and dining rituals, the centrality of the *ggeh* (revolving credit union) to the community, and the importance of Christianity in Korean culture, as well as an acknowledgement of the importance of the past. In a telling passage, that almost ventriloquises many of the Korean American authors of interest in this chapter, character John Kwang sermonizes:

> Recall the days over fifty years ago, when Koreans were made servants and slaves in their own country by the Imperial Japanese army. How our mothers and sisters were made the concubines of the very soldiers who enslaved us.
> I am speaking of histories that all of us should know. Remember, or now know, how Koreans were cast as the dogs of Asia, remember the way our children could not speak their own language in school, remember how they called each other by the Japanese names forced upon them, remember the public executions of patriots and the shadowy murders of collaborators, remember our feelings of disgrace and penury and shame, remember most of all the struggle to survive with one's own identity still strong and alive. (*Native Speaker*, p. 142)

John Kwang's passionate appeal to know and remember has not until recently applied to all those who suffered under the Japanese colonization of Korea. As the epigraphal quotations cited below graphically illustrate, one consitituency's story, that of the Korean Military Comfort Women, has largely remained unknown and unheard.

## CHŎNGSINDAE: THE KOREAN COMFORT WOMEN

> Silence has been a condition as well as a key component of representations of the Military Comfort Women issue
>
> —Hyunah Yang

> What cannot be uttered might at least be written—cloaked in the mask of fiction.
>
> —Suzette Henke

> I clawed through memory and story, denying what I heard and thought I remembered.
>
> —Beccah, *Comfort Woman*

> Even today, in an era where global consciousness around human rights, specifically the rights of women, has risen, survivors of sexual violence are largely denied redress.
>
> —Amnesty International

The particularly harrowing story of Korea's military comfort women illustrates the process of braiding together individual histories and human rights concerns which are of interest here. Comfort women were forcibly drafted into sex slavery to service the Japanese military at designated 'comfort stations', or brothels, during its occupation of Korea, between the late 1930s and 1945. Although there were also some Chinese, Taiwanese, Filipina and Dutch comfort women, and comfort stations were scattered across East Asia, Korean women were taken in the largest numbers (estimates reach 200,000 women), and it is thought that 80% of comfort women were young Koreans.[8] Although this constituted one of the most brutal organized mass rapes in history, until recently, the issue had hardly been discussed globally. The reasons for this silence are various: the combination of former comfort women's reluctance to speak of their ordeal (self-censorship may have occurred either because they were too traumatized or ashamed of their experiences), the dwindling numbers of survivors (the sheer brutality of the sexual slavery suffered by comfort women meant that few survived and those who did endured ongoing health problems, and the surviving comfort women are now in their eighties). Another factor was both Korean and Japanese cultural and political reticence on the issue (it was common for Korean government officials to refer to Korean history as *kwagŏsa* or "matters of the past", and the *Chŏngsindae* "comfort women" issue has been considered an assault upon Korean national pride[9]; the Japanese government also classified documents relating to its colonial involvement in Korea). This means that as Korean American academic Hyunah Yang puts it, there was virtually an "official move to freeze the history of Military Comfort Women" ("Re-membering the Korean Military Comfort Women", p. 123). Furthermore, since the sexual exploitation of Korean women by Japanese military personnel violated not only women's individual human rights, but has also been figured within Korea as the nationwide "contamination of Korean women's sexuality by foreign bodies" ("Re-membering the Korean Military Comfort Women", p. 131)—that is, the violation and shaming of Korean national pride itself—the issue extends the boundaries of victimhood in this case beyond the women themselves. Further, the story of the comfort women is also a gendered and embodied history, as well as a story of sexual corruption and the transgression of Korean sexual mores, that serves to deepen the perception within Korea of the comfort women as shamed and polluted: to tell the comfort women's story is to reveal the sullied body of the comfort woman herself. In short, it is a story noone has wanted to hear.

This all changed in August 1991 when one former Korean comfort woman, seventy- four-year-old Kim Hak-soon, chose to speak out, and thereby both raised international consciousness of the issue and publicly opened it to discussion. Consequently, in the 1990s and beyond, oral testimonies, written accounts and academic research have begun to appear, and political and media focus has gathered pace. Groups of former comfort women first began to speak out in significant numbers in 1992, and many subsequently came together to press for redress and for an official apology from Japan. Political interest has also surged in recent years. Japanese American congressman Mike Honda has also supported the campaign, by demanding publically that Japan "formally acknowledge, apologize and accept historical responsibility [ . . . ] for its Imperial Armed Forces' coercion of young women into sexual slavery". Testimonies by former comfort women have also begun to circulate. Apart from Nora Okja Keller's fictionalized account, there are now also several edited collections and books, including one by several former comfort women, entitled *The True Stories of the Korean Comfort Women* (1996), an edited collection of comfort women's testimonies, *Comfort Women Speak: Testimony by Sex Slaves of the Japanese Military* (2000), and two further book-length testimonies: Samuel Kimm's fictionalized *Cries of the Korean Comfort Women* (2004) and D. Kim-Gibson's oral histories *Silence Broken: Korean Comfort Women* (1999). The importance of these narratives is clear, as noted by Hyunah Yang:

> Testimonial narratives are sites where official memory, mediated by dominant discourse, can be contested. Thus, testimonies are employed as counter-discourses, even though they are also complex cultural products. ("Re-membering the Korean Military Comfort Women", p. 124)

These narratives have been supplemented by several scholarly studies: Elaine Kim's edited collection entitled *The Comfort Women: Colonialism, War, and Sex* (1997), George L. Hicks's *The Comfort Women: Japan's Brutal Regime of Enforced Prostitution in the Second World War* (1997) and Yoshiaki Yoshimi's *Comfort Women* (2002); (historian Yoshimi first exposed the Japanese Diet's awareness of the sex slavery system via his archival research). There are also a few websites devoted to the recording of the comfort women's experiences and pressing for redress. As I noted earlier, therefore, the global controversy over the very existence of the comfort women has thus been reignited, driven by some former comfort women's recent efforts to raise their visibility, split between an American-led campaign for compensation on one hand, and the Japanese government's attempts to suppress the topic on the other.

Coterminous with the emergence of comfort women's voices, in 1993 Tokyo formally acknowledged the comfort women issue for the first time, in Chief Cabinet Secretary Yohei Kono's statement of apology, which has subsequently become known as the "Kono Statement", in which it was declared that "in many cases [the women] were recruited against their will, through coaxing, coercion etc.", and that Japan extended "its sincere apologies and remorse to all those, irrespective of place of origin, who suffered immeasurable pain and incurable physical and psychological wounds as comfort women". However, Japan subsequently partly retracted this acknowledgement. In 1995 rightist politician Shinzo Abe suggested that the comfort women issue was "a made-up story", and then on March 3, 2007, as Japanese Prime Minister Abe, further contradicted the Kono Statement by claiming that women were not forced to be sex slaves for the military: "there is no evidence to prove that there was coercion, nothing to support it" he claimed, a comment that provoked an extensive global outcry. The issue reached the headlines again in June 2007, when a United States Congressional Committee chaired by Tom Lantos and supported by the Democratic Speaker Nancy Pelosi, passed a House Resolution introduced by Mike Honda calling for an "unambiguous" apology from Tokyo for the wartime sexual enslavement of women by the Imperial Japanese Army. Tom Lantos commented upon the imperative that Japan acknowledges "a horrible truth in order that this horror may never be perpetrated again". Debate before the House included the charged and poignant testimonies of several former Korean comfort women. In the same month a group of forty-four Japanese MPs put their signatures to a denial of the existence of sexual slavery during the Second World War, which was published, not in Japan, but in America, in *The Washington Post*.

It is significant, if not surprising, that despite the global dimension of this debate, it has largely been played out within the United States. Silvia Schultermandl ascribes the phenomenon of "the specific appropriation of the comfort women matter as an American issue" ("Writing Rape, Trauma, and Transnationality", p. 72), to American strategic interest in representing itself as the custodian of international human rights:

> The "Americanization" of the movement for redress for comfort women, that is, the emphasis on the U.S. government's role as political liberator and legal mediator in the matter of ongoing negotiations between Japan and the surviving comfort women who sue for financial compensation, operates with strategic discourses that portray America as the "defender of the free world". ("Writing Rape, Trauma, and Transnationality", p. 74)

Indeed, the strategic importance of America as the site of the emergence of comfort women's histories is a theme that repeatedly emerges in these narratives. The push for an apology and reparation for the former comfort women is ongoing, so these narratives are also engaged in exposing a human rights atrocity that Japan has yet to adequately acknowledge, and for which it has to date yet to categorically apologize.[10]

Hyunah Yang describes the complex history of the comfort women as a "history buried in darkness" ("Re-membering the Korean Military Comfort Women", p. 24). The very names by which comfort women have been variously known reflect a desire to both obscure and euphemize their role: in Japanese, therefore, we have the terms *"Jugun Ianfu"*—"comfort women"; and *"teishintai"* or *"daishindai"*—"team of offering bodies"; or in Korean *"Chŏngshindai"*—"battalion slave" or "volunteer". Likewise, the suffering of the comfort women occurs off-stage even in Korean expatriate literature. Whilst many books about Japan's colonial control of Korea make reference to the comfort women issue, it is especially remarkable that regardless of whether we turn to fiction or life writing, such references tend to occur obliquely. In one example, in Sook Nyul Choi's autobiographical fiction *Year of Impossible Goodbyes*, the child narrator Sookan describes a moment when she looks on puzzled as some local girls are rounded up to be taken by the Japanese to the front line. She recalls whispered references to their new role as "spirit girls" (*Year of Impossible Goodbyes*, p. 56), a phrase that despite its whimsical sound, seems to strike fear into all those women who hear it mentioned. The fictional gaze upon comfort women is one almost always cast askance, and the figure of the comfort woman, on the rare occasion when she does appear, is one lurking in the shadows. It is common, too, for writers to refer to comfort women as "ghostlike", that is, there but not quite there, and represented as figures hovering at the edges—literally haunting—Korean society.[11] In another instance, in Helie Lee's *Still Life with Rice*, Lee's grandmother, Hongyong Baek, refers to the comfort women as the "unmentionable" (p. 107), and recalls:

> Young unmarried women were recruited into the military under the euphemistic name of volunteers, *chungshindae*. In Japanese, they were called *daishindai*, meaning, literally, "team of offering bodies." Ordered to fill these positions, city governments notified families with eligible daughters. Husband deduced the true reason why women were being sent to the front lines. One hot, humid afternoon, he stormed into the courtyard as the children and I were resting in the cool shade. He stared at our baby daughter and his face reddened. [ . . . ] "I will never allow them to take her from us." He gritted his teeth. (*Still Life with Rice*, p. 107)

Against this backdrop of evasion and omission, Nora Okja Keller's *Comfort Woman* was the first, and to date, only book to approach the comfort women issue directly. Keller's writing is also overtly imbricated in the emergence of the comfort women's history as a human rights issue, and the transformation of the subject of Japanese military sex slavery as an

East Asian concern to an American one. Her purpose, like so many of the Korean American writers, is one of political intervention as well as full disclosure. Keller's initial motivation for writing stemmed from her attendance at a human rights symposium in 1993, where she heard the graphic and harrowing testimony of a former comfort woman, Keum Ja Hwang, who was captured and forced into prostitution by the Japanese military in 1941. In an interview in *AsianWeek*, she recalls her subsequent decision to record the testimony, almost as a psychological need:

> I went to a symposium on human rights at the University of Hawai'i. [ ... ] The former comfort woman spoke through a translator about her experiences as young girl when she was stolen by the Japanese army and forced into becoming a comfort woman, a sex slave. I couldn't believe that people didn't know about this, that we don't learn about this in history books. [ ... ]
>
> But the topic was too big. I couldn't even find the words to express how horrified I was, much less find the vocabulary to talk about the pain in this woman's life. But her story took hold of me. I felt so haunted. I began dreaming about images of blood and war, and waking with a start. Finally, I realized the only way to exorcise these dreams and the story from my mind was to write them down. So I got up one night and began to write bits and pieces of my dreams and the comfort woman's words. (*AsianWeek*, April 10th, 2002, p. 1)

Remarkably, Keller describes her own response to Keum Ja Hwang's story as a traumatic experience in its own right, a presence that continues to haunt her, refuses to be forgotten, and that may only be laid to rest via the act of textual inscription. Therefore, she adopts the issue as her own traumatic history and assumes responsibility for its exorcism, as well as raising global consciousness of this history, as she remarked in an interview: "You know we all wonder what effect any of our written words can have on the real world, so for me, it was incredible to be tied into that whole history and growing awareness" (Robert Birnbaum, Interview with Nora Okja Keller, www. identitytheory.com, April 2002). Her recognition that this trauma rendered her literally speechless, is an image that she employs extensively in *Comfort Woman* where, as Silvia Schultermandl observes, she "characterizes language and the desire to speak as subversive acts against sexual oppression and the imposed silence on rape victims" ("Writing Rape, Trauma, and Transnationality", p. 78). Schultermandl correctly reads this explicit linking of "voice" and "agency" as a significant move that breaks "the forced silence that colonial Japan, Korean society, and Western societies have imposed on the victims of this crime" ("Writing Rape, Trauma, and Transnationality", p. 82). Schultermandl recalls Kalí Tal's observation that the "raped female body is quite literally assumed to be 'unspeakable'" (*Worlds of Hurt*, qtd. "Writing Rape", p. 82), in order to suggest that Keller's project thus "restores the memory of a portion of history that has been largely suppressed" and thereby "re-establishes identity for the female bodies whose fates remain occulted and obscured because of their 'unspeakable' status as rape victims" (ibid., p. 83).

It might also be seen as something of a difficult project to make fiction from the stuff of such brutal exploitation; yet Keller not only achieved this, she produced a lyrical and meditative novel. Her fictionalized account of one woman's struggle with her memories explores ideas of the return of repressed memory, the bodily inscription of trauma, and the twin processes of revelation and recovery that occur both individually and across generations. Yet even Keller's fictional strategy highlights the problems of writing the comfort women's story directly. Keller chooses to reveal Akiko's past via her daughter, so that layers of narration serve to veil the hidden truth, and the telling occurs in measured stages. It is therefore also an example of generational storytelling and inter-generational dialogue in the best tradition of contemporary Asian American women's writing. Also, like so many other narratives of interest here: Helie Lee's *Still Life with Rice*, Linda Sue Park's *When My Name was Keoko*, and Elizabeth Kim's *Ten Thousand Sorrows*, to name but three, the first person voice of the "omma" or mother is reconstructed in conjunction with her daughter, and the women's voices sometimes merge. By means of this narrative structure, Keller underscores that access to women's stories cannot be taken for granted, and also that it is sometimes hard to hear such stories distinctly.

Akiko and her daughter Beccah's narratives alternate in *Comfort Woman*. The novel opens in Beccah's voice, which establishes the axes of the time and place of the narrative—the present of contemporary Hawaii—before turning to Akiko's story that is immersed in her memories of her past as a comfort woman. The reader is unceremoniously plunged into a quagmire of reminiscence, that is at once impressionistic yet horrifically detailed:

> When the missionaries found me [ . . . ] I responded to the simple commands they issued in Japanese: sit, eat sleep. Had they asked, I would also have responded to "close mouth" and "open legs." At the camps where the Japanese called us *Jungun Ianfu*, military comfort women, we were taught only whatever was necessary to service the soldiers. Other than that, we were not expected to understand and were forbidden to speak, any language at all. (*Comfort Woman*, p. 16)

As Akiko's telling continues, Keller takes considerable pains to depict the story in full, uncompromising detail, in order to convey the intricacies of the comfort women's daily degradations. This is evident when Akiko recalls her arrival at the comfort station and her first images of the caged women:

> I didn't see them right away; they were kept in their stalls, behind mat curtains, most of the days and throughout the night. Only slowly were

> they revealed to me as I delivered and took away their meals, as I emptied their night pots. Hanako 38, her name given because her face was once pretty as a flower. Miyoko 52, frail and unlucky as the Miyokos before her. Kimi-ko 3, with hair the color of egg yellow, which made the officers laugh when they realized the pun of her name: Kimi the sovereign, Kimi the yolk. Akiko 40, Tamayo 29, who told the men she loved them and received gifts and money that she, stubborn in her hopes for a future, would bury in the corner of her stall.
>
> Unless they had to visit the camp doctor, their freedom outside their stalls consisted of weekly baths at the river and scheduled trips to the outhouse. (*Comfort Woman*, pp. 19–20)

Keller augments Akiko's personal reminiscences like these with quasi-detached, almost forensic descriptions of the physical horrors of comfort station life:

> Though each shipment of women included boxes of condoms, and though the doctors tried to control outbreaks of syphilis through injections of 606, venereal disease spread through the camp, manifesting itself in the labia and the vaginas of the women. When the fist-sized eruptions swelled the women shut and spread to other body parts, climbing toward lips and eyes, the officers took the women out of the camp. (*Comfort Woman*, p. 147)

Akiko eventually replaces another woman,"the woman who was Akiko before me" (*Comfort Woman*, p. 20), as a comfort woman. Her induction involves firstly witnessing her predecessor's murder for insubordination:

> One night she talked loud and nonstop. In Korean and Japanese, she denounced the soldiers, yelling at them to stop the invasion of her country and her body. Even as they mounted her, she shouted: I am Korea, I am a woman, I am alive, I am seventeen, I had a family just like you do, I am a daughter, I am a sister. [ . . . ] Just before daybreak, they took her out of her stall and into the woods, where we couldn't hear her anymore. They brought her back skewered from her vagina to her mouth, like a pig ready for roasting. A lesson, they told the rest of us, warning us into silence. (*Comfort Woman*, pp. 20–1).

Followed by her first rape:

> That was my first night as the new Akiko. [ . . . ] Even though I had not yet had my first bleeding, I was auctioned off to the highest bidder. After that it was a free-for-all, and I thought I would never stop bleeding. [ . . . ] It was Akiko 41: it was me. (*Comfort Woman*, p. 21)

Akiko eventually escapes, via a missionary house, where she marries a missionary minister and travels with him to America. However, she continues to be wracked by her memories of her previous life, which also haunt the text:

> Invading my daily routine, shattering the gaps between movement and silence, were the gruntings of soldier after soldier and the sounds of flesh slapping against flesh. Whenever I stopped for a beat, for a breath, I heard men laughing and betting on how many men one comfort woman could service before she split open. (*Comfort Woman*, p. 64)

This description exactly matches trauma theorist Cathy Caruth's summary of the symptoms of post-traumatic stress disorder:

> There is a response, sometimes delayed, to an overwhelming event or events, which takes the form of repeated, intrusive hallucinations, dreams, thoughts or behaviors stemming from the event, along with numbing that may have begun during or after the experience [ . . . ] the experience of trauma repeats itself, exactly and unremittingly [ . . . ] it imposes itself again, repeatedly, in the nightmares and repetitive actions of the survivor. (*Trauma*, p. 4)

Furthermore, the sensory nature of the intrusive memories experienced by Akiko accurately match the pathological characteristics of such reminiscences as outlined by the practicing therapist Judith Lewis Herman in her work, *Trauma and Recovery*, which she describes less as coherent and linear, and more as recollections in the form of "vivid sensations and images" (*Trauma and Recovery*, p. 38). Yet, despite the explicit reverberations of Akiko's suffering in her own sections of the story, she never reveals this pain to her daughter. It is only towards the close of the novel, after her death, that her past is finally revealed to Beccah. Befitting Akiko's book-long outward reticence about her ordeal, it is finally via a recording made by the mother for her daughter that Beccah learns the truth, what she terms the "Beccah tape" (*Comfort Woman*, p. 191). Here, Akiko's confession comes through her daughter's words, rendered in the text in italics:

> *Chongshindae: Our brothers and fathers conscripted. The women left to be picked over like fruit to be tasted, consumed, the pits spit out as Chongshindae, where we rotted under the body of orders from the Emperor of Japan. Under the Emperor's orders, we were beaten and starved. Under Emperor's orders, the holes of our bodies were used to bury their excrement. Under Emperor's orders, we were bled again and again until we were thrown into a pit and burned, the ash from our thrashing arms dusting the surface of the river in which we had sometimes been allowed to bathe.* (*Comfort Woman*, p. 193)

As her daughter realizes, Akiko's "Beccah tape" memorializes all those who suffered as well as laying her own experience to rest:

> I rewound the tape where my mother spoke of the *Chongshindae*, listening to her accounts of crimes made against each woman she could remember, so many crimes and so many names that my stomach cramped. [ . . . ] I did not know how to place my mother, who sounded like an avenging angel recounting the crimes of men. [ . . . ] "Mommy—Omoni—is this you?" I cried, but my mother did not pause in her grief, her song for the dead. (*Comfort Woman*, p. 194)

Keller, a former student of psychology, weaves Akiko's traumatic memories into the very structure of the text. Many critics have drawn comparisons between Keller's novel and Toni Morrison's *Beloved*, a text that famously inscribed the traumatic return of the repressed and the suppressed memories of slavery. Keller's narrative in *Comfort Woman* also bears a striking resemblance to Suzette Henke's description of the workings of trauma and testimony in women's life writing, as outlined in her study *Shattered Subjects*, whereby the act of inscription itself becomes a mode of therapeutic intervention, that short-circuits the cycle of intrusive agonized memories and psychologically debilitative silence that characterizes the experience of the traumatized. Henke's own exploration of what she terms "scriptotherapy" life writing is, usefully for my purposes here, generically highly flexible:

> *life-writing* [ . . . ] challenge[s] the traditional limits of autobiography through the use of a category that encompasses memoirs, diaries, letters and journals, as well as the bildungsroman and other personally inflected fictional texts. This expanded genre embraces the flux and discontinuity that so frequently characterizes the orts, scraps, and fragments of self/life writing found in confessional novels, romans á clef, biomythography, and tantalizing autofictions [ . . . ] [and] every novel [also] incorporates shards of social, psychological, and cultural history into the texture of its ostensibly mimetic world. (*Shattered Subjects*, p. xiii)

For Henke, these forms characteristically share the features of "an author attempting to fashion an enabling discourse of testimony and self-revelation, to establish a sense of agency" (p. xvi); and as she notes, in an observation that exactly describes Keller's work, "both autobiography and autofiction offer a unique conflation of history and discourse, of verifiable fact and aesthetic fabulation" (ibid.). Henke writes that "Autobiography could [ . . . ] effectively mimic the scene of psychoanalysis" (*Shattered Subjects*, p. xii). My contention is that Keller's autofiction[12] recreates the scene of both the intrusion of traumatic memory via Akiko's narrative, and the scene of therapy, in Beccah's listening to and reception of her mother's story. Therefore, Keller's text shares with other forms of scriptotherapy the promotion of healing, enablement, and agency, through the outward re/articulation (testimony) of the traumatic past. Keller's fictionalized testimony also serves to begin to undo a history of silence and silencing. As Henke puts it, "what cannot be uttered might at least be written—cloaked in the mask of fiction" (*Shattered Subjects*, p. xix).

The Amnesty International report into the plight of the comfort women also observes that "Testimonies of the former 'comfort women' reveal that the trauma stays with them all their lives" (p. 6). Amnesty International identifies five measures that can promote "restorative justice" for the victims of human rights abuse:

- Restitution
- Compensation
- Rehabilitation
- Satisfaction
- Guarantees of non-repetition.

These five measures encompass the gamut of both symbolic and actual reparation, from monetary redress to the importance of full disclosure of "truthful facts", accurate historical documentation of the human rights violations that occurred and a push for wider educational initiatives. Facts and "truth" in historical representation and narrative have become widely and thoroughly debated notions. Dealing with a different yet nevertheless traumatic history of violence and repression, South Africa's Truth and Reconciliation Committee defined "truth" in four ways:

1. Factual or forensic truth
2. Personal or narrative truth
3. Social or "dialogue" truth
4. Healing or restorative truth.

In the Commission's words, these truths "reduce the number of lies that can be circulated unchallenged in public discourse".[13] In their campaign for redress and reparation, the former comfort women have called for a similar Truth and Reconciliation Commission that would "create a historical record of the gender based crimes committed during the war, transition, and occupation" ("Still Waiting", p. 12). One role of such a commission would be to provide "support for scholars and writers" who engage with the issue in order to "ensure the education of the population" ("Still Waiting", p. 12). This, then, is also the complex cultural and political work undertaken by *Comfort Woman*.

Keller's sequel, *Fox Girl*, extends her focus upon Korean women's tragic stories. Like *Comfort Woman*, the pattern of narrative emplotment is still temporal (here cyclical), as we follow the memories and maturation of Hyun Jin and Sookie, two young mixed race Korean girls—known in Korea as the "throwaway children"—who become "GI" prostitutes. *Fox Girl* continues Keller's project in her trilogy of exposing the exploitation of Korean women, in this text by placing America's entangled relationship with Korea into further relief by excavating the occluded history of American soldiers' violation of the Korean "GI girls".

## VOICES NORTH AND SOUTH I: HOME WAS THE LAND OF MORNING CALM

> *The Koreans who lived through the experience are the best witnesses, but they, for whatever reasons, have kept silent.*
> —K. Connie Kang, (p. 59)

K. Connie Kang's weighty Seoul-based memoir intertwines her personal memories of growing up in the wake of the Korean War with a consciousness of the importance of international intervention in human rights issues within Korea, and a fastidious record of Korean history. Somewhat unusually, her memoir is framed by a politically interventionist preface, that serves to set the overtly politicized tone of the narrative that follows, plus an epilogue calling for international support for Korean reunification, and a lengthy bibliography of academic source materials on Korean history and politics. Kang also includes a section of photographs marking key moments in her family's tale. Despite these rather scholarly-leaning contents, though, Kang manages to provide us with an immensely readable and detailed narrative. She does this partly by skillfully intertwining moments of pure history such as the following passage describing the U.S. response to the North Korean initiation of the Korean War:

> By Sunday evening when Truman returned to Washington, the UN Security Council, meeting in an emergency session at the behest of South Korean and U.S. officials, had passed a resolution condemning the North Korean attack and calling for the withdrawal of Kim's forces south of the thirty-eighth parallel. By late Monday (June 26), Truman committed U.S. air and naval forces to defend Korea—the first time the United States had come to Korea's aid since the signing of the treaty of Amity in 1882 (*Home Was the Land of Morning Calm*, pp. 108–9)

with political statements such as "The Japanese imperialism exacted a heavy toll on all Koreans. Then, as now, the voices of small countries fell on deaf international ears" (*Home Was the Land of Morning Calm*, p. 59), with her own family's fate at the hands of this history. Here Kang describes the end of the Korean War:

> As for our family, we lost everything for the second time. But we were lucky to be alive; so many people we knew had not been so fortunate. Our material possessions were gone, but our indomitable Korean spirit was intact. I would not be in Korea to see the signing of the agreement on July 1953. Eight months before the signing, when I was nine years old, my mother and I would move once again, to make another attempt to resume our lives. (*Home Was the Land of Morning Calm*, p. 125)

The oscillation between personal and national history is a hallmark of Kang's memoir; statements such as:

> It is Thanksgiving 1994. Five and a half years have passed since my return to the United States. These have been defining moments for Koreans back home and in America, and for me personally (*Home Was the Land of Morning Calm*, p. 292),

are common, and the text is replete with Kang's political opinions as well. Kang's narrative is also markedly multi-faceted in its trans-Korea focus, as she provides a perspective not just upon the South, but also her journey there during the Korean War, and the plight of her North Korean relatives before the War. In an early review of *Home Was the Land of Morning Calm*, Chunghee Sarah Soh remarked upon this, describing Kang's stories as both "like a historical novel, for Kang deftly interweaves them with the background narratives of the major political events", and the texture of "Kang's transnational migratory journeys" that propel the reader not just from North to South but also to the United States (Review of *Home Was the Land of Morning Calm, The Journal of Asian Studies* 55 [1996], pp. 1019–1020; p. 1019). This grand historical as well as geographical sweep stands in sharp contrast to the uniquely concentrated North Korea memoir I discuss next.

## VOICES NORTH AND SOUTH II: TEN YEARS IN THE NORTH KOREAN GULAG, YODOK AND THE AQUARIUMS OF PYONGYANG

> The only acceptable reunification is one that grants North Koreans the freedom to live a life worthy of human beings. They are now dying of hunger without the right to utter a protest, crushed by a system that walks all over their fundamental human rights.
>
> —Kang Chol-Hwan

*The Aquariums of Pyongyang* is arguably the most shocking and hard-hitting of all the literature under discussion here. In his introduction to Kang Chol-Hwan's memoir, writer and Kang's co-author Pierre Rigoulet puts it bluntly: "reading this book is a first step toward making the repression in

North Korea a major concern for human rights defenders around the world" (p. xxiv). It was as a result of reading Kang Chol-Hwan's *The Aquariums of Pyongyang* and his subsequent education in the North Korean regime's extensive abuse of individual human rights that impelled George W. Bush to turn his attention to the issue. Bush included North Korea in his 2002 "Axis of Evil" State of the Union Address, describing it as "a regime arming with missiles and weapons of mass destruction, while starving its citizens". In October 2004 he went further, when he signed into law the North Korea Human Rights Act, which sought to address human rights abuses and to support both defectors and those trapped and persecuted within North Korea's borders. *The Aquariums of Pyongyang* was initially recommended to him by the former Secretary of State Henry A. Kissinger. In turn, Bush recommended it to both his Secretary of State, Condoleeza Rice, and other senior White House aides. As a result, as *The New York Times* put it, "the book jumped to the top of the Bush administration's summer reading list". George Bush later met Kang Chol-Hwan at the White House in June 2005 in a highly publicized visit, together with the Vice President Dick Cheney and the national security advisor, Stephen J. Hadley. The White House's interest in Kang's story of human rights abuses in North Korea was both timely and expedient insofar as it enabled a beleaguered president to strengthen and underpin the theme of the promotion of democracy globally that formed so much of the substance of his speeches at the time. Yet the political benefits were by no means one-sided. In his Preface to *Aquariums*, worth quoting at length, Kang Chol-Hwan describes the remarkable and far-reaching political and personal consequences of his meeting with President Bush:

> On June 13, 2005, I met with President George W. Bush in the Oval Office for forty long minutes. I told the president about the plight of North Korean people, and we shared sincere opinions on how to save them.
> Throughout the meeting with President Bush, it dawned on me that [ . . . ] with one simple stroke [ . . . ] the bleak reality, in which nearly no one cared about the ghosts of three million famished souls and hundreds of thousands more in the concentration camps in my home country, was instantly changed.
> Since that meeting at the White House, I have received many emails from North Koreans hiding in China, all encouraging me and thanking the American president for caring about their fate. I don't have the slightest doubt that the good news has also traveled all across the country inside North Korea giving the 23 million people long-overdue hope and encouragement. For the 200,000 political prisoners in the gulag, the news must have struck them as if they had an encounter with the Savior himself. Some inside North Korea said that this single event could wipe out years of anti-American propaganda once and for all. [ . . . ]

> As for me personally, meeting with President Bush gave me such a visibility that I have been bombarded with requests for one public speech after another. I have been speaking out about human rights violations in North Korea with hundred-fold empowerment ever since.
>
> Furthermore, I've met with several members of the National Assembly in South Korea who all became acutely interested in the human rights issues in North Korea. South Korean Representative Kim Moon Soo has even begun a campaign to encourage South Koreans to read *The Aquariums of Pyongyang*. (*Aquariums*, pp. x–xi)

Kang links this statement to an explicit rallying call for intervention, asking "Are we to stand back and allow history to repeat itself? [ . . . ] I believe that the time has come for the collective conscience of our world to speak out against the barbarity of the Kim Jong Il regime" (*Aquariums*, p. xii). His call directly interpolates political co-activists: "I also want to thank the readers of this book who will partake with me of my kinsmen's sufferings. [ . . . ] I invite all of us to an unceasing prayer vigil for the early departed and for a hastened liberation followed by true democracy in my homeland" (*Aquariums*, pp. xii–xiii). In addition to these assertive and activist introductions to his memoir, Kang, who is the co-founder of the Democracy Network against the North Korean Gulag[14], also unashamedly engages in the politics of persuasion, in the best tradition of protest literature. He includes a pensive yet intellectually rigorous epilogue to the main text, "Pursuing Aid for North Korea", in which he provides detailed statistics (that due to the difficulties of penetrating North Korea are by necessity best estimates) of the numbers who are expected to have died in the latest famine, analyzes the politics and ethics of aid, and evaluates the possibilities for reunification. As with his preface, Kang short-circuits the intellectual fors-and-againsts of aid-giving with impassioned and hard-hitting interventions of personal testimony such as this: "Anyone who has stood as I have beside a person slowly dying of hunger—who has seen this horror with his own eyes—will never linger to debate the pros and cons of food aid" (*Aquariums*, p. 235). These testimonial statements attest to Kang's willingness to appeal to the authority of his own experience in aggressively contesting both versions of the North Korean situation in global circulation and North Korea's heavily censored versions of life under the Kim dictatorship.

The uniqueness of Kang's perspective lies in the fact that he is one of only a few people to escape North Korea to tell their story, and, to date, the only person to survive and escape the North Korean gulag and reveal details of its horror in book form. The sheer brutality of Kang's story is unquestionable: incarcerated at Yodok concentration camp in 1977 at the age of nine, Kang watches family members and friends die of hunger or as a result of execution, is near-starved and suffers repeated serious illness, relentless hard labour and deprivation for ten years, until his release in 1987. In a narrative that almost defies plausibility, Kang exposes life at the limits of humanity: executions, postmortem stonings, the desperate consumption of rats, roaches and snakes, and an appalling range of tortures. Yet Kang's narrative tone is often oddly measured and virtually devoid of emotion. He also explicitly interprets his own story solely through the possibilities of political transformation and intervention that its telling may offer. This quasi-detached perspective is revealed in his own evaluation of his life in the gulag: "from a human rights perspective, my case was shocking", he tells the reader simply (*Aquariums*, p. 206).

For the purposes of textual analysis though, Kang's memoir is complicated by two factors. The text is heavily mediated: Kang acknowledges that he is at times careful to conceal the identities of those who remain in danger in Korea; furthermore, the text is the result of a collaborative effort with the political historian and human rights activist Pierre Rigoulet, whose previous work has included the collaborative editing of *The Black Book of Communism*. The issue of this mediation raises the question of how far Kang's testimony can be taken at page value. Additionally, the text one reads—the text handed around the White House—has been translated from the original French by Yair Reiner in 2001, and it should not—indeed cannot—be assumed that such a translation is in any way either transparent or value-neutral. To suggest that these factors compromise any assumptions one is able to make about the referentiality and import of the text, is not to deny that similar factors are equally relevant to one's reading of the other texts explored in this chapter, nor is it to blunt the political dissonance and radicalism of Kang's text as artifact. From a generic perspective, *The Aquariums of Pyongyang* falls into at least two of the "Fifty-two Genres of Life Narrative" identified by Sidonie Smith and Julia Watson in their study, *Reading Autobiography*. The text obviously has affinities with the category of "collaborative life narrative", through the mode of co-production with Pierre Rigoulet and via Yair Reiner's translation; and thus, as Smith and Watson put it, *The Aquariums of Pyongyang* is "multiply mediated [ . . . ] [since] two or more parties are included in the production of the published story, particularly [ . . . ] [since] translation is required" (*Reading Autobiography*, p. 191). Smith and Watson warn that such texts may result in "assymetrical" (*Reading Autobiography*, p. 191) power relations between collaborators, and that while "readers cannot resolve either the psychodynamics or the politics of collaborative life writing" (*Reading Autobiography*, p. 178), they should nevertheless remain attentive to its possible consequences.[15] The text also clearly conforms to the category of "Survivor Narrative" as well, characterized by Smith and Watson as

> narratives by survivors of traumatic, abusive, or genocidal experience. Linda Martin Alcoff and Laura Gray-Rosendale propose this term to distinguish the political utility of self-referential discourse from the more limited discourse of confession. They note that, while "survivor discourse and the tactic of speaking out may often involve a confessional mode of

speech, including personal disclosure, autobiographical narrative, and the expression of feelings and emotions", effective voicing of certain kinds of trauma must go beyond the confessional to acts of witnessing. The confessional mode, they suggest, focuses attention on a victim's psychological state rather than the perpetrator's act and invests power in a confessor as interpreter and judge, stripping the survivor of authority and agency. Victims must be remade as survivors through acts of speaking out, telling their stories in ways that move beyond a concentration on personal feelings to testimony that critiques larger cultural forces. (*Reading Autobiography*, pp. 205–6)

Kang's text clearly testifies and bears witness to the acts of atrocity committed in the Yodok gulag, but his act of witnessing is also transformed from a simple statement of survival to another act, an intervention in the increasingly global debate over human rights in the Korean peninsula, in the manner described by Smith and Watson above. As Smith and Watson also emphasize, the act of witnessing in a politically active manner is a move that addresses another, and requires—indeed expects—a response, and so engenders a more active, alert relationship between witness/survivor/writer—text—reader.

## HELIE LEE: STILL LIFE WITH RICE AND IN THE ABSENCE OF SUN

> We must remember the women. The only way to remember these women and our ancestors is to write our story. By writing our story we dictate and influence what is considered history
> 
> —Helie Lee

The relation between the textual inscription of Korea's history and the push for human rights can sometimes work in reverse. Helie Lee's *Still Life with Rice* is one example in which her writing has unintentionally served to restrict the freedom of her North Korean relatives. Lee's bestseller, published in 1996, is an imaginative memoir that reconstructs the story of her grandmother, Hongyong Baek—known to Helie as "Halmoni" (grandmother)—through the recreation of her own voice, in Korea during the period between 1912 and 1991. Hongyong Baek's tale is immediately representative: she came of age in a socially repressive Korea, suffered family separation and tragedy during Japan's occupation and again during the Korean War, fled south, and then to the United States. However, her tale is also remarkable: Baek was an indomitable woman who supported her family single-handedly, built a profitable opium business after fleeing to China, then established a practice offering the ancient Korean healing therapy of *ch'iryo*, that she took to the sick leper colonies, before emigrating to the United States in 1976. In the present day of America, as the text opens, Helie Lee describes her own "unquenchable thirst to learn more" about her grandmother's past, a thirst that propels her to trawl family archives and travel around Korea in an effort to reconstruct her grandmother's story. The success of *Still Life with Rice* led to media appearances on Oprah Winfrey's show, coverage on CNN and in *Life* and *Time* magazines, *People* and *The Los Angeles Times*, and nationwide lecture tours and talks on university campuses. In June, 2002, Senator Ted Kennedy invited Helie Lee to testify at the Senate Subcommittee hearing on immigration, and she now serves on the U.S. Committee for Human Rights in North Korea (HRNK).

Yet while Lee was touring the United States to publicize her book, and enjoying her new-found fame, her book, which contained details of her North Korean family's identity and whereabouts, had attracted attention in Pyongyang, and Helie Lee found to her shock that she had unwittingly endangered the life of her North Korean relatives:

> By including details of my uncle's life in a book, I had alerted North Korea's enigmatic leadership to the identity of my relatives in a nation where it was better to remain invisible. [ . . . ] when I sat down at my computer and began writing about Halmoni's history [ . . . ] the past came crashing down on the streets of the present and a letter arrived from North Korea resurrecting my uncle's ghost. (*In the Absence of Sun*, pp. 5–6)

Lee becomes belatedly acutely conscious of the ethics of writing Halmoni's life narrative: both that the consequences of publication are far-reaching and potentially devastating, and that it is consequently encumbent upon her to right—to write—the wrong she has inadvertently caused. *In the Absence of Sun*, the 2002 sequel to *Still Life with Rice*, describes Lee's journey to find and rescue the North Korean family that she endangered by publishing her first book, a dangerous odyssey that took her to the shores of the Yalu river, China's border with North Korea, via the port city of Dalian and industrial Shenyang in China, and finally back to Seoul. It involved incredible danger and duplicity, as Lee described in an interview with Angie Kang in 2004:

> In 1997, when we rescued my uncle along with eight members of his family, nothing like that had been done before where an outside force or people had masterminded an escape of a family so large. There were a lot of things that went wrong with this rescue mission. There were a lot of scars, wounds, and family betrayal. It reads just like a thriller and I never thought we would actually get to the end. I never thought we would actually succeed. I thought at times someone was going to die or get hurt along the way. (*Asian Pacific Arts*, p. 3)

# Korean Expatriate Writing and the History of the Korean Peninsula

*Still Life with Rice* as an actual object of protest powerfully performs an eponymous role. Late on in *In the Absence of Sun* Helie Lee describes a moment when her North Korean relatives, on the cusp of escape, seem to lose their nerve. In a dramatic scene, part of *Still Life with Rice* is ripped out, folded, and smuggled across the Yalu River to the North Korean family members. Seeing their names in the print brings the dawning realization of the official state attention this will bring, and that they have no choice but to defect. This then gives them the motivation they need to act. Conscious of these possible consequences as a result of the publication *Still Life with Rice*, and wary of repeating the same mistake, Lee was initially reluctant to publish the subsequent story of her family's escape. However, she is urged to do so by her relatives, as her father tells her:

> Even if we all have to look over our shoulders for the rest of our lives, it's a small sacrifice. This story needs to be told, or all our efforts are just self-serving. Hae Ri must let people know what horrible hardships we endured and what desperate people will go through for the chance at freedom. (*In the Absence of Sun*, p. 329)

With this statement and at this juncture, Helie Lee accepts her role as a promoter of human rights in Korea, a role that she enacts through her writing. In a conclusion strongly reminiscent of Kang Chol-Hwan's closing lines, Lee writes:

> I understand now that I have a role, a responsibility, as an American, a Korean, a woman, and as a writer. I owe it to those who were left behind to take a stand. I haven't forgotten about them and will never forget them. By sharing my family's story with you, I hope to shine a bright light on North Korea's obscene dictatorship and what happens to people's humanity under such a regime.
>
> I believe one family, one person, one action can make a difference, because we are all connected. When we realize this connection, peace is possible. (*In the Absence of Sun*, p.342)

Implicit in this declaration is Lee's acceptance of the potentially far-reaching ethical ramifications of life-writing inscription, as well as her determination to promote a consciousness of the ethics attendant upon the practice of reading, on the part of her own readership. Lee, like Kang Chol-Hwan, expresses her hope that our own discomfort caused by reading about such suffering and deprivation in books like Lee's and Kang's will in turn initiate our own active engagement. Lee recognizes her story as a tale in microcosm of the struggle for human rights freedom in Korea:

> I felt it like it was Korea's history that I was seeing within my own family. The Korea War tragically divided my family in half and my parents

> and my grandmother have never stopped wishing and searching for her son and for the reunification of the country. That's why I think it's been so powerful and impactful for a lot of Koreans, Korean Americans, and Koreans all abroad. [ . . . ]
>
> I think my book is a testimony. My family's story is a testimony that there is a bright future for Korea with reunification. [ . . . ] You have to pay attention to what's going on in North Korea. [ . . . ] If someone is starving in North Korea, we are all affected. If there is a dictator somewhere, everybody is affected because we are now part of a global community. We cannot escape the pains of other countries. We have to be aware and be also active. [ . . . ] we've all become political activists. (*Asia Pacific Arts*, p. 4)

Lee's assignation of her work as "testimony" is significant if we recall Suzette Henke's designation of the possibilities of testimonial life-writing, which "allows the author to share an unutterable tale of pain and suffering, of transgression or victimization, in a discursive medium that can be addressed to everyone or no-one" (*Shattered Subjects*, p. xix). Furthermore, there is a clear connection between Lee's authorship and the historical moment. As attested by a plethora of recent newspaper reports, Lee's publication of what we might term her "defector narrative" coincides with a surge of media interest in the issue of North Korean defection, a phenomenon that itself emerges in conjunction with renewed efforts to move towards the reunification of the Korean peninsula, on the part of the United States (amongst whose vested interests may be George W. Bush's desire to belatedly claim a place as a global force for peace in the last months of his presidency); on the part of South Korea (whose President has been eager to further his so-called "Sunshine Policy" of reunification); on the part of China (who, as North Korea's sole ally, is increasingly embarrassed by its continuing isolation); and on the part of North Korea itself, a nation now desperate for more effective aid and increased overseas investment.

## CENTURY OF IMPOSSIBLE GOODBYES: SOOK NYUL CHOI'S KOREA TRILOGY

> Having a deep love and respect for Korean culture, and having grown up in Korea during a very turbulent time in its history, I wanted to share my knowledge and bring the culture and history of my native land to life for Americans.
>
> —Sook Nyul Choi

Despite the above observation, Sook Nyul Choi's Korea trilogy further illustrates some of the difficulties in successfully moulding the stuff of a traumatic past into an engaging narrative. Her books depict a by now familiar

# Korean Expatriate Writing and the History of the Korean Peninsula 123

trajectory: her feisty adolescent protagonist Sookan Bak flees from Pyongyang to Seoul in the wake of war, then travels onwards to Pusan in South Korea, eventually moving to the United States. This trajectory was also that trodden by Choi herself, who was born in Pyongyang in 1937, where with her family she endured life under Japanese control during WWII, and then fled the North as a young refugee during the Korean War; she subsequently emigrated to the United States in 1962.

As with Helie Lee, Nora Okja Keller and Kang Chol-Hwan, Choi's trilogy is generically complex, and these hybrid texts sit somewhat uneasily between several possible categories. She describes her trilogy as "fictional history", although it has elsewhere also been described as carrying "the tone of a memoir", and the majority of reviewers have approached it as adolescent fiction. Amy Ling described the trilogy as a catch-all "three-volume semi-autobiographical novel sequence" (*Yellow Light*, p. 46). As with Nora Okja Keller's trilogy, the narrative perspective is that of a maturing child, and Sookan's initiation into the horrors of an adult world at war is one of the title's main "goodbyes" into which she is forced. The overwhelming tendency to classify Choi's work as juvenile fiction may explain the relative paucity of critical material on her writing, despite many positive reviews and awards—*Year* received the ALA Best Book for Young Adults and Notable Book Awards amongst others—her work has received. Yet as a reviewer of *Year of Impossible Goodbyes* in the *Korean Quarterly* observed, "Choi's novels are anything but childlike and speak powerfully and intensely to older readers as well" (Jerry Winzig). *The New York Times Book Review* went further by recognizing that Choi's use of the childhood perspective in *Year* increased its potency as well as its potential to educate: "A glimpse into a young girl's mind and into a nation's heart—a tale of bearing witness to the plight of a people [ . . . ] should also be read by adults—both for its poignancy and for its capacity to illuminate". Robyn McCallum identifies the stages of childhood and adolescence as "a period during which notions of selfhood undergo rapid and radical transformation" (*Ideologies of Identity in Adolescent Fiction,* p. 3). Young adult fiction that depicts war and other psychologically traumatic experiences has an additional impact since the author is able to explore not only the dynamics of emerging selfhood, but also that of fledgling selfhood under stress. Furthermore, since writing both for and about children and young adults is commonly assumed to be a safe and protected space—if we can't protect the young from peril in real life then at least we can on the page—the appearance of potentially traumatic scenarios such as war, famine, or abuse, carries an additional import. That is, writers like Sook Nyul Choi can take emotional advantage of the startling disjuncture between the intended readership and the subject matter of the text.

It is no more surprising that critical attention has been concentrated upon the first book in the trilogy, *Year of Impossible Goodbyes* rather than *Echoes of the White Giraffe* or *Gathering of Pearls*. The resilient and beguiling heroine of *Year* appears in increasingly diluted form in the latter installments, and the depiction of Sookan's life as a student in America in *Gathering* is little short of a rather one-dimensional caricature of a "model Asian student". Furthermore, whilst *Year* is a substantial book with a gripping plotline, *Giraffe* and *Gathering* carry more than a whiff of simple potted history. The epic nature of *Year of Impossible Goodbyes* coupled with the unerring emphasis upon Sookan's personal childhood struggles sets a difficult precedent for the subsequent stories. *Echoes of the White Giraffe* documents Sookan's existence as a refugee in Seoul during the Korean War—no easy time, especially for a child—yet this experience scarcely matches the many extreme traumas endured by Sookan in *Year*. *Giraffe* is also significantly shorter.

As it opens, with Sookan's momentous sojourn in the United States, the final book *Gathering of Pearls* regains some of the momentum of *Year*, only to lose it again as the final installment dissolves into a virtual documentary of life at a Catholic boarding school for this young Korean student. Lengthy and turgid passages of Sookan's soul-searching over the sincerity of her desire to learn and her ability to dedicate herself wholeheartedly to her studies, leave the reader cold. The only triumph over adversity that we witness here is Sookan's resolve to study even harder by turning to her inner resources—the gathering of pearls of the text's title—in a rather superficial and disappointing conclusion to Sookan's odyssey. Despite this, Choi's trilogy must nevertheless be recognized as a notable achievement, and an important addition to the genre of Korean expatriate protest writing which, in common with the other texts discussed in this case study, fulfills her stated intention to "foster greater understanding about her homeland's 'sad history'" (Cathy Karlin Zahner, "Korean Girl's Travails Put Life in Perspective", *Kansas City Star*, March 1, 1992, p. 18). As such, along with the other narratives explored in this chapter, it helps to piece together what Bruce Cumings describes as "a fractured, shattered twentieth-century history".[16]

# Notes

## NOTES TO CHAPTER 1

1. The material available on Vietnam is too voluminous to mention here in any detail. For a sampling which includes writers of both Vietnamese and American ancestry, see Wayne Karlin, ed., *The Other Side of Heaven: Post-War Fiction by Vietnamese and American Writers* (Willimantic, Connecticut: Curbstone Press, 1995). Cambodia material includes Pin Yathay's *Stay Alive, My Son* (New York: Touchstone, 1988), Molyda Szymusiak et al., eds., *The Stones Cry Out: A Cambodian Childhood, 1975–1980* (Bloomington, Indiana: Indiana University Press, 1999); Darina Siv's *Never Come Back: A Cambodian Woman's Journey* (New York: The Writer Press, 2000); Loung Ung's *First They Killed My Father: A Daughter of Cambodia Remembers* (New York: Harper Perennial, 2006), Chanrithy Him's *When Broken Glass Floats: Growing Up Under the Khmer Rouge* (New York: Norton, 2001), Dith Pran's edited *Children of Cambodia's Killing Fields: Memoirs by Survivors* (New Haven, Connecticut: Yale University Press, 1999), and the 1984 film *The Killing Field*s, by Roland Joffé and directed by Haing S. Ngor (based upon Cambodian photojournalist Dith Pran's experiences). Kamikaze memoirs in English include *Kamikaze: A Japanese Pilot's Own Spectacular Story of the Famous Suicide Squadrons* by Yasuo Kuwahara (Clearfield, Utah: American Legacy Media, 2007) and Emiko Ohnuki-Tierney, *Kamikaze Diaries: Reflections of Japanese Student Soldiers* (Chicago: University of Chicago Press, 2007).
2. In this sense, I am concerned with both the role of the United States in the expression of human rights, and the role of texts as sources of significant political intervention in these debates.
3. Whilst I suggest that it is often women's narratives that provide key interventions and political resistance in global and state politics, in exploring this question, I am also particularly interested in the child's perspective, since this offers a significant political interrogatory framework, especially in the chapters on Korea and China.
4. www.un.org/Overview/rights.html. Also, see the United Nations Convention on the Rights of the Child (UNCRC), ratified in 1990. One hundred and ninety-three states are party to this. See UNICEF, www.unicef.org. I discuss the rights of the child specifically in the chapters on China and Korea.

## NOTES TO CHAPTER 2

1. Jung Chang and Jon Halliday, *Mao:The Unknown Story*, p. 259.

2. In, for example, his famous "Talks at the Yan'an Forum on Literature and Art" speech in 1942.
3. As Joseph Esherwick, Paul Pickowicz and Andrew Walder observe, the increased availability of what they call "unofficial sources": newspapers, pamphlets and posters, as well as oral histories and interviews with former Red Guards propelled Chinese historiography of the Cultural Revolution into a new phase in the post-1980s period. See *The Chinese Cultural Revolution as History*, pp. 10–11.
4. This is also mirrored within China. In *Mao's China* the editors observe that although "Oral histories, autobiographies and fictional accounts of the Red Guard generation have been appearing in China since the 1970s [ . . . ] far from abating, however, the outpouring of literature and film on this period seems to have gained momentum in the 1990s" (xi).
5. There are also a few texts by male authors, including *Gang of One* by Fan Shen (2004), Ma Bo's *Blood Red Sunset* (1995), *Red Land, Yellow River* by Ange Zhang (2004), and Da Chen's *Colors of the Mountain* (2001), *China's Son* (2001) and *Sounds of the River* (2002). Other fictional texts also address China's turbulent history, of course, and these include Amy Tan's *The Kitchen God's Wife*, Han Suyin's *Destination Chungking* and Aimee Liu's *Cloud Mountain*.
6. These narratives also further elide the distinctions between 'Asian American', 'Asian British' and 'Asian Asian' writing, which is becoming increasingly commonplace.
7. "Sour Sweet", *Bookcase*, Summer 1993, p. 7.
8. These, and the following quotations from reviews of *Wild Swans*, are taken from the book jacket.
9. Harriet Evans further suggests that the genre of popular history/memoir writing is not fit for its purpose here, and that we should be wary of turning to memoir writing as a means of explaining the past. See "Dangers of Arrogance", p. 29.
10. Jonathan Mirsky, "Literature of the Wounded", *The New York Review of Books*, March 5, 1992, pp. 6–10.
11. Kalí Tal, *Worlds of Hurt: Reading the Literatures of Trauma* (New York: Cambridge University Press, 1996).
12. See *Perspectives on the Cultural Revolution* for a discussion of Chinese language Cultural Revolution era novels, such as *The Path of Life*, *The Dividing Line* and *The Journey*, and Liyan Qin, "The Sublime and the Profane: A Comparative Analysis of Two Fictional Narratives about Sent-down Youth", in *The Cultural Revolution as History*, pp. 240–266.
13. As Lan Yang notes in *Chinese Fiction of the Cultural Revolution* "CR" (Cultural Revolution) literature is usually divided into pre-CR literature (1949–65), CR literature (1966–1976) and post-CR literature (1977–).
14. In viewing expatriate memoirs as unencumbered by the constraints of Chinese internal politics, and thus tending to be more overtly critical, I depart from the view expressed by Harriet Evans and Stephanie Donald, who write that "the autobiographical memoir, a genre of writing about the Cultural Revolution which has blossomed in the last decade or so [ . . . ] these contributions to rewriting the history of the Cultural Revolution do not tend to challenge the major premises of the official version" ("Introducing Posters in China's Cultural Revolution", p. 15).
15. See Joan Chen's Interview with Richard Corliss, "West to East", *Time Magazine*, vol. 153, issue 13, April 5, 1999; and also "The Sent Down Girl" by Steven Schwankert, *Beijing Scene*, Volume 5, issue 8, May 7, 1999.

16. Literature which deals with the subject of foot-binding in China, a common practice from the Tang dynasty until 1949, is becoming increasingly popular, as the success of Pang-Mei Natasha Chang's novel, *Bound Feet and Western Dress* illustrates. A more recent example is Kathryn Harrison's novel, *The Binding Chair*, published in 2000.
17. Work on these texts includes Ben Xu's "A Face that Grows into a Mask" (2004), Wenying Xu's "Agency via Guilt" (2000), Wendy Somerson's "Under the Mosquito Net" (1997), Cynthia F. Wong's "Remembering China" (1996), and my own work on Cultural Revolution memoirs in *Negotiating Identities* (2002).
18. Amy Ling, *Between Worlds: Women Writers of Chinese Ancestry* (New York: Pergamon, 1991), p. 85.
19. Despite the critical attention accorded to Chang's work, it should be noted, as C.T. Hsia does, that her writing never achieved the success of her contemporaries, the Chinese American writers Han Suyin or Pearl Buck, probably due to the serious subject of Chang's work. See C.T. Hsia, *A History of Modern Chinese Fiction* (Bloomington: Indiana University Press, 1999), p. 389. Chang is, however, enjoying something of a renaissance in popularity, especially since the republication of *The Rice Sprout Song* and *The Rouge of the North* by California University Press in 1998, as well as the success of the 2007 film *Lust, Caution*.
20. Jung Chang reviewed *The Rouge of the North* for the book-jacket, upon its republication. She said that "Eileen Chang beautifully and movingly evokes twentieth-century China and the hearts and minds of Chinese women".
21. In actual fact, within China in the 'Post-Mao' period (after 1976), several books have been published which are critical of the Cultural Revolution.
22. Preston Schoyer, "The Smell of a Hidden World", *Saturday Review*, May 21, 1955.
23. *A History of Modern Chinese Fiction*, p. 389.
24. The 'Orient' in this sense is used as a collective noun encompassing Asia, Africa and the Middle East.
25. Eileen Chang is not the only writer sponsored by the US information agency for propaganda purposes during this period. Following the success of her autobiography, *Fifth Chinese Daughter*, in 1953 Jade Snow Wong was sponsored by the US State Department to undertake a tour promoting her experiences of America.
26. However, as Han Suyin has noted, such memoirs are also appearing in China as well. She mentions Dai Houying's memoir, *Stones of the Wall*, and writes: "1978 also sees the advent of a new literature, called 'literature of the wounded'. The recital of the sufferings and humiliations endured by so many Party and non-Party intellectuals during the Cultural Revolution. Harrowing stories, which, after a while, stale because of a certain sameness" (Han Suyin, *Wind in My Sleeve: China, Autobiography, History* [London: Cape, 1992], p. 32).
27. Paradoxically, just as orientalism survives in various Western media perspectives, so its inverse, occidentalism, was—and continues to be—used by China as a strategy of containment as well.
28. Anhua Gao, letter to the author, 2001.
29. So-called "Post-Tiananmen Narratives" have begun to address this omission.
30. "Five of a Kind", *Editor*, December 5, 1998, p. 16.
31. "The East is Read: How the Orient Captivated the West", *Observer*, April 16, 2000, p. 16.
32. Ibid.

128  Notes

33. John McLeod, *Beginning Postcolonialism* (Manchester: Manchester University Press, 2000), p. 33.
34. Chang's latest project has been a collaborative book about Mao Zedong (with Jon Halliday).
35. Although they won't release the exact figures, Chang's publishers HarperCollins describe *Wild Swans* as "the biggest-selling non-fiction paperback in recent publishing history". It is estimated that the UK sales alone amount to two million copies.
36. HarperCollinsUK web site (see the works cited).
37. Hong Ying's reputation as a writer has been very uneven, especially in China. Her fictional stories have been attacked for their salacious content, and some critics have noted that Hong Ying's work panders to Western attitudes, and is tarnished by her descriptions of sexual activities. My thanks to Anhua Gao for pointing this out to me.
38. Adeline Yen Mah was also encouraged by Nien Cheng, whom she acknowledges in *Falling Leaves*.
39. It should be noted, however, that Adeline Yen Mah was born and raised in a rich family in Hong Kong, and this has inevitably influenced her perspective on the history of mainland Red China. My thanks to Adeline for reminding me of this.
40. See, for example, *Mao's Children in the New China: Voices from the Red Guard Generation* edited by Yafong Jiang and David Ashley (New York: Routledge, 2000). There is also a film of this experience, by Joan Chen, called *Xiu Xiu: The Sent-Down Girl*.
41. An interesting fictionalised account of the experiences of both rural and urban girlhoods should also be mentioned here: Xiaolu Guo's haunting 2005 book *Village of Stone*, translated from the Chinese, which was supported by Xinran.

## NOTES TO CHAPTER 3

1. Intercountry adoptions occur most frequently between Russia (and other areas of Eastern Europe) and the United States, closely followed by China and the United States. Smaller numbers come from Vietnam, Korea and Cambodia. Korean transracial adoption has a much longer history, as it started in the wake of the Korean War in 1953. Transethnic adoption, such as from Romania or Russia, is a much newer phenomenon.
2. Jing-Bao Nie, *Behind the Silence: Chinese Voices on Abortion* (Lanham, MD: Rowman and Littlefield, 2005), p.158.
3. This and the following testimonial evidence is taken from Section II of HRIC's report, "Caught Between Tradition and the State: Violations of the Human Rights of Chinese Women", New York, 1995. For the full text, see www.hrichina.org. Also see Susan Greenhalgh and Jiali Li, "Engendering Reproductive Policy and Practice in Migrant China: For a Feminist Demography of Reproduction", *Signs* 20 (Spring), pp. 601–641.
4. This testimonial evidence is taken from the Human Rights in China report cited above. Many experts on China have expressed a degree of skepticism about both the motivations and the conclusions of such reports, notably the Human Rights Watch report cited later, although not the testimonial evidence. See Kay Johnson, "Orphanage Care, 1989–1995" in *Wanting a Daughter, Needing a Son*, pp. 42–48 for a discussion of this criticism.
5. Johnson also notes that the Population and Family Planning Law implemented in September 2002 "strengthens protections against extreme and

illegal punishments," which may indicate a "symbolic change from coercion and punishment to voluntary compliance," *Wanting a Daughter, Needing a Son* (p. 207).
6. It should be made clear that "missing" here does not mean never born or aborted; rather this category also includes children who are "statistically missing" due to either underreporting or intentionally hiding children.
7. It should be noted though, that there is a difference between rural and city areas in the implementation of the one-child policy. Many rural areas have a de facto "one-son or two-child policy." Abandoned children also appear in greater proportion in areas south of the Yangtze River in Southeastern China.
8. As an anonymous reader of this chapter observed, however, human rights discourses often figure gender oppression in China simply and solely as an effect of Chinese traditional cultural mores, although this is not always accurate. For a critique of this tendency, see Arati Rao, "The Politics of Gender and Culture in International Human Rights" in Julie Stone Peters and Andrea Wolper, eds., *Women's Rights, Human Rights: International Perspectives* (New York: Routledge, 1995), pp. 167–175, and Chandra Talpade Mohanty et al., eds., *Third World Women and the Politics of Feminism* (Bloomington and Indianapolis: Indiana UP, 1991).
9. For a more detailed analysis of this "epidemic of abandonment," see Human Rights Watch/Asia report, *Death by Default: A Policy of Fatal Neglect in China's State Orphanages* (New York: Human Rights Watch, 1996).
10. For the full reports on China's population policy and its consequences, see the Human Rights in China website, www.hrichina.org, especially Articles 14 and 16.
11. An hour-long documentary directed by Phil Bertelsen on transracial international adoption, "Outside Looking In" was also aired on US television in February 2002, in which the stories of three generations of adoptees were traced.
12. For a succinct overview of this controversy, see the article by Michael Sheridan, "China Shamed by Forced Abortions", *Sunday Times,* 18 September 2005, p. 27.
13. John S. Aird, *Slaughter of the Innocents: Coercive Birth Control in China* (New York: AEI Press, 1990), p. 11; p. 2.
14. It should be noted, that in the wake of this phenomenon, international interest in China's orphanages has started to grow. The group Human Rights in China continues to document adoption and abandonment statistics, and the British and US media are increasingly reporting the phenomenon. A controversial and rather sensational 1995 documentary, "The Dying Rooms: China's Darkest Secret," which was aired on British television, on 14 June, 1995, came close to charging China's orphanages with abusing young children. It showed pictures of children tied to potty chairs, and one young girl near death. Although it incurred the wrath of the Chinese government, which responded with forceful indignation, and attracted criticism from Chinese experts as a poorly researched piece of journalism, it did serve to raise the profile of the issue internationally. An extensive review of books about transracial adoption appeared in *The Women's Review of Books* in January 2002 (vol. XIX, no.4). More recently in Britain, the broadsheet daily newspaper, *The Guardian,* published an in-depth and well-researched article on Chinese orphanages, "Lost Babies, Found Babies," in October 2002, and the *Times Higher Education Supplement* published a piece entitled "Child Trade on Rise", in August of the same year. As I mention above, February 2002 saw the airing of a television documentary, "Outside Looking In: Transracial

Adoption in America" on American national television, and in March 2003 a detailed article on the skewed gender ratio in China appeared in the British broadsheet, *The Guardian* (March 9, 2003). Articles have also appeared in *Reader's Digest*, *Life*, *Woman's Day*, *McCall's*, and the *Yale-China Review*. Many of these articles follow the theme of American adopting parents as "saviours" of abandoned baby girls languishing in horrific conditions in Chinese orphanages, and can be both quite biased and critical of the Chinese social welfare system.

15. This is by necessity only a sample of the material available. Interesting books not included in the discussion here, include: *Operation China* by Paul Hattaway (2000), *The Road Home* by Eliza Hall (1997), and *The Children Can't Wait* by Laura A. Cecere (1998). Children's books also include *Bullets on the Bund* by Steve Whan (2001), and studies of transracial adoption also include *Adopting in China* by Kathleen Wheeler and Doug Werner (1999), *West Meets East: Americans Adopt Chinese Children* by Richard Tessler, Gail Gamache and Liming Liu (1999), and *Intercountry Adoption from China: Examining Cultural Heritage and other Postadoption Issues* by Jay W. Rojewski and Jacy L. Rojewski (2001). *West Meets East* is particularly interesting, as it contains Richard Tessler's account of adopting his daughter Huling from Hefei in 1993, and as such, offers a unique male adopting parental perspective. Academic interest in the study has also continued to grow. See, for example, Barbara Yngvesson, "Going 'Home': Adoption, Loss of Bearings, and the Mythology of Roots", *Social Text* 21 (2003), pp. 7–27; Lisa Cartwright, "Photographs of 'Waiting Children': The Transnational Adoption Market", *Social Text* 21 (2003), pp.83–109; Toby Alice Volkman, "Embodying Chinese Culture: Transnational Adoption in North America", *Social Text* 21 (2003), pp. 29–55; Ann Anagnost, "Scenes of Misrecognition: Maternal Citizenship in the Age of Transnational Adoption", *Positions: East Asia Cultures Critique* 8 (2000), pp. 389–421; Laura Briggs, "Mother, Child, Race, Nation: The Visual Iconography of Rescue and the Politics of Transnational and Transracial Adoption", *Gender and History* 15 (2003), pp. 179–200; Alison Brysk, "Children across Borders: Patrimony, Property, or Persons?", in Alison Brysk and Gershon Shafir, eds., *People Out of Place: Globalization, Human Rights, and the Citizenship Gap* (New York: Routledge, 2004), pp.153–73; and Sara K. Dorow, "'China 'R' Us'? Care, Consumption, and Transnationally Adopted Children", in *Symbolic Childhood*, edited by Daniel Thomas Cook (New York: Peter Lang, 2002), pp. 149–168.

16. As one reader of this chapter pointed out to me, in contrast to the voluminous literature written by young adult Korean adoptees, the Chinese adoptee literature is virtually non-existent at this point due to the young age of the adoptees (though it is starting to develop). Thus, most of what we know about the outcomes of Asian American adoptions thus far comes from Korean experiences spanning the last twenty years. As the Chinese adoptees grow up, so their voices will be heard, and it may be that the children's perspectives prove very different from those of their parents. I am grateful for this observation.

17. The reader of this piece, who made these comments initially, also observed that entering adoptive motherhood in a society which undervalues adoptive parenting, and furthermore may specifically question the validity of transracial parenting, is a highly fraught endeavor.

18. Families with Children from China (FCC) also have an excellent website. Visit www.fwcc.org.

19. Many of the children's texts I discuss here 'soften' the difficult issues at stake–namely the central issue of abandonment—whilst at the same time striving for both honesty and some directness of explanation.

20. Children's transracial adoption narratives often focus upon visible differences between adopting parents and child adoptees as a metonym of the cross-racial differences at stake here. For other examples, see *I Don't Have Your Eyes* by Carrie A. Klitze (Warren, NJ: EMK Press, 2003), and *At Home in this World: A China Adoption Story* by Jean McLeod (Warren, NJ: EMK Press, 2003).
21. Ying-Ying Fry's publisher, Brian Boyd of Yeong and Yeong Books, told me that the young child remains very in touch with her background, and spent her first "fat" royalty cheque on eye exams and glasses for all the children still in her Chinese orphanage, and later for school tuition, a marvellous testament to the impact of this body of literature.
22. As one reader of this chapter pointed out to me, Ying Ying's perspective contrasts sharply with that of some young adult adoptees, such as Korean American Jane Jeong Trenka (*The Language of Blood*), who clearly and succinctly expresses her ambivalence and pain, asking, for instance: "How can an adoptee weigh her terrible loss against the burden of gratitude she feels for her adoptive country and parents?" (p. 201). As the Chinese American adoptee population matures, and starts to produce young adult or adolescent perspectives upon their experiences, then perhaps a different version of the adoption story will emerge.
23. Chinese domestic adoption involves a good deal of risk and expense relative to income, as it frequently pits the adoptive parents against the state. The information given in this section on domestic adoption is taken from Kay Johnson, Huang Banghan and Wang Liyao, "Infant Abandonment and Adoption in China", *Population and Development Review,* 24.3 (September 1998), pp. 469–510.
24. An interesting discussion of growing up with a bi/transracial identity can be found in counsellor Claire Chow's study, *Leaving Deep Water: Asian American Women at the Crossroads of Two Cultures*, (New York: Plume, 1998), especially Chapter 1, "Growing Up Asian, Growing Up American." See also *Growing Up Asian American: Stories of Childhood, Adolescence and Coming of Age in America from the 1800s to the 1990s*, edited by Maria Hong, (New York: Avon, 1995), and Helen Zia's *Asian American Dreams: The Emergence of an American People*, (New York: Farrar, Straus and Giroux, 2000).
25. Most adoptions have occurred between the Korean War and the 1988 Seoul Olympics, after which the South Korean Government largely halted adoptions, embarrassed by the international publicity and interest in the issue. The figures here are quoted by Jane Jeong Trenka, *The Language of Blood: A Memoir* (Minneapolis: Minnesota Historical Society, 2003), p. 225.
26. For a very interesting and somewhat unique perspective, see Hyun Sook Han's memoir, *Many Lives Intertwined* (Minnesota, Yeong and Yeong, 2004). Hyun Sook Han was born before and lived through the Korean War. She was a pioneer Korean social worker, who was involved with Holt International, one of the first international adoption agencies, and has a lifetime of experience of placing Korean children in American homes. Hers is, to my knowledge, the only professional Korean perspective on transracial adoption in English.
27. Also, see Mirim Kim, *Reconstructing Narratives of International Adoption: A Korean Adoptee Talks Back* (unpublished master's thesis, North Dakota State University, 2002); Sandra L. Patton, *Birthmarks: Transracial Adoption in Contemporary America* (New York: New York University Press, 2000); Susan Soon-keum, *Voices from Another Place* (Minnesota: Yeong and Yeong, 1999) and *I Wish for You a Beautiful Life: Letters from the*

Korean Birth Mothers of Ae Ran Won to Their Children ed., Sara Dorow (Minnesota: Yeong and Yeong, 1999).
28. Also see Joanna Catherine Scott, *The Lucky Gourd Shop* (New York: Pocket Books, 2000).
29. See www.wright.edu/~nancy.mack/transracial.pdf; and www.yeongandyeong.com.

## NOTES TO CHAPTER 4

1. See, for example, Japan scholar G. G. Rowley's translation of Sayo Masuda's autobiography for Columbia University Press in 2003.
2. These figures are taken from Lesley Downer's *Women of the Pleasure Quarters: the Secret History of the Geisha*, pp.79–80.
3. On Japanese funerals and geisha, see Liza Dalby, *Geisha*, page 174.
4. In her book, *Ko-uta: Little Songs of the Geisha World*, Liza Crihfield writes that "while conducting a socio-anthropological study as a traditional subculture within modern Japanese society [ . . . ] Part of the Study involved 'becoming a geisha' for a year" (Rutland: Charles E. Tuttle, 1979), p. 16.
5. This is the so-called "bi-confessional" or reflexive turn in cultural anthropology. See for example, James Clifford, *The Predicament of Culture: Twentieth-Century Ethnography, Literature, and Art* (Cambridge, Mass.: Harvard UP, 1988); George E. Marcus and James Clifford, eds., *Writing Culture: The Poetics and Politics of Ethnography* (Berkeley: University of California Press, 1986); and George E. Marcus and Michael M. J. Fischer, *Anthropology as Cultural Critique: An Experimental Moment in the Human Sciences* (Chicago: University of Chicago Press, 1986).
6. The study was originally published as Liza Crihfield's PhD thesis in 1978 in the Department of Anthropology, at Stanford, "The Institution of the Geisha in Modern Japanese Society". It was published by Liza Crihfield Dalby as *Geisha* by the University of California Press in 1983, then republished in the wake of what has been called "geisha fervor" in 1998, one year after the publication of Golden's *Memoirs of a Geisha*.
7. Another geisha study bears some mention here. Lisa Lewis's 1992 book, *Butterflies of the Night: Mama-sans, Geisha, Strippers, and the Japanese Men they Serve* (New York: Tengu Books, 1992), casts its gaze across the spectrum of the *mizu shobai* world, from the haughty highs of geishahood to the seedy lows of prostitution. Lewis has an extensive section on geisha, which covers geisha rituals, the geisha in history and an individual geisha's story. Lewis describes her own involvement in quasi-anthropological terms too: "Spending time in Japan's *mizu shobai* influenced me in many ways. The strongest feeling I have about it all now is that entering that world, as so many others have before and will in the future, provided me with an education that I could have obtained nowhere else. I learned about business, history, and an inner culture that profoundly affects the larger culture in which it is embedded" (p. 200). Despite this, Lewis has no formal training or indeed professional interest in the geisha world. Yet, she also describes a series of research questions which initiated her interest: "My career as a hostess was short by Japanese standards, but long enough to spark an interest in understanding the *mizu shobai*. How did these women feel about their work? What really motivated men to frequent these places? Could the industry survive the social and political changes sweeping the country? This book is the culmination of five years of firsthand interviews, exploration, and research. An outsider in

Japan, I had the chance to look at the club world from the inside, and receive an education in sociology and Japanese business techniques that no university can match" (pp. 24–5). The similarities between Lewis and Downer in particular are clear.

8. All subsequent studies of geisha culture proceed by acknowledging the influence of Dalby's study; Arthur Golden has said that reading Dalby's *Geisha* initially inspired him to write *Memoirs*.
9. www.lizadalby.com.
10. Lesley Downer has also written several books on Japanese cookery. See www.lesleydowner.com for details.
11. M. Cody Poulton, "Madame Sadayakko: the Geisha Who Seduced the West", *Asian Theater Journal*, 21 (2004), pp. 102–4.
12. See www.lesleydowner.com/abouttheauthor/htm for her autobiography.
13. See Mari Yoshihara's analysis of visual orientalism and the iconography of geishahood in the work of Bertha Lum, *Embracing the East: White Women and American Orientalism* (New York: Oxford UP, 2003), pp. 56–62.
14. See Narrelle Morris, "Innocence to Deviance: The Fetishisation of Japanese Women in Western Fiction, 1890s–1990s", intersections.anu.edu.au/issue7/morris.html.
15. This is a phenomenon also observed by Traise Yamamoto, who writes that "the body of the Japanese woman is conflated with and becomes a metonymic representation of Japan itself. The assignation of the feminine to Japan is thus literalized through the body of the Japanese woman, which is then metaphorized as a cultural/national landscape. The shifting interplay among metaphoric and literal registers—feminized nation/female body, geographic landscape/orientalized woman—rhetorically constructs a site that may alternately or simultaneously be inhabited by country and woman" (Traise Yamamoto, *Masking Selves, Making Subjects: Japanese American Women, Identity and the Body*, p. 23).
16. Yoshi Kuzume, "Images of Japanese Women in U.S. Writings and Scholarly Works, 1860–1990: Formation and Transformation of Stereotypes", *U.S.-Japan Women's Journal*, English Supplement 1 (1991), pp. 6–50.
17. Kuzume further traces the evolution of the images of the "geisha girl" and "devoted woman" from their emergence in the 1860s, through the appearance of stereotypes based on these images in America, which Kozume traces to 1899, via the transmutation of the images in the period 1910–1945, to the emergence of a postwar image in which "she was a person subjected to rigorous training according to exacting cultural standards, and a profession that was distinguished" (pp. 17–18).
18. Interestingly, as Sheridan Prasso notes, in contrast, the book has not sold well in Japan (where the title was simply *Sayuri*) because "the story itself was not appealing" (p. 221).
19. Noy Thrupkaew, "Going Geisha", www.zmag.org/ZSustainers/Zdaily/2001-04/14thrupkaew.htm.
20. www.fashion-era.com/Trends_2006/2006_spring_fashion_trends_looks.htm.
21. Liza Dalby, "Look of a geisha", *The Sunday Times*, 8 January 2006.
22. "Geisha guy seeks new date with the muse", *The Sunday Times*, 15 January 2006, p. 15.
23. See Sheridan Prasso, *The Asian Mystique: Dragon Ladies, Geisha Girls and our Fantasies of the Exotic Orient* (New York: Public Affairs, 2005), pp. 18–19.
24. Note, for instance, the current popularity of book-length biographies of Asians and of Asian historical novels.

25. A figure quoted by Sheridan Prasso, *The Asian Mystique*, p. 87.
26. This example clearly underscores the extent to which genre is implicated in orientalism.
27. Allison also views the device of Haarhuis as an "authenticating shadow" (p.3 89), as is the geisha Mineko Iwasaki, cited by Golden as an authority in his acknowledgements. She suggests that this meant that Golden had "anchored one foot of the book in Gion" and the other "in U.S. academia" (p. 389).
28. Spielberg eventually decided not to make the film and passed the project on to Lucy Fisher and Doug Wick, and to director Rob Marshall.
29. The plot similarities to the Cinderella fable lie in *Memoirs*' focus upon the poor fisherman's daughter Chiyo, who is sold to a geisha house, where she lives as an indentured child-maid, subject to vicious treatment from an older "sister" Hatsumomo, before being taken under the wing of another geisha, Mameha, and becoming the celebrated geisha Sayuri.
30. It is also the case that the Cinderella's fable's play upon disguise and revelation is echoed in Chiyo/Sayuri's story in *Memoirs* and of course is an important aspect of geisha allure as well. bell hooks notes that "Within commodity culture, ethnicity becomes spice, seasoning that can liven up the dull dish that is mainstream culture" *Black Looks: Race and Representation*, p. 21 (Boston: South End Press, 1992).
31. See, for example, S. Z. Ahmed's *I Am a Geisha* (Haverford, PA: Infinity Publishing, 2002); Bérénice Geoffroy-Schneiter's *Geishas* (New York: Assouline, 2002), and the *Geisha Secrets: A Pillow Book for Lovers* by Miranda Reigns (New York: Carroll and Graf, 2000).
32. An ancient Japanese form of assembled private writings, sometimes of explicit content.
33. See *the Life of a Geisha*, pp.42–3.
34. Caren Kaplan, "Resisting Autobiography: Out-Law Genres and Transnational Feminist Subjects", in Smith and Watson, eds., *De/Colonizing the Subject: The Politics of Gender in Women's Autobiography* (Minneapolis: University of Minnesota Press, 1992), especially pp. 208–9.

## NOTES TO CHAPTER 5

1. As Cumings elsewhere observes, it is also common to refer to the Korean War as a "forgotten war", almost as an "epitaph"; and, paraphrasing Nietzsche, Cumings calls Korean history "historia abscondita, concealed, secret or unknown history". See Bruce Cumings, "War is a Stern Teacher," in *Living Through the Forgotten War*, pp. 9–14; p. 13. Also see Paul M. Edwards, *To Acknowledge a War: the Korean War in American Memory* (Westport: Greenwood Press, 2000); Richard A. Peters and Xiaobing Li, *Voices from the Korean War* (Lexington: University Press of Kentucky, 2004); and Bruce Cumings ed. *Child of Conflict: the Korean American Relationship, 1943–1953* (Seattle: University of Washington Press, 1983).
2. See Seungsook Moon, "Begetting the Nation: The Androcentric Discourse of National History and Tradition in South Korea", in Choi and Kim, eds., *Dangerous Women*.
3. Two very recent books not included here, which provide slightly different perspectives are Hyok Kang's *This is Paradise! My North Korean Childhood* (London: Little Brown, 2005), and Richard M. Bassett, with Lewis H. Carlson, *And the Wind Blew Cold: the Story of an American POW in North Korea* (Kent, Ohio: Kent State University Press, 2002). Kang's book is

also mediated by translation, and pays homage to *The Aquariums of Pyongyang*.
4. Davis's analysis here is of memoirs of childhood penned by Cambodian survivors of the Khmer Rouge takeover, underpinned by Richard N. Coe's influential 1984 study, *When the Grass Was Taller: Autobiography and the Experience of Childhood* (Yale UP), and provides many useful parallels for my exploration of Korean American writings of war and occupation here, especially in her assertion that these narratives "may be read as an attempt to control, if not the past, then the narrativization of the past. When the past has been so exceptionally shattering [ . . . ] the loss of family members, the separation of the nuclear and extended family, the experience of being refugees and of forced immigration—the need to control the past by writing it becomes more imperative" (p. 74).
5. Ronald Takaki, *Strangers from a Different Shore: A History of Asian Americans* (New York: Penguin, 1989), p. 53.
6. Younghill Kang's work is increasingly attracting academic attention. For instance, in her study, *Assimilating Asians* (2000), Patricia Chu discusses Kang's writing alongside that of Carlos Bulosan, Milton Murayama, and John Okada.
7. See Elaine Kim's *Asian American Literature*, pp. 32–43.
8. For more detailed statistics, see "Still Waiting After 60 Years: Justice for Survivors of Japan's Military Sexual Slavery System", www.amnesty.org/library/Index.ENGASA220122005.
9. Hyunah Yang interestingly discusses the manner in which in Korea "the politics of apology is a twin of the politics of pride (*chajonsim*)" (p. 129).
10. See "Still Waiting After 60 Years" for a discussion of what would constitute an adequate apology.
11. See for example, Jun Jong Lee's fascinating essay on comfort women, shamanism, ghosts and Keller: "Princess Pari in Nora Okja Keller's *Comfort Woman*", *Positions: East Asia Cultures Critique* 12 (2004), pp. 431–456.
12. "Autofiction" is described by Sidonie Smith and Julia Watson as "fictional narrative in the first-person mode" (p. 186). It is therefore an apposite way to describe Keller's text.
13. See Truth and Reconciliation Commission: www.doj.gov.za/trc.
14. www.nkgulag.org.
15. Several possible questions are posed by Smith and Watson that readers need to ask, including "What kind of collaborative involvement has there been? Is this an 'as-told-to' or ghostwritten narrative? Has there been an editor, a transcriber, an amanuensis, or an interviewer involved in the project? What role has each person played in the making of the narrative? [ . . . ] Is there a preface, framing story, or notes that attend to the relationship between narrator/informant and editor/collaborator within the text?" (p. 178).
16. See Bruce Cumings, *Korea's Place in the Sun: A Modern History* (New York: Norton, 2005), p. 11. Cumings discusses the representation of Korea in the West, including in cultural representations. An especially interesting section deals with Ronyoung Kim's *Clay Walls*, which Cumings designates as a memoir of the colonial period. See pp. 178–9.

# Bibliography

Ahmed, S. Z., *I am a Geisha* (Haverford, PA: Infinity Publishing, 2002)
Aihara, Kyoko, *Geisha* (New York: Carlton, 2000)
Aiping Mu, *Vermilion Gate* (New York: Little, Brown, 2000)
Aird, John S., *Slaughter of the Innocents: Coercive Birth Control in China* (New York: AEI Press, 1990)
Allison, Anne, "Memoirs of the Orient", *Journal of Japanese Studies* Vol. 27.2 (Summer, 2001), pp. 381–398
Anagnost, Ann, "Scenes of Misrecognition: Maternal Citizenship in the Age of Transnational Adoption", *Positions: East Asia Cultures Critique* 8 (2000), pp. 389–421
Bassett, Richard M., and Lewis H. Carlson, *And the Wind Blew Cold: The Story of an American POW in North Korea* (Kent, Ohio: Kent State University Press, 2002)
Brada-Williams, Noelle, and Karen Chow, eds., *Crossing Oceans: Reconfiguring Asian Literary Studies on the Pacific Rim* (Hong Kong: Hong Kong University Press, 2004)
Briggs, Laura, "Mother, Child, Race, Nation: The Visual Iconography of Rescue and the Politics of Transnational and Transracial Adoption", *Gender and History* 15 (2003), pp. 179–200
Brysk, Alison, "Children across Borders: Patrimony, Property, or Persons?", in Alison Brysk and Gershon Shafir, eds., *People Out of Place: Globalization, Human Rights, and the Citizenship Gap* (New York: Routledge, 2004)
Cartwright, Lisa, "Photographs of 'Waiting Children': The Transnational Adoption Market", *Social Text* 21 (2003), pp. 83–109
Caruth, Cathy, *Trauma: Explorations in Memory* (Baltimore: John Hopkins University Press, 1995)
Cecere, Laura A., *The Children Can't Wait: China's Emerging Model for Intercountry Adoption* (Laura Cecere, 1998)
Chang, Eileen, *The Rice Sprout Song* (1955; Berkeley: University of California Press, 1998)
———. *The Naked Earth* (1956; Hong Kong: Union Press, 1964)
———. *Rouge of the North* (1967; Berkeley: University of California Press, 1995)
———. *The Golden Cangue* (1943), in *Modern Chinese Stories and Novellas, 1919–1949*, eds. Joseph S.M. Lau and C.T. Hsia (New York: Columbia University Press, 1981)
Chang, Pang-Mei Natasha, *Bound Feet and Western Dress* (New York: Bantam, 1996)
Chanrithy Him, *When Broken Glass Floats: Growing Up Under the Khmer Rouge* (New York: Norton, 2001)
Chen, Joan, Interview with Richard Corliss, "West to East", *Time Magazine*, 153(13), April 5, 1999, pp. 60–62
Cheng, Nien, *Life and Death in Shanghai* (New York: Flamingo, 1987)

Choi, Sook Nyul, *Year of Impossible Goodbyes* (Boston: Houghton Mifflin, 1991)
———. *Echoes of the White Giraffe* (New York: Bantam Doubleday, 1993)
———. *Gathering of Pearls* (Boston: Houghton Mifflin, 1994)
Chow, Claire, *Leaving Deep Water: Asian American Women at the Crossroads of Two Cultures* (New York: Plume, 1998)
Chu, Patricia, *Assimilating Asians: Gendered Strategies of Authorship in Asian America* (Durham: Duke University Press, 2000)
Chun Yu, *Little Green: Growing Up During the Chinese Cultural Revolution* (New York: Simon and Schuster, 2005)
Chunghee Sarah Soh, Review of *Home Was the Land of Morning Calm*, The Journal of Asian Studies 55 (1996), pp. 1019–1020
Choi, Chungmoo, and Elaine H. Kim, eds., *Dangerous Women: Gender and Korean Nationalism* (New York: Routledge, 1997)
Choi, Yearn Hong, and Haeng Ja Kim, eds. *Surfacing Sadness: A Centennial of Korean-American Literature 1903–2003* (Dumont, NJ.: Homa and Sekey Books, 2003)
Clifford, James, *The Predicament of Culture: Twentieth-Century Ethnography, Literature, and Art* (Cambridge, Mass.: Harvard University Press, 1988)
Coe, Richard N., *When the Grass Was Taller: Autobiography and the Experience of Childhood* (Yale: Yale University Press, 1984)
Crihfield, Liza, *Ko-uta: Little Songs of the Geisha World* (Rutland: Charles E. Tuttle, 1979)
Cumings, Bruce, *Korea's Place in the Sun, A Modern History* (New York: Norton, 2005)
———. "War is a Stern Teacher," in *Living Through the Forgotten War: Portrait of Korea* edited by Patrick Dowdey (Middletown, Conn.: Wesleyan University Press, 2003)
———. ed., *Child of Conflict: the Korean American Relationship, 1943–1953* (Seattle: University of Washington Press, 1983)
Da Chen, *Colors of the Mountain* (New York: Anchor, 2001)
———. *China's Son: Growing Up In the Cultural Revolution* (New York: Laurel Leaf, 2001)
———. *Sounds of the River* (New York: Harper Perennial, 2002)
Dalby, Liza, *Geisha* (New York: Vintage, 2000)
———. "Look of a geisha", *Sunday Times*, January 8, 2006. http://women.timesonline.co.uk/tol/life_and_style/women/beauty/article783644.ece. Accessed May 19 2008.
Darina Siv, *Never Come Back: A Cambodian Woman's Journey* (New York: The Writer Press, 2000)
Davis, Rocío G., *Begin Here: Reading Asian North American Autobiographies of Childhood* (Honolulu: University of Hawaii Press, 2007)
Dith Pran, ed., *Children of Cambodia's Killing Fields: Memoirs by Survivors* (Yale: Yale University Press, 1999)
Dorow, Sara K., "'China 'R' Us'? Care, Consumption, and Transnationally Adopted Children", in *Symbolic Childhood*, edited by Daniel Thomas Cook (New York: Peter Lang, 2002)
———. ed., *I Wish for You a Beautiful Life: Letters from the Korean Birth Mothers of Ae Ran Won to Their Children* (Minnesota: Yeong and Yeong, 1999)
———. *When You Were Born in China: A Memory Book for Children Adopted from China* (St. Paul, Minnesota: Yeong and Yeong Book Company, 1997)
———. *Transnational Adoption: A Cultural Economy of Race, Gender and Kinship* (New York: New York University Press, 2006)
Dowdey, Patrick, and Wei Hsin Gui, *Living Through the Forgotten War: Portrait of Korea* (Middletown, Conn.: Wesleyan University Press, 2003)

Downer, Lesley, *Geisha: The Secret History of a Vanishing World* (London: Headline, 2000)
———. *Women of the Pleasure Quarters: The Secret History of the Geisha* (New York: Broadway, 2001)
———. *Madame Sadayakko: The Geisha Who Seduced the West* (London: Headline, 2003)
Edwards, Paul M., *To Acknowledge a War: the Korean War in American Memory* (Westport: Greenwood Press, 2000)
Eidse, Faith, and Nina Sichel, eds., *Unrooted Childhoods: Memoirs of Growing Up Global* (London: Nicholas Brealey Publishing, 2004)
Esherwick, Joseph W., et al, *The Chinese Cultural Revolution as History* (Stanford: Stanford UP, 2006)
Evans, Harriet and Stephanie Donald, eds., *Picturing Power in the People's Republic of China: Posters of the Cultural Revolution* (London: Rowman and Littlefield, 1999)
Evans, Harriet, "Dangers of Arrogance", *TLS* 4918 (1997), p. 29
Evans, Karin, *The Lost Daughters of China: Abandoned Girls, Their Journey to America, and the Search for a Missing Past* (New York: Penguin Putnam, 2000)
Fairbanks, Jessica EunYung et al, eds., *The Letter Never Sent I* and *II* (Seoul: IECEF, 2004; 2005)
Fan Shen, *Gang of One: Memoirs of a Red Guard* (Nebraska: University of Nebraska Press, 2004)
Feng Jicai, *Voices from the Whirlwind: An Oral History of the Chinese Cultural Revolution* (New York: Pantheon, 1991)
Fenkl, Heinz Insu, and Walter Lew, eds., *Kŏri: The Beacon Anthology of Korean American Fiction* (Boston: Beacon Press, 2001)
Fry, Ying-Ying, *Kids Like Me in China* (St. Paul: Yeong and Yeong Book Company, 2001)
Gallagher, John, *Geisha: A Unique World of Tradition, Elegance, and Art* (London: PRC Publishing, 2003)
Gao, Anhua, *To the Edge of the Sky* (New York: Viking, 2000)
Geoffroy-Schneiter, Bérénice, *Geishas* (New York: Assouline, 2002)
Gillan, Audrey, "Lost Babies, Found Babies", *The Guardian Weekend*, October 12, 2002, pp. 18–30
Golden, Arthur, *Memoirs of a Geisha* (New York: Vintage, 1997)
Greenhalgh, Susan and Jiali Li, "Engendering Reproductive Policy and Practice in Migrant China: For a Feminist Demography of Reproduction", *Signs*, 20 (Spring), pp. 601–641
Grice, Helena, *Negotiating Identities: An Introduction to Asian American Women's Writing* (Manchester: Manchester University Press, 2002)
Guo Sheng, *Tears of the Moon* (London: Penguin, 2003)
Haaken, Janice, *Pillar of Salt: Gender, Memory, and the Perils of Looking Back* (London: Free Association Books, 1998)
Han Suyin, *Destination Chungking* (London: Jonathon Cape, 1943)
———. *Wind In My Sleeve: China, Autobiography, History* (London: Cape, 1992)
Harris, Sara, *House of 10,000 Pleasures: A Modern Study of the Geisha and of the Streetwalker in Japan* (1962; London: Pan, 1999)
Harrison, Kathryn, *The Binding Chair* (London: Fourth Estate, 2000)
Hattaway, Paul, *Operation China: Introducing All the People of China* (Pasadena: William Carey Library Publishing, 2000)
Henke, Suzette, *Shattered Subjects: Trauma and Testimony in Women's Life-Writing* (New York: Palgrave Macmillan, 1998)
Herman, Judith Lewis, *Trauma and Recovery: From Domestic Abuse to Political Terror* (London: Rivers Oram Press/Pandora's List, 2001)

Hicks, George L., *The Comfort Women: Japan's Brutal Regime of Enforced Prostitution in the Second World War* (New York: Norton, 1994)
Hodgson, John, *The Search for the Self: Childhood in Autobiography and Fiction since 1940* (Sheffield: Sheffield Academic Press, 1993)
Hong, Maria, ed., *Growing Up Asian American: Stories of Childhood, Adolescence and Coming of Age in America from the 1800s to the 1990s* (New York: Avon, 1995)
Hong Kingston, Maxine, *The Woman Warrior* (London: Picador, 1979)
Hong Ying, *Daughter of the River* (London: Bloomsbury, 1997)
hooks, bell, *Black Looks: Race and Representation* (Boston: South End Press, 1992)
Hsia, C.T., *A History of Modern Chinese Fiction* (Bloomington: Indiana University Press, 1999)
Human Rights in China, *Caught between Tradition and the State: Violations of the Human Rights of Chinese Women* (New York: HRIC, 1995)
Human Rights Watch/Asia, *Death by Default: A Policy of Fatal Neglect in China's State Orphanages* (New York: Human Rights Watch, 1996)
Hyok Kang, *This is Paradise! My North Korean Childhood* (London: Little Brown, 2005)
Hyun, Peter, *Man Sei! The Making of a Korean American* (Honolulu: University of Hawaii Press, 1986)
Hyun Sook Han, *Many Lives Intertwined* (Minnesota: Yeong and Yeong, 2004)
Hyunah Yang, "Re-membering the Korean Military Comfort Women: Nationality, Sexuality and Silencing" in Elaine H. Kim and Chungmoo Choi, eds., *Dangerous Women: Gender and Korean Nationalism* (New York: Routledge, 1998), pp. 123–140
Iwasaki, Mineko, *Geisha: A Life* (New York: Washington Square Press, 2002)
———. *Geisha of Gion* (London: Pocket Books, 2003)
Ji-Li Jiang, *Red Scarf Girl: A Memoir of the Cultural Revolution* (New York: Harper Collins, 1991)
Jing-Bao Nie, *Behind the Silence: Chinese Voices on Abortion* (Lanham: Rowman and Littlefield, 2005)
Johnson, Kay, *Wanting a Daughter, Needing a Son: Abandonment, Adoption, and Orphanage Care in China* (St Paul, Minnesota: Yeong and Yeong, 2004)
———. "The Politics of the Revival of Infant Abandonment in China, with Special Reference to Hunan", *Population and Development Review*, 22 (1996), pp. 77–98
Johnson, Kay, Huang Banghan and Wang Liyao, "Infant Abandonment and Adoption in China", *Population and Development Review*, 24 (1998), pp. 469–510
Joseph, William A., Christine P. W. Wong and David Zweig, *New Perspectives on the Cultural Revolution* (Harvard: Harvard University Press, 1991)
Jun Jong Lee, "Princess Pari in Nora Okja Keller's *Comfort Woman*", *Positions: East Asia Cultures Critique* 12 (2004), pp. 431–456
Jung Chang and Jon Halliday, *Mao: The Unknown Story* (New York: Vintage, 2007)
Jung Chang, *Wild Swans: Three Daughters of China* (London: Harper Collins, 1993)
———. 'Sour Sweet', *Bookcase*, Summer 1993, p. 7
Kang Chol-Hwan, *The Aquariums of Pyongyang* (New York: Basic, 2001)
Kang, Connie K., *Home Was the Land of Morning Calm* (Cambridge, Mass.: Da Capo, 1995)
Kang, Younghill, *The Grass Roof* (1931; New York: Norton, 1975)
———. *East Goes West* (1937; New York: Kaya, 1997)
Kaplan, Caren, "Resisting Autobiography: Out-Law Genres and Transnational Feminist Subjects", in Smith and Watson, eds., *De/Colonizing the Subject: The*

*Politics of Gender in Women's Autobiography* (Minneapolis: University of Minnesota Press, 1992), pp. 115–138

Karlin,Wayne ed., *The Other Side of Heaven: Post-War Fiction by Vietnamese and American Writers* (Connecticut: Curbstone Press, 1995)

Karnow, Stanley, *Mao and China: A Legacy of Turmoil* (New York: Penguin, 1990)

Keller, Nora Okja, *Comfort Woman* (New York: Penguin, 1997)

———. *Fox Girl* (New York: Penguin, 2002)

Keller, Nora Okja, Brenda Kwon, Sun Namkung, Gary Pak and Cathy Song, eds. *Yobo: Korean American Writing in Hawaii* (Honolulu: Bamboo Ridge, 2003)

Kelsky, Karen, *Women on the Verge: Japanese Women, Western Dreams* (Durham: Duke University Press, 2002)

Kim, Elaine, *The Comfort Women: Colonialism, War, and Sex* (Durham: Duke University Press, 1997)

———. *Asian American Literature: An Introduction to the Writings and Their Social Context* Philadelphia: Temple University Press, 1982)

———. "Korean American Literature", in *An Interethnic Companion to Asian American Literature*, ed. King-kok Cheung (New York: Cambridge University Press, 1997), pp. 156–191

Kim, Elaine H. and Eui-Young Yu, eds., *East to America: Korean American Life Stories* (Derby, PA.: Diane Publishing Company, 1996)

Kim, Elaine H. and Laure Hyun Yi Kang, eds., *Echoes upon Echoes: New Korean American Writings* (Philadelphia: Temple University Press, 2002)

Kim, Elizabeth, *Ten Thousand Sorrows* (New York: Doubleday, 2000)

Kim-Gibson, D., *Silence Broken: Korean Comfort Women* (Parkersburg, Iowa: Mid-Prairie Books, 1999)

Kimm, Samuel, *Cries of the Korean Comfort Women: The Vivid Testimony of a Korean Teenage Girl During World War II* (Philadelphia: Xlibris, 2004)

Klitze, Carrie A., *I Don't Have Your Eyes* (Warren, NJ: EMK Press, 2003)

Klatzin, Amy, ed., *A Passage to the Heart: Writings from Families with Children from China* (St. Paul: Yeong and Yeong Book Company, 1999)

Kolosov, Jacqueline, *Grace from China* (St. Paul, Minneapolis: Yeong and Yeong, 2004)

Kuzume, Yoshi, "Images of Japanese Women in U.S. Writings and Scholarly Works, 1860–1990: Formation and Transformation of Stereotypes", *U.S.–Japan Women's Journal*, English Supplement, 1 (1991), pp. 6–50

Kyoko Aihara, *Geisha* (New York: Carlton, 2000)

Lee, Chang-Rae, *Native Speaker* (New York: Riverhead, 1995)

Lee, Helie, *Still Life with Rice* (New York: Touchstone, 1996)

———. *In the Absence of Sun: A Korean American Woman's Promise to Reunite Three Lost Generations of Her Family* (New York: Harmony, 2002)

Lee, Mary Paik, *Quiet Odyssey: A Pioneer Korean Woman in America* (Seattle: University of Washington Press, 1990)

Lee, Myung-Ok Marie, *Somebody's Daughter* (Boston: Beacon Press, 2005)

Lewis, Lisa, *Butterflies of the Night: mama-sans, geisha, strippers, and the Japanese men they serve* (New York: Tengu Books, 1992)

Lewis, Rose, *I Love You Like Crazy Cakes* (Boston: Little, Brown, 2000)

Li, Moying, *Snow Falling in Spring: Coming of Age in China During the Cultural Revolution* (New York: Farrar, Straus and Giroux, 2008)

Lim, Shirley Geok-lin, John Blair Gamber, Stephen Hong Sohn and Gina Valentino, eds., *Transnational Asian American Literature: Sites and Transits* (Philadelphia: Temple University Press, 2006)

Ling, Amy, *Between Worlds: Women Writers of Chinese Ancestry* (New York: Pergamon, 1991)

Liu, Aimee, *Cloud Mountain* (New York: Warner, 1997)

Liu Hong, *Startling Moon* (London: Headline, 2001)
Liyan Qin, "The Sublime and the Profane: A Comparative Analysis of Two Fictional Narratives about Sent-down Youth", in Joseph W. Esherwick et al, eds., *The Cultural Revolution as History* (Stanford: Stanford University Press, 1996), pp. 240–266
Long, Jeffrey E., *Remembered Childhoods: A Guide to Autobiography and Memoirs of Childhood and Youth* (Libraries Unlimited, 2007)
Loung Ung, *First They Killed My Father: A Daughter of Cambodia Remembers* (New York: Harper Perennial, 2006)
Ma Bo, *Blood Red Sunset: A Memoir of the Cultural Revolution* (New York: Penguin, 1994)
Ma Yan, *The Diary of Ma Yan: The Life of a Chinese Schoolgirl* (London: Virago, 2002)
McLeod, Jean, *At Home in this World: A China Adoption Story* (Warren, NJ: EMK Press, 2003)
Marchetti, Gina, *Romance and the "Yellow Peril": Race, Sex, and Discursive Strategies in Hollywood Fiction* (Berkeley: University of California Press, 1994)
Marcus, George E., and James Clifford, eds., *Writing Culture: The Poetics and Politics of Ethnography* (Berkeley: University of California Press, 1986)
Marcus, George E., and Michael M. J. Fischer, *Anthropology as Cultural Critique: An Experimental Moment in the Human Sciences* (Chicago: University of Chicago Press, 1986)
Masuda, Sayo, *Autobiography of a Geisha*, trans., G. G. Rowley (New York: Columbia University Press, 2003)
McCallum, Robyn, *Ideologies of Identity in Adolescent Fiction* (New York: Garland, 1999)
McClellan, Anita D., "Bridging the Ocean", *The Women's Review of Books*, 19 (2002), pp. 7–9
McLeod, John, *Beginning Postcolonialism* (Manchester: Manchester University Press, 2000)
Millet, Catherine, *The Sexual Life of Catherine M.* (New York: Corgi, 2003)
Min, Anchee, *Red Azalea* (London: Victor Gollancz, 1993)
Mineko Iwasaki, *Geisha of Gion* (New York: Pocket Books, 2002)
Mirim Kim, *Reconstructing Narratives of International Adoption: A Korean Adoptee Talks Back* (Unpublished Master's Thesis, North Dakota State University, 2002)
Mirsky, Jonathan, "Literature of the Wounded", *The New York Review of Books*, 39(5), March 5, 1992, pp. 6–10
Mohanty, Chandra Talpade, and others, eds., *Third World Women and the Politics of Feminism* (Bloomington: Indiana University Press, 1991)
Molyda Szymusiak and others, eds., *The Stones Cry Out: A Cambodian Childhood, 1975–1980* (Bloomington: Indiana University Press, 1999)
Morris, Narrelle, "Innocence to Deviance: The Fetishisation of Japanese Women in Western Fiction, 1890s–1990s", intersections.anu.edu.au/issue7/morris.html. Accessed January 10, 2008.
Nanchu, *Red Sorrow* (New York: Arcade Publishing, 2002)
Ohnuki-Tierney, Emiko, *Kamikaze Diaries: Reflections of Japanese Student Soldiers* (Chicago: University of Chicago Press, 2007)
Okihiro, Gary, *Common Ground: Reimagining American History* (Princeton: Princeton UP, 2001)
Pai, Margaret K., *The Dreams of Two Yi-Min* (Honolulu: University of Hawaii Press, 1989)
Park, Linda Sue, *When My Name Was Keoko* (New York: Yearling/Random House, 2002)

Patton, Sandra L., *Birthmarks: Transracial Adoption in Contemporary America* (New York: New York University Press, 2000)

Peacock, Carol Antoinette, *Mommy Far, Mommy Near: An Adoption Story* (Morton Grove, Illinois: Albert Whitman and Company, 2000)

Perkins, P. D., *Geisha of Pontocho* (Tokyo: Tokyo News Service,1954)

Peters, Richard A., and Xiaobing Li, *Voices from the Korean War* (Lexington: University Press of Kentucky, 2004)

Pin Yathay, *Stay Alive, My Son* (New York: Touchstone, 1988)

Prager, Emily, *Wuhu Diary: On Taking My Adopted Daughter Back to Her Hometown in China* (New York: Random House, 2001)

Prasso, Sheridan, *The Asian Mystique: Dragon Ladies, Geisha Girls and our Fantasies of the Exotic Orient* (New York: Public Affairs, 2005)

Poulton, M. Cody, "Madame Sadayakko: the Geisha Who Seduced the West", *Asian Theater Journal* 21, (2004), pp. 102–4

Rao, Arati, "The Politics of Gender and Culture in International Human Rights", in Julie Stone Peters and Andrea Wolper, eds., *Women's Rights, Human Rights: International Perspectives* (New York: Routledge, 1995), pp.167–175

Register, Cheri, *Are Those Kids Yours? American Families with Children Adopted from Other Countries* (St. Paul, Minnesota: Yeong and Yeong, 1990)

———. *Beyond Good Intentions: A Mother Reflects on Raising Internationally Adopted Children* (St. Paul, Minnesota: Yeong and Yeong, 2005)

Reigns, Miranda, *Geisha Secrets: A Pillow Book for Lovers* (New York: Carroll and Graf, 2000)

Robinson, Katy, *A Single Square Picture: A Korean Adoptee's Search for Her Roots* (New York: Penguin, 2002)

Rojewski, Jay W., and Jacy L. Rojewski, *Intercountry Adoption from China: Examining Cultural Heritage and other Postadoption Issues* (New York: Greenwood, 2001)

Ronyoung Kim, *Clay Walls* (Seattle: Washington State University Press, 1987)

Said, Edward W., *Orientalism* (New York: Penguin, 1978)

Sansan, *Eighth Moon: True Story of a Young Girl's Life in Communist China* (New York: Sphere, 1984)

Schoyer, Preston, "The Smell of a Hidden World", *Saturday Review*, May 21, 1955

Schultermandl, Silvia, "Writing Rape, Trauma, and Transnationality" *Meridians: Feminism, Race, Transnationalism* 7.2 (2007), pp. 71–100

Scott, Adolphe, *The Flower and Willow World: The Story of the Geisha* (London: Heinemann, 1959)

Scott, Joanna Catherine, *The Lucky Gourd Shop* (New York: Pocket Books, 2000)

Seungsook Moon, "Begetting the Nation: The Androcentric Discourse of National History and Tradition in South Korea", in Choi and Kim, eds., *Dangerous Women: Women and Korean Nationalism* (New York: Routledge, 1998), pp. 33–66

Sheridan, Michael, "China Shamed by Forced Abortions", *Sunday Times,* September 18, 2005 Online www.timesonline.co.uk. Accessed January 30, 2006.

Slaughter, Joseph R., *Human Rights, Inc.: The World Novel, Narrative Form and International Law* (New York: Fordham University Press, 2007)

Smith, Sidonie, and Julia Watson, *Reading Autobiography: A Guide for Interpreting Life Narratives* (Minneapolis: University of Minnesota Press, 2002)

Somerson, Wendy, "Under the Mosquito Net" *College Literature* 24.1(February, 1997), pp. 98–115

Soon-keum, Susan, *Voices from Another Place* (St. Paul, Minnesota: Yeong and Yeong, 1999)

Steinberg, Gail, and Beth Hall, *Inside Transracial Adoption* (Indianapolis: Perspectives Press, 2000)

Sterngold, James, "Spielberg Looks to the East", *New York Times*, September 11, 1998. http://topics.nytimes.com/top/reference/timestopics/people/s/james_sterngold/index.html. Accessed May 14, 2007.
Sun Shuyin, *Ten Thousand Miles Without a Cloud* (New York: Harper Perennial, 2003)
Takaki, Ronald, *Strangers from a Different Shore: A History of Asian Americans* (New York: Penguin, 1989)
Tal, Kalí, *Worlds of Hurt: Reading the Literatures of Trauma* (New York: Cambridge University Press, 1996)
Tan, Amy, *The Joy Luck Club* (London: Minerva, 1989)
———. *The Kitchen God's Wife* (London: Flamingo, 1992)
Tessler, Richard, Gail Gamache and Liming Liu, *West Meets East: Americans Adopt Chinese Children* (Westport: Bergin and Garveg, 1999)
Thorpe, Vanessa, 'The East is Read: How the Orient Captivated the West', *Observer*, Sunday April 16, 2000. www.guardian.co.uk/uk/2000/apr/16/books.booksnews. Accessed December 19, 2000.
Trenka, Jane Jeong, *The Language of Blood: A Memoir* (Minneapolis: Minnesota Historical Society/Borealis, 2003)
Underwood, Eleanor, *The Life of a Geisha* (New York: Smithmark Publishers, 1999)
Volkman, Toby Alice, "Embodying Chinese Culture: Transnational Adoption in North America", *Social Text* 21 (2003), pp. 29–55
Whan, Steve, *Bullets on the Bund* (Vancouver: Autumn Jade, 2001)
Winzig, Jerry, "Discovering Sook Nyul Choi's Autobiographical Novels for Young Adults", *Korean Quarterly* (Winter, 1997), www.koreanquarterly.org. Accessed August 8, 2008
Wong, Jan, *Red China Blues* (London: Bantam, 1996)
Wong, Cynthia F., "Remembering China in *Wild Swans* and *Life and Death in Shanghai*", *Homemakers: Women Writers and the Politics and Poetics of Home*, eds. Catherine Wiley and Fiona R. Barnes (New York: Garland, 1996), pp. 15–133
Xiaolu Guo, *Village of Stone* (New York: Vintage, 2005)
Xiaomei Chen, "Growing Up with Posters in the Maoist Era", *Picturing Power in the People's Republic: Posters of the Cultural Revolution* eds. Harriet Evans and Stephanie Donald (Boulder, CO.: Rowman and Littlefield, 1999), pp. 101–122
Xu, Ben, "A Face that Grows into a Mask: A Symptomatic Reading of Anchee Min's *Red Azalea*" *MELUS* 29.2 (Summer, 2004), pp. 157–180
Xu, Meihong, *Daughter of China: The True Story of Forbidden Love in Modern China* (London: Headline, 1998)
Xu, Wenying, "Agency via Guilt in Anchee Min's *Red Azalea*" *MELUS* 25.3(Autumn/Winter 2000), pp.203–219
Xue, Xinran, *The Good Women of China: Hidden Voices* (London: Vintage, 2003)
———. *What the Chinese Don't Eat* (New York: Vintage, 2006)
———. *China Witness: Voices from a Silent Generation* (New York: Pantheon, forthcoming 2009)
Yafong Jiang and David Ashley, eds., *Mao's Children in the New China: Voices from the Red Guard Generation* (New York: Routledge, 2000)
Yamamoto, Traise, *Masking Selves, Making Subjects: Japanese American Women, Identity, and the Body* (Berkeley: University of California Press, 1999)
Yang, Rae, *Spider Eaters* (Berkeley: University of California Press, 1997)
Yasuo Kuwahara, *Kamikaze: A Japanese Pilot's Own Spectacular Story of the Famous Suicide Squadrons* (Clearfield, Utah: American Legacy Media, 2007)
Ye, Ting-xing, *A Leaf in the Bitter Wind* (New York and London: Bantam, 2000)

Yen, Maria, *The Umbrella Garden; A Picture of Student Life in Red China* (New York: Macmillan, 1954)
Yen-Mah, Adeline, *Falling Leaves: The True Story of an Unwanted Chinese Daughter* (New York: Penguin, 1997)
———.*Chinese Cinderella: The Secret Story of an Unwanted Daughter* (NY: Puffin, 1999)
Ying Ying Fry, *Kids Like Me in China* (St. Paul, Minnesota: Yeong and Yeong, 2001)
Yngvesson, Barbara, "Going 'Home': Adoption, Loss of Bearings, and the Mythology of Roots", *Social Text* 21 (2003), pp. 7–27
Yoshiaki Yoshimi, Comfort *Women* (New York: Columbia UP, 2002)
Yoshihara, Mari, *Embracing the East: White Women and American Orientalism* (New York: Oxford UP, 2003)
Yuan-tsung Chen, *The Dragon's Village: An Autobiographical Novel of Revolutionary China* (New York: Penguin, 1981)
Yun, Mia, *Translations of Beauty* (New York: Washington Square Press, 2004)
———. *House of the Winds* (New York: Penguin, 1998)
Zhang, Ange, *Red Land, Yellow River* (Berkeley: Groundwood, 2004)
Zia, Helen, *Asian American Dreams: The Emergence of an American People* (New York: Farrar, Straus and Giroux, 2000)

## WEB RESOURCES

"Geisha guy seeks new date with the muse" (2006, January 15), *The Sunday Times* http://timesonline.co.uk/article/o,,2088-1985861,00.html
Noy Thrupkaew, "Going Geisha",
www.zmag.org/ZSustainers/Zdaily/2001-04/14thrupkaew.htm
www.wright.edu/~nancy.mack/transracial.pdf
Families with Children from China www.fwcc.org
Human Rights in China NGO www.hrichina.org
United Nations—Declaration of Human Rights www.un.org/Overview/rights.html
Unicef NGO www.unicef.org
Harper Collins Publishers www.harpercollins.co.uk
www.lesleydowner.com/abouttheauthor/htm
www.lizadalby.com
www.fashion-era.com/Trends_2006/2006_spring_fashion_trends_looks.htm
Amnesty International NGO www.amnesty.org/library/Index.ENGASA220122005
Truth and Reconciliation Commission South Africa www.doj.gov.za/trc
Democracy in North Korea Network www.nkgulag.org
Yeong and Yeong Books www.yeongandyeong.com
www.washingtonpost.com (Nov. 12, 2008)
www.uscis.gov (United States Immigration)

## DOCUMENTARIES

Kate Blewett and Brian Woods, "The Dying Rooms: China's Darkest Secret", aired 1995, Channel 4, UK.

# Index

## A
Abe, Shinzo, 5, 106
abortion, 34, 129n6; enforced, 46–7, 48–9, 129n12
abuse, 10, 118–19; childhood, 15, 37, 41, 100–101, 123, 129n14; domestic, 15, 31; sexual, 6–7, 104, 108–9, 110–111. *See also* rape
adoption. *See* Chinese Americans, adoptees; domestic adoption; international adoption; Korean American, adoptees; transethnic adoption; transracial adoption
aesthetics, 8–9, 12, 112
Ahmed, S.Z., *I am a Geisha*, 90, 134n31
Aihara, Kyoko, *Geisha*, 68
Aiping Mu, 3; *Vermilion Gate*, 12
Aird, John S., 44, 49
Aizaburo, Akiyama, *Geisha Girl*, 67
Akasaka (geisha district), 69
Alcoff, Linda Martin, 118–19
Allison, Anne, 81–3, 84, 88, 89, 134n27
Amis, Martin, 13
Amnesty International, 10, 104, 113
anthropology, 68, 71–2, 74, 90, 132–3nn4–7. *See also* ethnography
anti-Communism, 22
*AsianWeek*, 108
autobiography. *See* life writing

## B
Bantam (publishers), 18, 19
*Barbarian and the Geisha, The* (film), 78
Bassett, Richard M., *And the Wind Blew Cold*, 134n3
Behr, Edward, 13
Beijing: Lu Xun Literature Academy for Writers, 34; National Beijing University, 20; Olympic Games (2008), 22
Belgrade, 51
Bertelsen, Phil, 129n11
Bhabha, Homi, 18
Birnbaum, Robert, 108
birth control, 46–9
*Black Book of Communism, The*, 118
Boyd, Brian, 131n21
Brada-Williams, Noelle, 7
Britain: Asian British writing, 126n6; and Chinese expatriate writing, 3, 12, 14, 19, 24–5, 28, 31; and Chinese human rights abuses, 3, 63, 129n14
Brown, Jane, 53
Buck, Pearl, 127n19
Bush, George W., 48, 116–17, 122

## C
California, 97, 102
Cambodia, 2, 100, 125n1, 128n1, 135n4
Canada, 13, 19
Caruth, Cathy, 10, 15, 111
CBC News, 88–9
censorship, 3, 6, 10, 12, 15, 27, 28, 117
Cha, Theresa Hak Kyung, *Dictee*, 5, 96
Chan, Sucheng, 97, 101, 102
Chang, Eileen, 20–22, 43, 127nn19–20; *The Golden Cangue*, 20, 21; *Lust, Caution*, 21, 127n19; *The Naked Earth*, 20, 21; *The Rice Sprout Song*, 20, 21, 22, 127n19; *The Rouge of the North*, 20, 127nn19–20

## Index

Chang, Pang-Mei Natasha, *Bound Feet and Western Dress*, 13, 18–19, 25, 26, 127n16
Changsha, 55
Chen, Da, 126n5
Chen, Joan, 3, 18, 24, 126n15, 128n40
Cheney, Dick, 116
Cheng, Nien, 6, 12, 32, 128n38; *Life and Death in Shanghai*, 20, 21, 23
Chengdu, 28
children: child abandonment, 3, 44, 45–6, 48, 49, 50, 54, 60, 62–3, 129n7, 129n9, 129–30n14, 130n19; childhood abuse, 15, 37, 41, 100–101; and Chinese Cultural Revolution, 37, 38–43, 128nn40–41; Chinese "missing" children, 47–8, 129n6; cruelty of, 41; in Korea, 100–101, 123; and trauma, 40, 100–101; UN Convention on the Rights of the Child, 101, 125n4. *See also* domestic adoption; international adoption; one-child policy; transethnic adoption; transracial adoption
children's books, 10, 37–8, 39, 49, 50, 53–7, 123, 130n15, 130n19, 131n20
China: adoption policy, 60, 131n23; atrocities in, 2, 12, 22, 27; censorship, 3, 12, 15, 27, 28; Communist Party, 12, 18, 20, 21, 26, 27, 28, 31, 127n26; Deng Xiaoping's reforms, 24, 28, 37; emigration, 11; famine, 12, 14, 30, 33, 34; human rights abuses, 2, 10, 12, 22, 27, 46, 48–9, 63–4, 127n26, 129n8, 129n14; Japanese occupation, 26, 27; and Korea, 122; Kuomintang, 26, 27, 37; orphanages, 3, 45, 51, 54, 56, 60, 63, 129n9, 129–30n14, 131n21; peasants, 21, 27, 32, 33; population policy, 2, 3–4, 6, 44–9, 51, 54, 56, 58, 60, 62–4, 129n7, 129n10; 'Post-Mao' period, 12, 16–17, 24, 32–4, 126n3–4, 127n21; prisons, 8, 31; Red Guard, 26, 27, 29, 40, 41, 126nn3–4; and Taiwan, 1; Tiananmen Square protests (1989), 2, 22, 127n29; Western view of, 2, 11, 20, 22–3; Young Pioneers, 29, 41. *See also* Cultural Revolution, Chinese
Chinatown, 59, 61
Chinese Americans: adoptees, 45–6, 49–64, 65, 129n11, 130n16, 131n22; and racial identity, 49, 50, 53, 54, 55–6, 59–63; women's writing, 13, 18–19, 20–22, 24–5, 25–6, 127n19
*ch'iryo* (healing therapy), 119
Choi, Chungmoo, 93
Choi, Sook Nyul, 96–7, 122–4; *Echoes of the White Giraffe*, 94, 96, 100, 124; *Gathering of Pearls*, 94, 96, 124; *Year of Impossible Goodbyes*, 94, 96, 100, 107, 123–4
Chongqing, 32
*Chŏngsindae*. *See* comfort women
Chow, Claire, *Leaving Deep Water*, 131n24
Chow, Karen, 7
Christianity, 79, 103
Chu, Patricia, 135n6
Chun Yu, *Little Green*, 12, 38
Chunghee Sarah Soh, 115
Cinderella story, 37, 77, 89, 134nn29–30
Clinton, Bill, 81
CNN, 120
Cobb, Katherine, 52–3
Coe, Richard N., *When the Grass Was Taller*, 135n4
Cold War, 2, 22
colonialism: Japanese, 5; neo-colonialism, 26; Western, 81
'comfort stations' (brothels), 8, 104, 109–110
comfort women, 2, 5, 95, 98, 103–114
*Comfort Women Speak* (edited collection), 105
*Common Ground* (Okihiro), 7
Communism: atrocities of Communist regimes, 2; *The Black Book of Communism*, 118; in China, 2, 3, 11, 12–13, 20–22, 29–30; in North Korea, 2; in Russia, 22
Communist Party (Chinese), 12, 18, 20, 21, 26, 27, 28, 31, 127n26
Confucius, 93
*Courtship of Eddie's Father, The* (film), 77
Cowan, Laura, 53

*Crossing Oceans* (Brada-Williams and Chow), 7
*Cry for Happy*, 78
Cultural Revolution, Chinese (1966–1976), 6, 11–12; and aesthetic production, 12; 'Anti-Rightist Campaign', 30; childhood perspectives on, 34–43, 128nn40–41; Chinese accounts of, 3, 11, 12, 16–18, 24, 32, 126nn3–4, 126n12, 127n21, 127n26; "criticize Lin Biao" campaign, 15; expatriate memoirs of, 3, 12–16, 17, 18–19, 20–22, 23, 24–31, 43, 126n14; and famine, 12, 14, 30; film representations of, 3; The Great Leap Forward, 15, 29–30; Move to the Country campaign, 15; Red Guard, 26, 27, 29, 40, 41, 126nn3–4; Rustification campaign, 15; Western view of, 2, 3
Cumings, Bruce, 92, 124, 134n1, 135n16

**D**
Dai, Houying, *Stones of the Wall*, 127n26
*Daily Telegraph*, 80
Dalby, Liza, 6, 73–4, 75, 76, 80, 90, 91; *Geisha*, 4, 68, 69, 71–3, 74, 84–5, 86, 87, 132n6, 133n8
Dalian, 120
*danna* (geisha patrons), 70, 84, 87
Davis, Rocío G., 1, 37–8, 100–101, 135n4
Democracy Network Against the North Korean Gulag, 10, 117
Deng Xiaoping, 16–17, 24, 28, 37
Deyang, 27
domestic adoption, 60, 63, 131n23
Donald, Stephanie, 12, 126n14
Dorow, Sara K., 44, 50, 64, 65, 130n15; *When You Were Born in China*, 49, 53, 55
Dowdey, Patrick, 95
Downer, Lesley, 74–7, 84, 86, 91, 133n7, 133n10; *Geisha*, 4, 68, 69; *Madame Sadayakko*, 74, 75, 76, 80; *Women of the Pleasure Quarters*, 4, 68, 69, 70, 74–5, 80, 85, 132n2
"Dying Rooms, The" (documentary), 63, 129n14

*Dynasty* (soap opera), 13

**E**
Eady, Toby, 35
*East to America* (Kim and Yu), 5, 94
*Echoes upon Echoes* (Kim and Kang), 93
Egypt, 81
Esherwick, Joseph, 17, 126n3
ethnicity, 4, 10, 43, 44, 45, 61, 103, 134n30; inherited, 59; symbolic, 60; transethnic adoption, 128n1
ethnography, 72–3, 76–7, 82, 84, 91; 'interpretive ethnography', 72. *See also* anthropology
Evans, Harriet, 11, 12, 22, 126n9, 126n14
Evans, Karin, *The Lost Daughters of China*, 45, 49, 50, 51–2, 57, 58, 59, 60, 62

**F**
Families with Children from China (FCC), 45, 52, 130n18
famine, 12, 14, 30, 33, 34, 117, 123
fashion, 80
feminism, 18, 74, 79, 129n8
Feng Jicai, *Voices from the Whirlwind*, 14
Fenkl, Heinz Insu, 92, 98–9
film: and Chinese Cultural Revolution, 3; representations of geisha culture, 4, 67, 68, 77, 78, 80, 88–9, 91; and "sent down youth", 128n40
Fisher, Lucy, 134n28
foot-binding, 26, 27, 29, 35, 36, 48, 127n16
Fry, Ying Ying, 55, 131nn21–2; *Kids Like Me in China*, 49, 53, 55–6

**G**
Gallagher, John, *Geisha*, 90
Gamache, Gail, 44, 46, 130n15
Gao, Anhua, 3, 23, 24, 32, 43, 128n37; *To the Edge of the Sky*, 12, 14, 15, 29–31, 32
geishas and geisha culture: American women and, 4, 68, 71–7; anthropological and ethnographical analyses of, 68, 71–4, 76–7, 82, 84, 90, 91, 132–3nn4–7; *danna*, 70, 84, 87; decline of, 2, 69; fictional

150  Index

accounts of, 72, 77–8, 80–81, 82–4, 85–6, 87–8; film representations of, 4, 67, 68, 77, 78, 80, 88–9, 91; and gender commodification, 8, 67, 89–91, 133n15; *hanadai*, 70; *hanamachi*, 68, 69, 75, 76; historical role of, 69–70, 73, 76–7, 132n3; *maiko*, 70, 71, 84–5; *minarai*, 71, 72; *mizuage*, 4, 68, 70, 84–8, 90; mystery and secrecy of, 4, 67–8, 68–70, 73–4, 75–6; *ochaya*, 71; *okasan*, 76, 85; *okiya*, 69, 70, 71; *onsen* geisha, 69, 87–8; and orientalism, 68, 76, 81–2, 83, 89, 133n13, 134n26; revivification of interest in, 6, 69, 80–81; and sexuality, 67, 68, 70, 74–5, 77–8, 81, 84–8, 89–91; Western observers of, 4, 67–8, 71–2, 76, 77–82, 88–9, 90–91; *zashiki*, 70, 76, 84
gender: and adoption, 44–6, 49, 55, 56, 62–3, 128n3; and child abandonment, 44, 45–6, 48, 62–3; commodification, 8, 67, 89–91, 133n15; and human rights, 6, 10, 48, 49, 129n8; and infanticide, 47–8; and trauma, 14, 15
Geoffroy-Schneiter, Bérénice, *Geishas*, 67, 90, 134n31
*ggeh* (revolving credit union), 103
"GI girls", 114
Gion (geisha district), 69, 85–6, 134n27
Gion Higashi (geisha district), 69
globalization, 6, 9–10
Golden, Arthur, 6, 80–81, 88, 90, 91, 133n8; *Memoirs of a Geisha*, 4, 19, 25, 68, 69, 72, 74, 80–84, 85–6, 87–8, 133n18, 134n27, 134nn29–30
Gong Li, 88
Gray-Rosendale, Laura, 118–19
Great Leap Forward, The, 15, 29–30
*Guardian, The* (newspaper), 24–5, 42, 129–30n14
gulag, 8, 10, 94, 115–19
Guo Sheng, *Tears of the Moon*, 12
Guo, Xiaolu, *Village of Stone*, 128n41

H
Haaken, Janice, 1, 10
Hadley, Stephen J., 116
Hall, Beth, 49, 61, 62

Halliday, Jon, 12, 35, 128n34
Han Suyin, 21, 127n19; *Destination Chungking*, 126n5; *Wind in My Sleeve*, 127n26
*hanadai* (geisha 'flower money'), 70
*hanamachi* (geisha districts), 68, 69, 75, 76
Harris, Sara, *House of 10,000 Pleasures*, 68
Harrison, Kathryn, *The Binding Chair*, 127n16
Hawaii, 96, 97, 101, 102, 108, 109
Heller, Richard, 13
Henke, Suzette, 10, 103, 112, 113, 122
Hicks, George L., 105
Hodgson, John, 40
Hollywood, 67, 77, 78, 79, 89, 91
Holocaust, 3, 15, 16
Holt International (adoption agency), 131n26
Honda, Mike, 105, 106
Hong Kingston, Maxine, 13, 38; *The Woman Warrior*, 13, 24–5
Hong Kong, 13, 27, 35, 37, 128n39
Hong Ying, 3, 31, 128n37; *Daughter of the River*, 12, 15, 19, 31–4, 43
hooks, bell, 67, 82, 88, 134n30
House UnAmerican Activities Committee, 20
Hsia, C.T., 22, 127n19
Hu Jintao, 48
Hughes-Hallett, Lucy, 13
human rights: in China, 2, 10, 12, 22, 27, 46, 48–9, 63–4, 127n26, 129n8, 129n14; discourses on, 2, 6, 7–9, 10, 101, 125n1, 129n8; and gender, 6, 10, 48, 49, 129n8; in Korea, 5, 101, 114, 115–19, 120, 121–2; and 'restorative justice', 113; Universal Declaration of Human Rights, 7–8
Human Rights in China (HRIC), 46, 48, 128nn3–4, 129n10, 129n14
Human Rights Watch, 10, 48, 128n4, 129n9
Hwang, David Henry, *M. Butterfly*, 68
Hyok Kang, *This is Paradise!*, 5, 134–5n3
Hyun, Peter, *Man Sei!*, 93
Hyun Sook Han, *Many Lives Intertwined*, 5, 94, 131n26
Hyunah Yang, 103, 104, 105, 107, 135n9

## I

immigration (to United States): Chinese, 11; Japanese, 101; Korean, 94, 96, 97, 101–3, 123
indenture, 6–7, 8, 87, 134n29
*Independent, The* (newspaper), 13
infanticide, 47–8
international adoption, 2, 3–4, 10, 44–5, 49, 60–66, 128n1, 129n11, 131nn25–7
'interpretive ethnography', 72
Iwasaki, Mineko, 85–6, 88, 91, 134n27; *Geisha: A Life*, 70, 86; *Geisha of Gion*, 4, 68

## J

Japan: atrocities, 2; colonial rule in Korea, 1–2, 5, 92, 93, 94, 98, 101, 103, 104, 107, 114, 119; economy, 78, 79–80; and Korean comfort women, 95, 104, 105–7; occupation of China, 26, 27; Western representations of, 88–9, 91. *See also* geishas and geisha culture
Japanese Americans, 101, 105
Ji-Li Jiang, 3, 17, 24; *Red Scarf Girl*, 12, 26, 38, 41–2
Jing-Bao Nie, 46, 47, 48–9
Johnson, Kay, 44, 45–6, 47, 63, 128–9nn4–5, 131n23
Joseph, William A., 16
Jun Jong Lee, 135n11
Jung Chang, 3, 6, 17, 24, 32, 35, 127n20; on Mao, 12, 128n34; *Wild Swans*, 12, 13–14, 18–19, 23, 25, 26–9, 32, 34, 35, 38, 128n35

## K

Kamikaze pilots, 2, 125n1
Kamishichiken (geisha district), 69
Kang, Angie, 120
Kang Chol-Hwan, 94–5, 116, 123; *The Aquariums of Pyongyang*, 5, 94, 98, 100, 115–19, 121, 135n3
Kang, K. Connie, 5, 94–5; *Home Was the Land of Morning Calm*, 93, 94, 98, 99, 100, 114–15
Kang, Younghill, 101–2, 135n6; *East Goes West*, 102; *The Grass Roof*, 102
*Kansas City Star*, 124
Kaplan, Caren, 91

Karnow, Stanley, 40
*kary-kai*. *See* geishas and geisha culture
Keller, Nora Okja, 5, 96, 108, 112, 123; *Comfort Woman*, 5, 93, 95, 99, 100, 104, 105, 107–113, 135n11; *Fox Girl*, 93, 95, 100, 113–14
Kelsky, Karen, 91
Kennedy, Ted, 120
Keum Ja Hwang, 108
Khmer Rouge, 100, 125n1, 135n4
Kim, Elaine H., 5, 96–7, 98, 101–2; *The Comfort Women*, 105
Kim, Elizabeth, *Ten Thousand Sorrows*, 94, 100, 109
Kim Hak-soon, 105
Kim Il Jong, 5, 117
Kim Il Sung, 5, 92, 98
Kim Moon Soo, 117
Kim-Gibson, D., 105
Kimm, Samuel, 105
Kissinger, Henry, 116
Klatzin, Amy, 49, 52, 53, 55
Kolosov, Jacqueline, *Grace from China*, 49, 53
Kono, Yohei, 106
Korea: American military presence, 64, 93, 95, 98, 114; comfort women in, 2, 5, 95, 98, 103–114; division of, 5, 92, 93, 95, 98, 99; human rights in, 5, 101, 114, 115–19, 120, 121–2; Japanese colonial rule, 2, 5, 92, 93, 94, 98, 101, 103, 104, 107, 114, 119; reunification efforts, 94, 114, 115, 117, 122. *See also* North Korea; South Korea
Korean Americans: adoptees, 56, 64–6, 128n1, 130n16, 131–2nn26–7; and Japanese colonialism in Korea, 5, 94, 101, 103; racist treatment of, 5, 64, 94, 102; and twentieth-century Korean history, 5, 92–6, 98–101, 102–3, 119–20, 121–2, 124, 135n4; women's narratives, 96–7, 102, 108, 109
*Korean Quarterly*, 123
Korean War, 2, 5, 6, 7, 64, 92, 93, 95, 98, 114–15, 119, 123, 124, 128n1, 134n1
Korean Women's Patriotic Society, 97
Korean Women's Relief Society, 97
*Kŏri* (Fenkl and Lew), 92, 93, 98–9
Kuo, Helena, 21

## 152   Index

Kuomintang, 26, 27, 37
Kuzume, Yoshi, 78–9, 133n17
Kyoto, 69, 71, 73, 76, 85, 87

## L

language, 59, 61, 98
Lantos, Tom, 106
Lee, Ang, 21
Lee, Chang-Rae, *Native Speaker*, 92, 102–3
Lee, Helie, 5, 121–2, 123; *In the Absence of the Sun*, 93, 96, 120–21; *Still Life with Rice*, 93, 96, 98, 100, 107, 109, 119–21
Lee, Mary Paik, *Quiet Odyssey*, 5, 93, 97, 98, 101, 102
Lee, Myung-Ok Marie, *Somebody's Daughter*, 64–5
lesbianism, 15, 18
*Letter Never Sent* (Fairbanks et al), 94
Lew, Walter, 92, 98–9
Lewis, Lisa, *Butterflies of the Night*, 132–3n7
Lewis, Rose, *I Love You Like Crazy Cakes*, 49, 53–4, 55
Li, Moying, 3, 17; *Snow Falling in Spring*, 12, 38–9
Liang Xiaosheng, *Snowstorm Tonight*, 17
libricide, 12
*Life* (magazine), 120, 130n14
life writing: and agency and guilt, 23–4, 91, 112; and authority and authenticity, 83–4, 91, 118–19; "collaborative life narratives", 118, 135n15; and empowerment, 10; and ethics, 120–21; expatriate women's, 13; and human rights, 6, 9, 10, 121–2; testimonial narratives, 15, 105, 122; and traumatic experience, 10, 23, 101, 112–13, 118–19, 122–3
Lin, Hazel, 21
Ling, Amy, 20, 21, 22, 26, 123
Liu Binyan, 23
Liu Hong, *Startling Moon*, 12
Liu, Liming, 44, 46, 130n15
Liu, Lucy, 77
Liyan Qin, 17, 24, 126n12
Long, Jeffrey E., 1
Long, John Luther, "Madame Butterfly", 68
*Lord of the Flies, The* (Golding), 40
Los Angeles, 102

*Los Angeles Times*, 120
Loti, Pierre, *Madame Chrysanthème*, 68
Lu Xun Literature Academy for Writers, 34
*Lust, Caution* (film), 21, 127n19

## M

Ma Bo, *Blood Red Sunset*, 39, 126n5
Ma Yan, *The Diary of Ma Yan*, 42–3
*McCall's* (magazine), 130n14
McCallum, Robyn, 123
McCarthy, Joseph, 20
McClellan, Anita D., 56, 57
McLeod, Jean, *At Home in this World*, 49, 53, 131n20
McLeod, John, 25
*Madama Butterfly* (Puccini), 4, 68, 77
Madonna (entertainer), 80
*maiko* (apprentice geishas), 70, 71, 84–5
Manchuria, 27
Mao Zedong, 11–12, 14, 16, 28, 29–30, 32, 37, 39, 40, 128n34
March First Movement, 97
Marchetti, Gina, 67, 77–8, 79–80
Marrin, Minette, 13–14
Marshall, Rob, 88, 134n28
Masuda, Sayo, *Autobiography of a Geisha*, 68, 87–8, 132n1
*Memoirs of a Geisha* (film), 4, 68, 77, 80, 81, 88–9, 134nn28–30
memory, 1, 8, 10, 28, 38–9, 42, 95, 99, 104, 109, 111, 112; collective, 1, 87, 101; cultural, 92, 99; official, 105
Middle East, 81, 88, 127n24
Millet, Catherine, *The Sexual Life of Catherine M.*, 90
Min, Anchee, 3, 17, 18, 32, 38; *Red Azalea*, 12, 15, 18, 19, 23, 26
*minarai* (geisha training process), 71, 72
Mirsky, Jonathan, 14, 15
*Miss Saigon* (musical), 77
Miyagawa-cho (geisha district), 69
*mizu shobai* ('water trade'; prostitution), 86, 132n7
*mizuage* (geisha ceremony), 4, 68, 70, 84–8, 90
Moorehead, Caroline, 13
Morris, Narelle, 77, 78, 79, 80, 133n14
Morrison, Toni, *Beloved*, 112
Move to the Country campaign (Chinese), 15
*My Geisha* (film), 78

## N

Nanchu, 17; *Red Sorrow*, 12, 38, 40–41
Nanking, 2
National Beijing University, 20
NATO, 51
*Negotiating Identities* (Grice), 3, 68, 80, 89, 127n17
neo-colonialism, 26
neo-orientalism, 13, 22, 25–6, 81–2
New York, 37, 61
*New York Review of Books*, 14
*New York Times*, 18, 81, 116
*New York Times Book Review*, 123
North Korea: aid to, 117, 122; atrocities in, 2, 8, 117–18, 119; and "Axis of Evil", 116; defection from, 122; gulag, 8, 10, 94, 117–18; human rights in, 115–19, 120, 121–2; and Korean War, 114, 115; repression in, 5, 8, 92, 94, 98, 115–16, 120–21; Western view of, 2, 116

## O

*Observer, The* (newspaper), 25
occidentalism, 127n27
*ochaya* (geisha teahouses), 71
*okasan* (geisha house mothers), 76, 85
Okihiro, Gary, 7
*okiya* (geisha houses), 69, 70, 71
Olympic Games: Beijing 2008, 22; Seoul 1988, 131n25
one-child policy (Chinese), 2, 3–4, 6, 44–9, 51, 54, 56, 58, 60, 62–4, 129n7, 129n10
*onsen* geisha, 69, 87–8
orientalism, 3, 11, 22, 25, 127n24, 127n27; and geisha culture, 68, 76, 81–2, 83, 89, 133n13, 134n26; neo-orientalism, 13, 22, 25–6, 81–2
orphanages, 3, 45, 51, 54, 56, 60, 63, 129n9, 129–30n14, 131n21
"Outside Looking In" (documentary), 129n11

## P

Paek Ki-wan, 92
Pai, Margaret K., *The Dreams of Two Yi-Min*, 5, 93, 102
Park, Linda Sue, 5; *When My Name Was Keoko*, 93–4, 98, 100, 109
participant observation, 71–2

*Passage to the Heart, A* (ed. Klatzin), 49, 52–3, 55
Peacock, Carol Antoinette, *Mommy Far, Mommy Near*, 49, 53, 54–5, 57, 62
Pearl River Delta, 51
Pelosi, Nancy, 106
*People* (magazine), 120
Perkins, P.D., *Geisha of Pontocho*, 67
Pickowicz, Paul, 17, 126n3
pillow books, 89, 90, 134n32
Pontocho (geisha district), 69, 71, 73
pornography, 81, 89–90
post-traumatic stress disorder, 111
Poulton, M. Cody, "Madame Sadayakko", 75, 80
Prager, Emily, *Wuhu Diary*, 49, 50–51, 52, 55, 57–9, 61, 62
Prasso, Sheridan, 67, 77, 80, 81, 86–7, 89, 133n18, 133n23, 134n25
prostitution, 6–7, 26, 37, 64, 114; and geisha culture, 70, 74, 77, 84, 85, 86–7, 89; *mizu shobai*, 86, 132n7. *See also* comfort women
Puccini, Giacomo, *Madama Butterfly*, 4, 68, 77
Pusan, 123
Pyongyang, 120, 123

## Q

*Quiet American, The* (Greene), 77

## R

race: racial difference, 18, 25, 54, 62, 64, 91, 131n20; racial identity, 49, 50, 53, 54, 55–6, 59–63, 64–6, 131n24; racial self-esteem, 52, 61–2; racial slur, 4, 45; racial stereotyping, 4, 45, 91, 133n17; and representation, 88–9. *See also* transracial adoption
racism, 5, 50, 61–2, 94, 102
rape, 6–7, 100, 104, 108–9, 110
*Reader's Digest*, 130n14
reading, 9, 10, 25–6
*Reading Autobiography* (Smith and Watson), 83, 91, 118–19, 135n12, 135n15
Red Guard, 26, 27, 29, 40, 41, 126nn3–4
Register, Cheri, 65–6
Reigns, Miranda, *Geisha Secrets*, 90, 134n31
Reiner, Yair, 118

'restorative justice', 113
Rice, Condoleeza, 116
Rigoulet, Pierre, 115–16, 118
Robinson, Katy, *A Single Square Picture*, 65
Ronyoung Kim, *Clay Walls*, 5, 93, 100, 102, 135n16
Rowley, G.G., 87, 88, 132n1
Russia, 22, 98, 128n1
Rustification campaign (Chinese), 15

S

Sada Yakko, 74, 75
Said, Edward, 13, 22, 81, 83
San Francisco, 96
*San Francisco Chronicle*, 80
Sansan, *Eighth Moon*, 20
*Sayonara* (film), 77
"scar literature", 17
Schultermandl, Silvia, 106, 108–9
Schwartz, Vera, 1
Scott, Adolphe, *The Flower and Willow World*, 67–8
scriptotherapy, 112, 113
Second World War, 2, 3, 69, 79, 98, 106, 123
See, Carolyn, 13
"sent down youth": films, 128n40; novels, 17, 24, 126n12, 126n15
Seoul, 94, 114, 120, 123, 124; Olympic Games (1988), 131n25
sexual abuse, 6–7, 104, 108–9, 110–111
Shanghai, 32, 35, 36
Shen, Fan, *Gang of One*, 126n5
Shenyang, 120
Sheridan, Michael, 129n12
Shimbashi (geisha district), 69
*Shogun* (Clavell), 77
*shunga* (prints), 76, 90
Slaughter, Joseph R., 7, 9
slavery, 7; child slaves, 37; female slaves, 48. *See also* comfort women
Smith, Sidonie, 10; *Reading Autobiography*, 83, 91, 118–19, 135n12, 135n15
Somerson, Wendy, 15, 18, 22, 127n17
South Africa, 113
South Korea, 1, 5, 93, 98, 114, 115, 117, 122, 123, 131n25
Spielberg, Steven, 80, 89, 134n28
Steinberg, Gail, 49, 61, 62
stereotyping, 4, 11, 25–6, 45, 76, 77–9, 91, 103, 133n17

sterilisation, 46, 47
Stone, Oliver, 3
Sugimoto, Etsu, 101
Sun Shuyin, *Ten Thousand Miles Without a Cloud*, 12
*Sunday Times*, 80, 88, 129n12
*Surfacing Sadness* (Choi and Kim), 93

T

*Taehan Puin Kuje-hoe* (Korean Women's Relief Society), 97
*Taehan Yoja Aikuk-dan* (Korean Women's Patriotic Society), 97
Taiwan, 1, 27, 104
Takaki, Ronald, 101
Tal, Kalí, 10, 15
Tan, Amy, 13, 18, 19; *The Joy Luck Club*, 19; *The Kitchen God's Wife*, 18, 25, 126n5
*Teahouse of the August Moon* (film), 78
Tessler, Richard, 44, 46, 130n15
Thorpe, Vanessa, 25
Tiananmen Square protests (1989), 2, 22, 127n29
Tianjin, 36, 37
*Time* (magazine), 48, 120, 126n15
*Times, The*, 19
Tokyo, 69, 87, 89
torture, 8, 23, 30
transethnic adoption, 128n1
*Transnational Asian American Literature* (Lim et al), 10
transracial adoption, 6, 128n1, 129n11, 129–30n14, 130n15, 130n17; and birth heritage, 57–60; and gender, 44–6, 49, 55, 56, 62–3; and naming of children, 58–9; narratives of, 4, 45, 49–60, 61, 64–6, 130nn15–6, 131n20, 131n22; and racial identity, 49, 50, 53, 54, 55–6, 59–63, 64–6, 131n24; rise of, 2, 3–4, 44–5, 51, 60
trauma: and childhood, 40, 100–101; and gender, 14–15; post-traumatic stress disorder, 111; and writing, 6, 8–9, 10, 14–15, 28, 99–101, 112–13, 118–19, 122–3
Trenka, Jane Jeong, *The Language of Blood*, 64, 131n22, 131n25
*True Stories of the Korean Comfort Women, The* (edited collection), 5, 95, 105
Truman, Harry S., 114

Truth and Reconciliation Committee (South African), 113

**U**
Underwood, Eleanor, *The Life of a Geisha*, 90
United Nations, 48; Convention on the Rights of the Child, 101, 125n4; Security Council, 114; Universal Declaration of Human Rights, 7–8
United States: Asian immigration, 11, 94, 96, 97, 101–3, 123; and China, 20, 22–3, 48–9; Committee for Human Rights in North Korea, 120; House UnAmerican Activities Committee, 20; international adoption in, 4, 10, 44–5, 52–3, 63, 64, 128n1; and Japan, 79–80; and Korea, 64, 93, 95, 98, 114, 116–17, 120, 122; and Korean comfort women, 105, 106; treatment of Korean Americans, 5, 64, 94, 102
United States Information Agency, 21, 127n25
United States State Department, 45, 127n25
Universal Declaration of Human Rights, 7–8
*Unrooted Childhoods* (Eidse and Sichel), 10

**V**
venereal disease, 110
Vietnam, 2, 3, 125n1, 128n1
voyeurism, 26

**W**
Walder, Andrew, 17, 126n3
Wang Xiaobo, *Golden Age*, 17
*Washington Post*, 48, 88, 106
Watson, Julia, *Reading Autobiography*, 83, 91, 118–19, 135n12, 135n15
Wawaqiao, 31
Wei Hsin Gui, 95
Wells, H.G., 9
Wick, Doug, 134n28
Winfrey, Oprah, 120
*Woman's Day*, 130n14
women: in China, 8, 26, 28–9, 32, 33–4, 35–6, 43, 46–9, 63; Chinese American, 13, 18–19, 20–22, 24–5, 25–6, 43, 127n19; in Japan, 67, 76, 77–80, 89–91, 133nn15–17; in Korea, 93, 96–7, 119; Korean American, 96–7, 102; orientalization of Asian women, 81–2, 89; stereotyping of, 26, 77–9, 91, 133n17. *See also* comfort women; geishas and geisha culture
*Women's Review of Books*, 129n14
Wong, Christine P.W., 16
Wong, Jade Snow, *Fifth Chinese Daughter*, 127n25
Wong, Jan, 12–13; *Red China Blues*, 12, 18, 19
"Words on the Night Breeze" (radio programme), 42
*World of Suzie Wong, The* (film), 77
World War II, 2, 3, 69, 79, 98, 106, 123
Wuhu City, 50

**X**
Xi'an, 47
Xiaomei Chen, 16, 22–3, 24
Xu, Ben, 11, 38, 127n17
Xu, Meihong, 3, 32; *Daughter of China*, 12, 19, 31
Xu, Wenying, 11, 16, 23, 127n17
Xue, Xinran, 35, 42, 43, 128n41; *China Witness*, 42; *The Good Women of China*, 42; *What the Chinese Don't Eat*, 42
Xue Zhi-Heng, General, 26, 27

**Y**
Yachiyoko, 89
*Yale-China Review*, 130n14
Yalu River, 120, 121
Yamamoto, Traise, 67, 79, 90–91, 133n15
Yang, Rae, 3; *Spider Eaters*, 12, 38, 42
Yangtze River, 19, 32–3, 50, 129n7
Ye, Ting-xing, 3; *A Leaf in the Bitter Wind*, 12
Yen Mah, Adeline, 6, 13, 31, 32, 34, 128n39; *Chinese Cinderella*, 37; *Falling Leaves*, 13, 14, 19, 25, 26, 34–7, 128n38
Yen, Maria, *The Umbrella Garden*, 20, 22
Yeoh, Michelle, 88
Yeong and Yeong Book Company, 65, 131n21

Yibin, 26
*Yobo* (Keller et al), 93
Yodok concentration camp, 94, 117–18, 119
Yoshihara, Mari, 77, 133n13
Yoshimi, Yoshiaki, 105
Young Pioneers, 29, 41
Yu, Eui-Young, 5
Yu-fang, 27
Yuan-tsung Chen, 21; *The Dragon's Village*, 20, 22
Yun, Mia: *House of the Winds*, 93, 96, 99, 100; *Translations of Beauty*, 93

## Z

Zahner, Cathy Karlin, 124
*zashiki* (geisha event), 70, 76, 84
Zhang, Ange, *Red Land, Yellow River*, 38, 126n5
Zhang Ziyi, 88
Zhao, Henry, 17
Zhao Lin, 31
Zhou Enlai, 16, 39
Zhu De, 39
Zinn, Howard, 26
ZNet (website), 80
Zweig, David, 16

For Product Safety Concerns and Information please contact our EU
representative  GPSR@taylorandfrancis.com
Taylor & Francis Verlag GmbH, Kaufingerstraße 24, 80331 München, Germany

www.ingramcontent.com/pod-product-compliance
Lightning Source LLC
Chambersburg PA
CBHW070619300426
44113CB00010B/1584